Vineta

The Phantom City

E. Werner

(Translator: Frances A. Shaw)

Alpha Editions

This edition published in 2024

ISBN : 9789362994462

Design and Setting By
Alpha Editions
www.alphaedis.com
Email - info@alphaedis.com

Contents

CHAPTER I.

THE WIDOW AND HER SON.

The hot summer afternoon neared its close. The sun had already set, but the twilight glow still lingered in the western sky, and was mirrored in the sea, which, scarcely rippled by a zephyr's breath, caught the last splendors of the dying day.

At some distance from the shore along which ran the great promenade of the fashionable watering-place of C----, usually thronged with visitors at this hour, stood a solitary country house, modest and unpretending, but distinguished from the large and splendid villas of the neighborhood by the beauty of its situation and its outlook over the sea to the horizon's verge. It was a quiet, secluded spot, well fitted to be the abode of people seeking retirement and desiring no part in the gay, excited life around them. At an open glass door leading out upon a balcony stood a lady in deep mourning. Her stature was tall and imposing, and although she had reached the meridian of life, she was still beautiful. This face with its firm, regular outlines could never have possessed the charm of gentleness and amiability, but years had robbed it of little of its cold, severe beauty. The black dress with its heavy crape trimmings indicated a recent bereavement, but the eyes bore no trace of tears; there was no touch of sensibility in the resolute features. If sorrow had come near this woman, she had not felt it deeply, or she had conquered it.

At the lady's side stood a gentleman of equally imposing appearance; although very near her in age, he seemed ten years her senior, for time and life had left deep traces as they swept over his head. The grave, expressive face bore that impress which the world's storms and conflicts leave behind them; the dark, abundant hair was tinged with gray, the brow was furrowed, and the profound melancholy of the glance was in keeping with that look of sadness stamped upon all the features. He had been intently gazing out upon the sea, but he now turned away with an impatient gesture.

"They are not yet in sight," he said; "they will not be likely to return before dark."

"You should have announced your arrival," replied the lady. "We did not expect you for some days. The boat never comes in sight until it has doubled that wooded point yonder.--Go down to the beach, Paul," she added, speaking to a servant, "and as soon as the boat lands, inform your young master and mistress that Count Morynski has arrived."

The servant left on his errand, and the count, abandoning his watch on the balcony, entered the house with the lady and seated himself at her side. "Forgive my impatience, sister," he said; "your society ought to content me for the present, but it is a year since I have seen my little girl."

The lady smiled. "You will see a little girl no longer," she said. "A year counts much at her age, and Wanda gives promise of great beauty."

"And has her intellectual culture kept pace with her physical development? Your letters have always expressed great satisfaction in her progress."

"Her mental attainments are beyond her years; she always outstrips her tasks, and in this respect needs to be restrained rather than urged on. But I must tell you that Wanda has one great fault: self-will. I have sometimes been compelled to enforce the obedience she was inclined to deny me."

The father smiled as he answered: "This is a strange reproach from *your* lips, Maryna. Self-will, you are aware, is a distinguishing trait of your own character; it is in fact an especial trait of our family."

"But it is not to be tolerated in a young girl of sixteen," replied the sister. "I tell you once for all, Wanda's obstinacy must be controlled."

This assertion did not seem to please the count, and he tried to change the subject. "I feel sure that I could commit my child to no better hands than yours," he said, "and I am doubly rejoiced that now I have come to take Wanda home, she will still be near you. I did not count upon your return so soon after your husband's death. I supposed you would remain in Paris until Leo had completed his studies."

"I did not feel at home in Paris," replied the lady; "you know from your own experience that exile is an unenviable lot. Although my husband was banished for life from his native land, return was not denied his widow and son. Leo is the last of his race; he must represent the family. I wished to educate him at home, so that he might become in thought and feeling a true son of his fatherland. He is still very young, but the duties which are required of him are beyond his years, and he must learn to fulfil them."

"Where do you think of making your home?" asked Count Morynski; "you know that my house is at all times open to you."

"I know it," returned the princess, "and I thank you; but my great object in life is to secure a future for my Leo worthy of the name he bears. You understand our pecuniary circumstances; we have sacrificed nearly all for our country and its lost cause, and our life in exile has been full of privations. Some better fortune must be in store for us. For Leo's sake I have decided upon a step which for myself alone I would not have taken. Can you divine the reason why I have chosen C---- for a summer residence?"

"No, I cannot; your choice surprises me. Herr Witold's estate lies only ten miles distant from here, and I should suppose you would wish to avoid such proximity. Have you lately been corresponding with Waldemar?"

"No," replied the princess, coldly. "During our absence in France I scarcely heard from him; in all these years he has made no inquiries after his mother."

"And has his mother inquired after him?" asked the count.

"If I had done so, it would have been to subject myself to repulsion and humiliation," replied the princess, excitedly. "Herr Witold has always hated me, and has asserted his unlimited rights as guardian of my eldest son in the most annoying ways. Here I am powerless."

"A mother's rights stand so high that if you had asserted them with your wonted decision, Witold would not have ventured to deny you all intercourse with your child. But you have not done this; be honest, Maryna, you have never loved your eldest son!"

The princess leaned her head upon her hand, and was silent. She felt the truth of her brother's words.

"I well know why Waldemar does not hold the first place in your heart," continued the count; "he is the son of an unloved husband whom you were forced to accept; he reminds you of an unblest marriage. Leo is the child of your heart and of your love."

"And his father never gave me the slightest cause for complaint," added the princess.

"You had entire influence over your last husband," said the count; "but we will waive this subject. You have a plan, it seems. Do you propose to assert a mother's claims over Waldemar?"

"I propose at least to assert the right of which my first husband's will robbed me; that unjust will, every line of which was dictated by hatred, and a resolve that the widow, as well as the mother, should be disinherited. Until now, the will has remained in full force, but it declares Waldemar of age in his twenty-first year. He has reached that age, and is now his own master. I want to put it to the test--if he will allow his mother to seek an asylum with relatives, while he is reckoned among the wealthiest proprietors of the country, and it will cost him but one word to secure an honorable existence to his mother and brother upon one of his estates."

Count Morynski shook his head. "If you reckon upon any filial sentiments in this son, I fear you delude yourself. He has been separated from you since infancy, and you may be very sure that he has been taught no love for his mother. I have seen him only once; he was then a boy of some ten years of age, and he impressed me favorably. But I remember perfectly that he was not at all pliant in disposition."

"You may well say that," returned the princess. "He is his father's own son, and must be, like him, rough, uncontrollable, and unsusceptible to high and noble influences. I think I fully understand Waldemar's character, but he will allow me to control him. Inferior natures always yield to intellectual superiority, if it is only asserted in the right way."

"Could you control the boy's father?" asked the count, gravely.

"You forget, Bronislaw, that I was at the time of my first marriage a young girl of seventeen, without experience and without knowledge of human nature. I should now know how to deal with such a character, and to mould it to my will. Besides, in dealing with Waldemar, I have a mother's authority; he will yield to me."

The count thought differently, but ere he had time to reply, a light, quick step echoed on the balcony. The door flew open, a young girl bounded into the room, and the next moment was clasped in her father's arms.

The princess rose and advanced to meet her son who stood in the doorway. "You have been absent a long while, Leo," she said; "we have waited a full hour for your return."

"I beg your pardon, mamma; the sunset upon the water was so beautiful that we wanted to gaze at it until the last moment."

With these words, Leo Zulieski took his mother's hand, and leading her to the sofa, sat down by her side. He was very young, perhaps seventeen or eighteen years of age, and bore a striking resemblance to his mother; but the cold, severe expression of that older face was absent from these youthful features, where all was warmth and animation, and from the dark, fiery eyes, which indicated an ardent, impulsive temperament. The young fellow was such a picture of youthful strength, grace, and beauty, that the pride with which his mother took his hand and led him to his uncle might well be pardoned.

"Leo has no father," she said, sadly. "Whenever he needs a man's advice and guidance, I rely upon you, Bronislaw."

The count embraced his nephew warmly and cordially, but his glances as well as his thoughts were centred upon his daughter. The joy of meeting her again overruled all other emotions.

Wanda did not bear the slightest resemblance to her father; she seemed a being unique and unlike all others. Her graceful figure, which was still that of a child, had not attained its full stature or development; her features were those of a child, although their expression was firm and resolute. Her face was pale, but not with illness: it bore the impress of perfect health; a faint flush, called forth by the least excitement or emotion, came and went on her lips and cheeks. The abundant, deep black hair made the exceeding fairness of the complexion still more striking, and the large, dark, liquid eyes were shaded by long black lashes. Wanda indeed gave promise of great beauty. She could not now be called beautiful, but she possessed that indefinable fascination we see in many young girls when standing upon that charmed boundary,

"Where the brook and river meet,
Womanhood and childhood sweet."

In this young girl's whole appearance there was a delightful blending of the petulance and innocence of the child with the gravity of the young lady, who every now and then calls to mind her sixteen years, and feels that her childhood has passed. The halo of early youth, which surrounded her like the fragrant odor around a half-opened rosebud, made her doubly enchanting.

The first joy and surprise of reunion were over, and the conversation began to flow in quiet channels. The count drew his daughter closer to his side, and playfully chided her for not having returned sooner.

"I did not know you had come, papa," she said; "and, besides, I had an adventure in the forest."

"In the forest?" interrupted her aunt. "Were you not with Leo upon the sea?"

"Only upon our return, Aunt Maryna. We had planned a sail to Buchenholm; Leo thought the distance by water less than that by the forest-path; I maintained the contrary. We disputed a while, and at last concluded to prove which was right. Leo sailed away alone, and I took the path through the forest."

"Who guided you?" asked the count.

Wanda smiled archly. "O, some satyr!--one of those old giant-ghosts which now and then flit around here. But you must question me no further, papa. Leo is dying of curiosity to know; he tormented me with questions all the way home, and for this very reason I will not tell him a syllable."

"This is all a made-up story," cried Leo, laughing; "a subterfuge to explain your late return. You would invent a whole fairy-tale rather than own I was in the right."

"Subterfuge or not," interposed the princess, "this solitary walk was highly improper. I gave you permission to take a short sail with Leo, but I had no idea he would leave you for hours alone in the forest."

"Wanda insisted upon it," replied Leo. "She was determined to settle our dispute about the distance."

"Yes, Aunt Maryna, I *would* have my own way," said Wanda, emphatically, "and Leo knew that he could not keep me back."

The princess was about to reprimand her niece for this new exhibition of self-will, but her brother said, hastily, "I feel somewhat fatigued with my journey, and would like to retire to my room. I would also speak with Wanda alone. Good night."

He rose, took his daughter's arm, and left the room.

"My uncle seems perfectly bound up in Wanda," said Leo, as the father and daughter disappeared.

The princess gazed after the two retreating forms, and said, half audibly,--

"He will spoil her. He idolizes her blindly, as he once idolized her mother. Wanda will all too soon learn her power and exercise it. I feared this before his return; I now see that my apprehensions were just. What about this forest adventure, Leo?"

"I do not know. It is very likely one of Wanda's jests. She first roused my curiosity by all sorts of hints, then obstinately refused to explain, and made herself merry over my resentment. You know her way."

"Yes, I know it," the princess said, with a slight frown. "Wanda loves to make sport of us all. You should not let this be so easy for her, Leo, where you are concerned."

Leo flushed to the forehead. "*I*, mamma? I often quarrel with Wanda."

"And yet you allow yourself to be a mere tool for her caprices. I am well aware, my son, who wins in all your quarrels. But this is mere childishness. I wish to speak with you of serious matters. Close the balcony door, and sit down by me."

Leo obeyed, but his face and manner showed that he was offended, perhaps less at his mother's reprimand than at the word "childishness."

Without taking the slightest notice of her son's mood, the mother began: "You know that I was a widow when I married your father, and that there is a son of the first marriage still living. You also know that he has been reared in Germany. You will soon see him and make his acquaintance."

"Do you mean my brother Waldemar?"

"Yes, Waldemar Nordeck. He lives here in the neighborhood, upon his guardian's estate. I have written to him of our arrival, and hope to see him in a few days."

Leo's ill-humor vanished, and he showed deep interest in the subject of conversation. "Mamma," he said, hesitatingly, "will you not tell me something definite concerning these family matters? I only know that your first marriage was unhappy, that you had a falling out with Waldemar's relatives and his guardian, and I learned this by hints from my uncle and the old servants of our house. I never questioned my parents; I saw that this topic wounded my father and angered you, and that you both strove to banish its remembrance."

The lady's features assumed a rigid expression, and her voice was hard and cold as she replied,--

"We do best when we shroud mortifications and humiliations in forgetfulness, and I have sought to do so in regard to that unhappy marriage, which was full of both. Do not ask an explanation from me, Leo; you know the sequel,--let that suffice. I cannot and I will not initiate you into this family tragedy, which I never recall, even at this late day, without hatred toward the dead. I have striven to blot those three years from my life; I did not dream that I should be forced to recall them."

"And what forces you to recall them?" asked Leo, excitedly. "My uncle has offered us his protection; are we not going to his house?"

"No, my son; we are going to Villica."

"To Villica!" echoed Leo, in surprise. "That is Waldemar's estate."

"It should have been my widow's dower," said the princess, resentfully; "it is now the property of my son, and ought to afford his mother a refuge."

Leo started. "What does this mean?" he said, excitedly. "I know that we are poor, but I will endure all privations and renounce all worldly advantages, rather than allow you for my sake--"

The princess rose majestically. Her glance and bearing were so imperious that her son was awed into silence. "Do you think your mother capable of humiliating you?" she asked. "Do you know her so superficially? Leave to me, my son, the care of your position, and of my own. You certainly need not define limits for my actions; I alone understand them."

Leo cast down his eyes and ventured no reply. His mother drew near him and took his hand.

"Will this fiery head never learn to think dispassionately?" she said, gently. "You have great need of calm deliberation before entering upon the life before you, my son. I shall carry out alone my plans concerning Waldemar; you, my Leo, shall experience none of the bitterness which is perhaps in store for me. You must keep your vision clear and your courage unshaken for the future that awaits you. This is your task; mine shall be to secure that future at any price. Trust your mother."

She clasped her son to her heart, and he pressed his mother's hand to his lips, as if in mute entreaty for forgiveness. As she bent to kiss the handsome young face, so bright with hope, so radiant with the promise of high achievement, it was evident that this cold, proud woman possessed all the self-forgetful care and tenderness of a mother, and that, in spite of the rigor with which she treated him, Leo was still her idol.

CHAPTER II.

WALDEMAR.

"Doctor, will you have the kindness to stop once for all these everlasting complaints! Nothing can be done with the lad, I tell you. I have tried often enough to make him change his ways, and have called in six private tutors to help me. We could not manage him, and you can not; so let him have his own way!"

It was the rich proprietor, Herr Witold of Altenhof, who gave this advice to his ward's tutor. Both gentlemen sat in the large corner room of the Altenhof dwelling. The windows were wide open on account of the heat, and all the surroundings showed that the people who dwelt here held such things as elegance and comfort superfluous if not disgraceful. The shabby, old-fashioned furniture was shoved here and there as convenience demanded, and without the least regard to taste or order. On the walls hung a confused medley of fowling-pieces, hunting implements, and deer-horns. Wherever a vacant space offered, a nail had been driven, and some nondescript object had been hung upon it without the least concern for appearances. Upon the writing-desk lay household accounts, tobacco-pipes, spurs, and half a dozen new riding-whips; a pile of daily newspapers upon the floor afforded a luxurious couch to the large hunting-dog, and gave evidence of frequent use. Nothing was in its place; but there was one article in the room which gave a hint of the artistic tastes of the inmates of the house; this was a very gaudy, highly-colored hunting-piece which hung over the sofa, occupying the place of honor upon the blank, grimy wall.

Herr Witold sat in his arm-chair at a window, but his face and head were quite lost in dense clouds of smoke from his meerschaum pipe. In spite of his white hair and his sixty years, he had a fresh, youthful look, and was in the fulness of strength and health. The very tall figure showed a proportionate rotundity; the ruddy face did not indicate great intelligence, but it bore the unmistakable impress of good-nature. The dress, a combination of house and hunting costume, was rather negligent, and the powerful frame and loud voice formed a striking and almost painful contrast to the slender form and timid accents of the tutor.

The doctor was evidently a little past thirty; he was of medium height, although his bowed form made him appear shorter; his face was not really plain, but it bore so marked an impress of ill health and of a subordinate place in life, that it could not be called attractive. His complexion was pale and sallow, his brow was wrinkled, and his eyes had that absent, uncertain glance peculiar to people whose thoughts seldom or never descend to the level of real and practical things. His black suit betrayed the most scrupulous care, and there was something timid and anxious in the man's whole appearance. This timidity and anxiety pervaded the tones of his voice, as he answered, mildly,--

"You know, Herr Witold, that I come to you only in cases of extreme necessity; this time I must ask you to assert your authority; I see no other way."

"What has Waldemar been doing?" asked the guardian, in a tone of great annoyance. "I know as well as you that he is ungovernable, but I cannot help you. The youngster has outgrown my authority, he no longer obeys any one. You say he runs away from his books, preferring to drive around with the hunters; that is nothing; I did the same thing when I was a lad, and I could never get this learned nonsense into my head any better than he can. You say also that he has no manners; well, they are not at all necessary. We live here all by ourselves, and if we happen to meet our neighbors, we feel no embarrassment; our manners are as good as theirs. You must admit this, doctor, if you do take to your heels whenever we have our hunting and drinking parties."

"But these are only companies of men; supposing Waldemar, with his uncultivated manners, should enter other circles and the society of ladies; supposing he should some day marry--"

"*Marry!*" echoed Herr Witold, really wounded at such a supposition. "He will not do that. Why need he marry? I have lived a bachelor all my life, and I am very happy and comfortable. My deceased relative, Nordeck, would have done far better to remain single. But we need not trouble ourselves about Waldemar's marrying, Heaven be praised! He runs away from all the girls, and there he is right!"

The old bachelor leaned back in his arm-chair with an air of supreme comfort and satisfaction. The doctor drew nearer.

"To return to the first topic of conversation," he said, hesitatingly; "you must admit that my pupil has passed entirely beyond my control, and it is high time he was sent to the university."

Herr Witold gave such a violent start that the affrighted tutor stepped back several paces.

"I thought you were coming round to the university! You have talked of nothing else for a month. And what will Waldemar do at the university? Let the professors cram his head with more learning? I thought he had already learned quite enough from you; you have taught him all a clever landlord needs to know. He is just as capable of managing an estate as my inspector; he understands better than I how to make his tenants respect him, and none excel him in riding and hunting. He is a splendid young fellow."

The tutor did not seem to share the guardian's enthusiasm for his ward, but he ventured no opinion; he only summoned up his little stock of courage, and said, very timidly,--

"The heir of Villica requires something more than the knowledge which fits a man to be a good steward or inspector; a university education seems to me highly desirable for Waldemar."

"I do not at all agree with you," replied Herr Witold. "Is it not enough that this boy who has grown so near my heart must soon leave me to take charge of his estates in that accursed Poland? Shall I send him from me to the university when he does not want to go? Don't mention the subject again, doctor; he will remain here until he goes to Villica."

He resumed his pipe in grim displeasure, taking such enormous puffs that his face again disappeared behind clouds of smoke. The tutor sighed and was silent, but even this quiet resignation seemed to annoy the tyrannical master of Altenhof.

"You may as well be content, doctor, to give up that idea of the university," he said, in a more conciliating tone. "You will never, never persuade Waldemar to go there, and as for yourself, it is far better for you to remain in Altenhof. Here you are right in your element among these giants' graves and runic stones, and whatever else you call that sort of stuff you are studying all day long. I can't for the life of me understand what you find so remarkable in this old heathen rubbish, but every living mortal has his own idea of pleasure, and I allow you yours with all my heart, for Waldemar often makes your lot hard enough; and so do I, for that matter."

"O, no, Herr Witold--" began the doctor, deprecatingly.

"No protestations," interrupted the old man, good-naturedly. "I know you must abhor our outlandish way of life here; you would long ago have left us as your six predecessors did, if it had not been for this old pagan trash to which your heart clings, and from which you cannot tear yourself away. You know I am, upon the whole, a rather good sort of a man, although I flare up now and then; and as your thoughts constantly prowl around those old barbarous times, you must feel yourself at home in Altenhof, which is so full of relics of past ages. How can you set such store by the people of those times, when they had such execrable manners? Why, the best of friends among them used to beat each other to death just for pure amusement."

Herr Witold's historical knowledge quite confounded the doctor. "I beg your pardon," he said; "the old Germans--"

"Were not at all like you, doctor," interposed Herr Witold, laughing. "I think of all people I know, Waldemar most resembles them, and I can't understand why you find so much fault with him."

"But, my dear sir, in the nineteenth century--" began Doctor Fabian; he went no further, for at this moment a shot whizzed through the open window, and the huge antlers which hung over the writing-desk fell with a crash.

Herr Witold sprang from his chair. "What does this mean? Is the young upstart going to shoot us right here in our sitting-room? Wait, I'll see about that!"

He was about to rush out of doors, but at this moment a young man burst into the room. He was in hunting costume, a large hound followed him, and he carried a fowling-piece in his hand. Without greeting or apology, he marched up to his guardian, planted himself right before him, and said, triumphantly, "Well, who was right, you or I?"

The old gentleman was really angry. "What do you mean by shooting over people's shoulders, and endangering their lives?" he cried, excitedly. "Did you really want to shoot the doctor and me?"

Waldemar shrugged his shoulders. "O, by no means! I wanted to win my wager. You declared yesterday, that I could not, firing from outside, hit that nail from which the deer-antlers hung. There is the ball!"

"Yes, there it is to be sure," reiterated Witold, admiringly and quite pacified. "But what is the matter with *you*, doctor?"

"Doctor Fabian has one of his nervous attacks," said Waldemar, with a contemptuous shrug, laying aside his gun, but making no effort to help his tutor who had sunk half fainting upon the sofa, and trembling from head to foot. The good-natured Witold held him upright and tried to reassure him.

"Don't faint because a little powder has been fired off," he said; "it isn't worth minding. We did lay a wager, but I had no idea that the youngster would decide it in that preposterous way. There, you are better now, thank God!"

Doctor Fabian rose and made an unavailing effort to control his trepidation. "You might have shot us, Waldemar," he said, with white lips.

"No, doctor, I could not have done that," replied Waldemar, unconcernedly. "You stood with my uncle at the window to the right, I shot through the window to the left, at least five paces distant. You know I never miss my aim."

"But you must stop all such foolhardy actions," said the guardian, with an effort at asserting his authority. "Henceforth I forbid your shooting in the yard."

The young fellow folded his arms, and gazed defiantly at his guardian. "You can forbid, uncle, but I shall not obey," he said. "I shall shoot wherever like."

He stood before his foster-father, the very personification of self-will and defiance. Waldemar Nordeck was moulded after the Germanic type, and bore no trace of his Polish origin. The tall, almost giant figure towered even above Witold's stately form, but it lacked symmetry; its outlines were sharp and angular. The heavy mass of blonde hair seemed a burden to his head, for it fell low over the forehead, and was every now and then thrown back with an impatient movement; the blue eyes had a sullen expression, and in moments of exasperation, like this, an almost malignant glare; the face was decidedly plain, having neither the delicate lineaments of the boy, nor the decided features of the man. The transition period from youth to manhood in Waldemar Nordeck assumed an almost repellent form, and his lack of polite culture, his entire disregard of all social customs, served to heighten the unfavorable impression produced by his appearance.

Herr Witold was one of those men whose physique indicates an energy they do not possess. Instead of resolutely opposing and correcting the obstinacy and rudeness of his ward, he passively yielded to his will in all things. "I tell you, doctor, that boy is more than a match for me," he said, with a tranquillity which showed that this was the usual conclusion of all differences between them, and that if Waldemar insisted upon having his own way, the guardian was powerless as the tutor.

The young man took no further notice of either; he threw himself on the sofa entirely oblivious to the fact that his boots, which were soaked through with ditch-water, rested on the cushions. The dog, also drenched with water, followed the example of his master, and with the same unconcern made himself comfortable on the carpet.

An ominous pause followed. Herr Witold, muttering to himself, sought to re-light his pipe; Doctor Fabian had fled to a window and was contemplating the sky with an absent, restless glance which expressed more plainly than words his exceeding discomfort in the life around him. Herr Witold, finding his pipe empty, was meantime searching for his tobacco-box, which he presently found on the writing-desk under the spurs and riding-whips. While drawing the box from beneath a mass of rubbish, an unopened letter fell into his hands. He took it up, saying, "I had quite forgotten, Waldemar; here is a letter for you."

"For *me*?" asked Waldemar, indifferently, and yet with that accent of surprise which accompanies an unusual event.

"Yes; and there is a coronet on the seal, and a shield with all sorts of armorial bearings. It must be from your princess-mother. It is a long time since she has honored us with a specimen of her dainty handwriting."

Young Nordeck broke the seal and read the letter. It contained only a few lines, but his brow darkened as he read.

"Well, what is it?" asked the guardian. "Is the princess still in Paris? I did not notice the postmark."

"The Princess Zulieski is with her son at C----," returned Waldemar, who seemed to have an aversion to the names mother and brother. "They wish to see me there, and I shall ride over to-morrow."

"You will do no such thing!" said Herr Witold. "Your princely relatives have for years ignored you, and now you may ignore them. We care no more for them than they for us. You shall not go."

"Uncle Witold, I have had enough of your everlasting commands and prohibitions," cried Waldemar so savagely that his guardian stared at him in open-mouthed wonder. "Am I a schoolboy who must ask permission for every step I take? At twenty-one years of age, have I not a right to decide whether I will go and see my mother? I have already decided. I shall ride over to C---- to-morrow morning."

"Tut! tut! don't be so furious about it," said the old gentleman, more astonished than angry at this sudden outbreak of a fury he could not understand. "Go where you like for all me, but I will have nothing to do with this Polish gentry, I tell you that!"

Waldemar found refuge in an indignant silence, and ere long, taking his fowling-piece and whistling to his dog to follow him, he left the house. Herr Witold gazed after his ward, shaking his head dubiously, but all at once a new idea seemed to dawn upon him; he took up the letter Waldemar had carelessly flung upon the table, and read it through. His brow grew dark in turn, as he read, and his voice broke out into fury.

"I thought so!" he exclaimed, striking with his clenched hand upon the table, "this is just like our lady-princess. In half a dozen lines she goads the young fellow on to revolt against me; I now see what all at once made him so defiant. Doctor, just listen to this precious epistle."

"'MY SON: Years have passed since I received a word or sign of life from you,'--('As if she had given him one!' interpolated the reader.)--'I know only through strangers that you are living at Altenhof with your guardian. I am at present in C----, and it will delight me to see you there and introduce you to your brother. I do not really know'--, ('Listen, doctor, now comes the sting')--'I do not really know whether you will be allowed to make this visit, as I am told that, although you have attained your majority, you are still entirely under your guardian's control.'--('Doctor, you yourself can testify how that young scoundrel defies and overreaches us every day.')--'I do not question your willingness to come, but I doubt whether you can obtain the required permission. I have thought best to write to you, and I shall see if you possess independence enough to gratify this wish of your mother, the first she has ever expressed to you, or if you *dare* not attempt it'--('This *dare* is underlined.')--'In the former case, I expect you immediately, and close with kindest greetings from your brother and myself.

"'Your MOTHER.'"

Herr Witold was so exasperated that he flung the letter upon the floor. "This is a fine piece of strategy in the princess-mother," he said. "She knows as well as I what a self-willed fellow Waldemar is; and if she had studied him for years, she could not have approached him on a weaker side. The mere thought of compulsion enrages him. I might now move heaven and earth to keep him here, and he would go, merely to prove that he has his own way. What have you to say on the subject?"

Doctor Fabian seemed fully to understand the family relations, and to regard the approaching interview with an alarm quite equal to that of Herr Witold; but it arose from entirely different reasons. "Heaven help us!" said he, anxiously. "If Waldemar, with his uncultivated manners, goes to C---- and appears before the princess, what will she think of him?"

"She will think that he resembles his father and not her," was the emphatic answer. "And as soon as she sees Waldemar, it will become clear to her that she can make him no pliable tool for her intrigues; for I will wager my head that she has some intrigue on hand. Either the princely purse is empty--I believe it has never been any too full--or a little government conspiracy is on the tapis, and Villica, which lies close to the Polish boundary, is a very convenient place. Heaven only knows what she wants of my boy, but I will find out her plans and open his eyes in season."

"But, Herr Witold," remonstrated the doctor, "why widen this unfortunate breach in your family just now, when the mother offers her hand in reconciliation? Would it not be better to make peace at last?"

"You do not understand the situation," replied the guardian, with a bitterness very unusual to him. "No peace can be made with this woman without entire submission to her authority; and because my deceased relative would not yield up his will to hers, he had continual discord in his house. But I do not hold him guiltless; he had serious faults, and made his wife's life very wretched; but this Princess Maryna was no wife for him. Another and a different woman might perhaps have won unbounded influence over him, and have wrought a change in his whole character; but affection alone could have such power, and this woman has never cared for any one but herself. She is by nature heartless and arrogant. Well, she atoned for the supposed humiliation of her first marriage by a second union to a Polish prince, but the one supreme grievance of her life has been her expulsion from Villica, which would have been her widow's dower if Nordeck had not cut her off in his will. He left his entire fortune to Waldemar, and we have educated the lad in such a way that he will not be likely to make a fool of himself."

"We!" cried the doctor, in consternation. "Herr Witold, I have honestly tried to do my duty to my pupil, but I have not been able to effect the least improvement in his manners. If I had--" He stopped short.

"They would have been different," added Witold, laughing. "Well, you need have no twinges of conscience about that. The lad suits me perfectly just as he is now. If you prefer to have it so, say that I have educated him; I shall be delighted if he does not prove a suitable instrument for his mother's intriguing plans, and if my training and her Parisian culture are at loggerheads to-morrow, it will delight me still more. This, at least, will be a revenge for that malicious letter."

With these words, Herr Witold left the room. The doctor picked up the letter from the floor, folded it carefully, and murmured, with a deep sigh,--

"After all, it will be said that a certain Doctor Fabian educated the young heir. O, righteous heaven!"

CHAPTER III.

VILLICA.

Villica, the inheritance of Waldemar Nordeck, was situated in one of the eastern provinces of Germany, and consisted of several large estates whose central point was the old castle of Villica. The manner in which the late Nordeck had come into possession of this estate, and had finally won the hand of the Princess Maryna, affords only a new example of the spectacle so often repeated in our day,--the decline of an old, noble, and once wealthy family, and the rise of a new, plebeian element, with whose wealth comes also the power which once belonged wholly to the aristocracy.

Count Morynski and his sister had been left orphans in childhood, and had lived under the guardianship of their relatives. Maryna was educated in a convent, and before she left its walls a marriage had been arranged for her. Among noble families this is nothing unusual, and the young countess would have made no protest if the husband chosen for her had been her equal in birth, or a son of her own people. She had, however, been selected as a passive instrument for the carrying out of family plans.

In the neighborhood where the Morynski family had lived for generations, a certain Nordeck suddenly appeared. He was a German of plebeian birth, but he had amassed great wealth,--enough to acquire large landed possessions in these troublous times, when the old nobility were fugitives or impoverished in consequence of the sacrifices they had made for their country. He had purchased several incumbered estates at half their value, and had all at once become one of the richest proprietors in the country.

Although the new-comer was a man of narrow culture, rough manners, and questionable morality, his immense possessions gave him very great influence, which he used unscrupulously against the Poles and their cause. Through some secret means this wily stranger gained an insight into certain party schemes, which made him a most dangerous enemy, and his friendship must be won at any price. As the millionnaire could not be approached with a bribe, it was thought best to flatter his vanity by the proposal of a marriage alliance with some noble Polish family. Villica manor had once been in the possession of the Morynski family, and for this reason the now penniless daughter of a once wealthy house was chosen as the sacrifice. The uncouth parvenu, who needed no dowry with his bride, and who felt flattered at the proposal of an alliance with a countess, eagerly consented to the plan. And so Maryna, when she left the cloister, found a destiny arranged for her at which her whole soul rebelled.

Her first step was a decided refusal. But what availed the No of a girl of seventeen years, in a matter urged on by policy as well as necessity? When commands and threats proved useless, persuasion and flattery were tried. She was reminded of the brilliant role she could play as mistress of Villica; of the absolute sway so young, beautiful, and high-born a wife must gain over the mind of her plebeian husband. Would it not be a satisfaction to her to become mistress of the estates wrested from her ancestors; to change the dreaded enemy into a friend,--into a pliant tool of the party which was seeking the liberation of her native land? Persuasion triumphed where compulsion failed. The life of a poor, dependent relation was not at all to the taste of the young countess. She was exceedingly ambitious, and her heart knew nothing as yet of love. Nordeck seemed very much in love with her, and she had reason to believe that her power over him would be boundless. So she finally yielded, and the marriage took place. All parties were doomed to disappointment; Nordeck proved to be no such man as they had thought. Instead of yielding to the will of his young wife, he asserted his own authority, and could neither be cajoled nor intimidated. When he discovered that Maryna had designed to use his interest and his property for the benefit of her family and friends, his love was turned to hatred. The birth of an heir made no change in the situation; the breach between the husband and wife seemed rather to widen. Nordeck's character was not one to win a wife's respect, and this wife showed her contempt in ways that would have exasperated any man. Terrible scenes followed, after one of which the young mistress of Villica left the castle and fled to the protection of her brother.

The child, Waldemar, now scarcely a year old, was left with his father. Nordeck, furious at his wife's departure, imperiously demanded her return; Bronislaw did what he could to protect his sister, and the consequences would have been serious if death had not unexpectedly dissolved this unholy marriage. Nordeck was fatally injured by a fall from his horse while hunting. But even when dying, he retained strength and presence of mind enough to dictate a will, debarring his wife from any share in his property, or any part in the education of the child. Her flight from his house gave him the right to disinherit her, and he used it pitilessly. Waldemar was placed under the guardianship of Herr Witold, his father's chosen friend and distant relative, who was given full control of the boy during his minority.

The new guardian proved his sincere friendship for his deceased relative by rigidly executing the conditions of the will, and by rejecting all the widow's claims. Witold was then proprietor of Altenhof, and not disposed to reside at Villica; he therefore took his ward to Altenhof, and from infancy to majority the young heir visited his estates but seldom, and then in his guardian's company. The immense income of Villica, of which no use could be made during the boy's minority, was added to the original inheritance, and upon becoming of age, Waldemar Nordeck found himself one of the wealthiest citizens of the country.

For a time, Nordeck's widow lived with her brother, who had meantime married; but a frequent visitor at the house, Prince Zulieski, fell passionately in love with the young, handsome, and gifted woman, and at the expiration of the conventional year of mourning they were married. This second marriage proved very happy; and yet it was truly asserted that the prince, who possessed a chivalrous but not energetic nature, was entirely under his wife's control, his all-absorbing love for his wife and son making even submission a delight.

The happiness of this union was not to remain long unclouded; but the storm that now threatened came from without. Leo was an infant at the outbreak of that great revolution which ere long overspread half of Europe. In this Polish province, insurrection, so often quelled, broke out with renewed fury. Zulieski and Morynski were true sons of Poland; they flung themselves ardently into the strife for the independence of their country. This revolt, like so many previous ones, was forcibly suppressed, and the Polish provinces were treated with especial severity. Prince Zulieski and his brother-in-law fled to France, where they were soon joined by their wives and children. The Countess Morynski, a delicate, sickly woman, did not long endure the sojourn in a foreign land. She died at the expiration of a year, and Count Morynski placed his young daughter in his sister's care.

He could not remain in Paris, where everything reminded him of the loss of his idolized wife. He wandered to and fro, without any fixed abode, coming only at long intervals to see his daughter. Finally a declaration of amnesty permitted him to return home, where a large estate had fallen to him by the death of a relative. Here he settled down permanently. Prince Zulieski, having been one of the leaders of the insurrection, and not being included in the amnesty, was obliged to remain in exile. After his death, his wife and son, who had shared his banishment to the last, returned to their native land.

CHAPTER IV.

THE MEETING.

The hour of noon had not yet struck. The Princess Zulieski sat alone in that room of her summer villa which opened upon the balcony. She held in her hand a letter received an hour previous, containing the announcement of Waldemar's immediate coming. She gazed intently at the letter, as if from its curt, chilling words, or from its handwriting, she would read the character of the son who had become so entirely estranged from her. During the time of her residence in France she had neither seen nor heard from him. She retained in memory a distinct picture of the child she had left behind her when she fled from her husband's house, and as the infant even then resembled his father, the picture was repulsive and seemed to correspond with all she had learned of the youth. Now it was for her interest to win over this unloved son, and the princess was not the woman to shrink from a difficult undertaking. She rose, and, absorbed in thought, was walking up and down the room, when she was suddenly arrested by the sound of heavy and hurried footsteps in the hall. Paul at once opened the door, and announced, "Herr Waldemar Nordeck." The young man entered, the door closed behind him, and the mother and son stood face to face.

Waldemar advanced a few steps and then paused suddenly. The princess sought to approach him, but she felt all at once like one paralyzed. At this first moment of meeting it seemed as if a broad chasm had opened between mother and son, as if the old estrangement had widened and deepened. This moment of silence and mutual repulsion spoke more distinctly than words; it showed that no tie of affection united these two who should have been so near and yet were so far apart. The princess was first to break the spell. "I thank you for coming, my son," she said, extending her hand.

Waldemar slowly approached his mother; he held the proffered hand for an instant only, and then let it fall. There was no attempt at an embrace on either side. As the princess stood there in the sunlight, her mourning apparel falling around her like a cloud, her figure was imposingly beautiful; but although the young man gazed at her intently, her grace and majesty did not seem to make the slightest impression upon him. The mother's gaze also rested upon her son's face, but she vainly sought a single feature like her own. This son was the living image of his father--of the man she hated even in death.

"I was sure you would come," the princess said, as she sat down and motioned for Waldemar to take a place near her side. Waldemar remained standing. "Will you take a seat?" she asked, and the question reminded the young man that he could not conveniently stand during his whole visit. He drew up a chair and sat down opposite his mother, the place at her side remaining vacant.

The mother could not misunderstand this action. She set her lips firmly together, but her face betrayed no emotion. Waldemar wore, as usual, a sort of hunting costume, which, although it bore no marks of the chase, was ill-fitting and negligent, and differed widely from an elegant riding-suit. He wore no gloves, and in his left hand he held a round hat and a riding-whip. His boots were dusty, and his manner of seating himself betrayed entire ignorance of the etiquette of the *salon*. His mother saw all this at a glance, and she also marked the defiance in his compressed lips and his blue eyes. She felt that her task would be no easy one.

"We have become estranged from each other, Waldemar," she began; "and at this first meeting I cannot ask a son's embrace from you. I was forced to commit you in your childhood to the care of strangers; I have never been allowed to fulfil a mother's duties to you, nor to exercise her rights."

The angry expression which accompanied these words enraged Waldemar. "I allow no reproaches to be cast upon my Uncle Witold," he cried, furiously; "he has been a second father to me, and if you have summoned me here to listen to attacks upon him, I will leave at once. You and I can never be more than strangers."

The princess saw her error in thus giving way to animosity against the hated guardian, but it was too late to repair it. Waldemar would in all probability go away in a rage, and yet everything depended upon his remaining. At this critical juncture, help came from an unexpected source. A side door opened, and Wanda entered the room. She had just returned from a walk with her father, and knew nothing of the young man's visit.

Waldemar, who had already risen to go, stopped suddenly as if rooted to the spot. His face flushed so deeply that its intense glow seemed kindled by some inward flame; all its anger and defiance vanished, and he stood there willess and motionless, his eyes fixed intently upon the beautiful young girl. Wanda had been on the point of leaving the room when she perceived that her aunt had a visitor, but as this stranger's glance met hers, she uttered a half audible exclamation of surprise. She did not lose her self-control, however, and was not in the least embarrassed. On the contrary, she was seized with an uncontrollable desire to laugh. It was too late to retire, so she closed the door behind her and took her station near her aunt.

"My son, Waldemar Nordeck. My niece, Countess Morynski," said the princess, looking with a puzzled expression from one to the other. Wanda had quickly overcome her childish excitement, and recalled the fact that she was a young lady and must maintain the dignity of that position. Her graceful bow was in strict accordance with society etiquette, but a tell-tale smile lurked around her mouth when Waldemar acknowledged the introduction with a movement evidently intended for a bow, but which was only a jerk and a grimace.

"You seem to have already met your cousin," said the mother in an inquiring tone. Reference to the cousinly relation disconcerted the young man still more.

"I do not know," he replied, with the greatest embarrassment. "In fact, I have--a few days ago--"

"This young gentleman was so kind as to be my guide when I lost my way in the forest," said Wanda, coming to the rescue. "It was day before yesterday, on our way to the beech-holm."

The princess had considered this solitary walk through the forest a most improper proceeding; but now she had not a word of censure. She answered, very graciously,--

"It was indeed a singular meeting. But why are you both so formal? Among relatives this is quite unnecessary. Give your cousin your hand, Wanda."

The young girl extended her right hand without the least embarrassment. Her cousin Leo was gallant enough to kiss this hand when given in reconciliation after a dispute; the elder brother possessed no such gallantry. He took the delicate lingers timidly and hesitatingly as if scarce daring to touch them; then he all at once pressed them so tightly that the young lady could scarce repress a cry of pain. This new cousin was quite as much a stranger to her as to his half-brother Leo, and they had looked forward with equal curiosity to the expected visit. It was evident that Waldemar's manners and appearance surprised her greatly.

"And so you met in the woods?" resumed the princess. "Was no name mentioned by either that would have made you known to each other?"

"Unfortunately I took Herr Nordeck for a satyr," said Wanda, heedless of her aunt's warning glance; "and he did his utmost to confirm me in this belief. Dear aunt, you haven't the least idea how interesting our conversation was! During our half-hour's companionship he did not make it clear to me whether he belonged to the human race of our own day, or to the old-world prodigies of myth and fable. You must see that, under the circumstances, a formal introduction was unnecessary."

Her words had an unmistakably mocking tone, but Waldemar, who had just shown himself so excitable, did not take the least offence. His eyes rested intently on the young girl, whose satire he scarcely seemed to hear.

The princess considered it necessary to put a stop to Wanda's jests ere they ended in downright impertinence. She turned to her son with the most stately composure, and said, "Waldemar, you have seen neither your brother nor your uncle. I will take you to them. You will, of course, pass the day with us?"

"If you desire it," replied Waldemar, hesitatingly. The former defiance had vanished; he evidently had not the least idea of going.

"Most certainly I desire it. Remember this is your first visit, and it must not be broken off abruptly. Come, Wanda."

Young Nordeck still hesitated; but when Wanda seconded her aunt's request, he had no difficulty in deciding. He laid the hat and whip he had until now persistently held in his hand upon the chair which in the irritated mood of a few minutes before he had thrust from him, and passively followed the ladies. A scarcely perceptible, but still a triumphant smile played around the lips of the princess. She was too good an observer not to know that she already had the game in her own hands.

CHAPTER V.

THE BROTHERS' FIRST MEETING.

Count Morynski and Leo were in the sitting-room of the princess. They had been informed of Waldemar's arrival, but did not wish to intrude upon this first meeting between mother and son. The count appeared somewhat surprised at seeing Wanda enter with both, but refrained from questioning his daughter. Young Nordeck for the moment riveted his whole attention.

The princess took the hand of her younger son and led him to the elder. "You two have never met before," she said, "but from this day I hope that the estrangement may end. Leo meets you in warm brotherly love, Waldemar, and I believe he will find a brother in you."

Waldemar measured his brother with a hasty glance, but it had no hostility. The beauty of the young prince fascinated him, and he cordially grasped the hand Leo extended, with a half bashful reserve. Count Morynski now approached to greet his sister's son, but Waldemar answered all his questions in monosyllables. The conversation which, out of regard to Waldemar, was in German, would have been forced and insipid if the princess had not skilfully led it. She avoided every unpleasant topic and every offensive allusion. So admirable was her tact that for half an hour there seemed to exist the most perfect harmony between all present. Leo stood close to Waldemar, and the contrast between the two brothers was very striking. The young prince, also, had just outgrown his boyhood, and had not yet arrived at manhood; but how different was the transition state in the two brothers! The elder never appeared to greater disadvantage than when near this slender, elastic, youthful figure, with perfect symmetry in every outline, and easy assurance in every posture and movement, with the handsome head so well poised upon the graceful shoulders. Young Nordeck, with his sharp, irregular features, with his sullen eyes peering forth from under the mass of blonde hair that fell low over his forehead, justified his mother's feeling as her glance rested upon both,--upon her idol, her handsome, spirited boy, and upon that other one, who was also her son, but to whom she was united neither by similarity of feature nor by one emotion of the heart. Waldemar to-day appeared more repulsive than usual. His rude, imperious nature ordinarily corresponded with his outward appearance, and was at least characteristic; but now for the first time in his life he was timid and embarrassed, for the first time he felt himself among people superior to him in all respects. It was the presence of Wanda, more than all the others, which gave him this timidity and self-distrust. He had come prepared for a hostile encounter, but he now helplessly gave up the contest. Count Morynski's questioning glance every now and then seemed to ask if this blushing, embarrassed youth was really the Waldemar Nordeck of whose rude, ungovernable disposition he had heard so much.

When Paul came to announce dinner, the princess said, as she rose and took her brother's arm, "Leo, you will allow your brother to be Wanda's escort."

"Well, how do matters stand?" asked the count in Polish, as they passed on in advance to the dining-room.

The princess smiled significantly, then she glanced back at Waldemar who was timidly approaching Wanda, and replied in Polish, "Do not fear; he can be led, you may be sure of that."

Young Nordeck returned to Altenhof at nightfall. Leo accompanied him to the porter's gate, and then returned to the drawing-room. The princess and her brother were no longer there. Wanda stood alone on the balcony to see her cousin ride away.

"Good heavens, what a monster this Waldemar is!" she exclaimed. "How was it possible, Leo, for you to keep a sober face the whole time? See here! I have torn my handkerchief in pieces trying to keep from laughing, but now I can control myself no longer; if I do I shall suffocate!" And throwing herself upon a chair, Wanda indulged in peal after peal of merry laughter.

"We were prepared for Waldemar's peculiarities," said Leo, coming to the defence of his brother. "After all I had heard, I was certainly most agreeably disappointed in him."

"O, you have only seen him in his parlor guise," returned Wanda. "Supposing you had, like me, met this savage in his primitive forest: I tremble at the very thought of that meeting."

"But you haven't told me about it yet," Leo replied, excitedly. "It was Waldemar, then, who guided you to the beech-holm day before yesterday; at least, I infer this from your words. But why need you make such a secret of the affair?"

"Just to tease you. You were so irritated when I spoke of that delightful meeting with a stranger, supposing, of course, that my escort was some chivalrous gentleman, that I just let you go on thinking so. Now, Leo," she added, almost convulsed with laughter, "you see there was no danger of a love-affair."

"Yes, I see," replied Leo, laughing. "But Waldemar seems to have been gentleman enough to act as your guide."

"O, yes; and I shall always be grateful to him. I all at once lost the path--a path that I had often travelled and thought I knew perfectly. At every attempt to regain it I went deeper into the forest, and finally found myself in a spot entirely new to me. I did not even know the direction of the sea, for there was no breeze, and I could not hear the roar of the waves. I stood there perfectly helpless and irresolute, when all at once I heard a loud crashing in the bushes as if a whole hunting party were driving through. Suddenly a figure stood before me which I could take for nothing but a satyr. It seemed to have risen from the swamp, for it was covered with mud to the knees. A young deer just slain dangled from its shoulders, and the warm blood was trickling down over the clothes of this grotesque being. A sort of huge, tawny lion's mane,--I could scarce call it hair,--torn by the bushes, hung down over the satyr's face. Thus the apparition stood before me, rifle in hand, and a snarling hunting-hound at its heels. Could I possibly regard this sylvan monster as a man and a hunter?"

"No doubt you were terribly frightened," said Leo, teasingly.

Wanda lifted her head in scorn. "Frightened, *I*? You know I am not cowardly. Any other girl would no doubt have run away; but I held my ground, and inquired the direction to the beech-holm. I repeated the question, but received no answer. Instead of answering me, the monster stood there as if petrified, and stared at me with his great, wild eyes, not uttering a single word. I began to feel uncomfortable, and turned to go; but he came up to me in two strides, pointed to the right, and showed an unequivocal intention of guiding me."

"But it was not all in pantomime?" asked Leo. "He must have spoken to you."

"Yes, he spoke; that is, along the whole distance he honored me with a dozen words, but no more. When we started, I heard him say, 'We must go to the right;' when we had reached our goal, he added, 'There is the beech-holm.' We were a whole half-hour on the way, and these are the only words he spoke. And what a walk it was! My amiable guide went ahead through the thicket, breaking and treading down all the bushes like a bear. I really believe he laid waste half the forest making a path for me. We then came to a clearing, and pretty soon to a piece of marshy ground. Without a single word, my companion took me up under one arm as if I had been a feather's weight, and carried me safely over. I really began to be afraid, and when I glanced up in the face bending over me, I felt more uncomfortable than ever. The look in those eyes startled me. I made up my mind that this strange apparition had just risen from some giant's grave, and was going to carry off the first human being he met, to offer up upon some old heathen altar as a sacrifice to the pagan gods. Just as I had given up all for lost, I caught a glimpse of the blue sea shimmering through the trees, and recognized the vicinity of the beech-holm. My cavalier paused, stared at me with open eyes and mouth, as if ready to devour me on the spot, and turning a deaf ear to my trembling words of gratitude, incontinently vanished among the trees. The next minute I was on the strand, where I found you and your boat awaiting me. Imagine my surprise, on returning home to-day, to find my satyr, my giant-spectre,--whom I had supposed back again in his old resting-place, the bowels of the earth,--in my aunt's reception-room, and my utter astonishment in having this monster introduced to me as my cousin Waldemar! He was really upon his good behavior to-day; he even escorted me to dinner. But, good heavens, how embarrassed he was! This must have been the first time he had ever offered a lady his arm. Did you notice how he bowed, and how awkward he was at table? Don't be offended, Leo; this new brother of yours is a true son of the wilderness; he cannot appear among civilized people without convulsing everybody with laughter. And this is the future master of Villica!"

Leo shared Wanda's opinion, but he felt in duty bound to take his brother's part. Fully conscious of his own superiority in manners and appearance, he could afford to be magnanimous. "It is not Waldemar's fault that his education has been so entirely neglected," he said; "mamma thinks that his guardian has let him run wild on purpose."

"That does not matter,--he is a monster. If such an escort to dinner is again given me, I shall decline to appear at table."

As they talked, Wanda's handkerchief had fallen, and lay under the ivy branches encircling the balcony. Leo politely stooped to pick it up; in order to reach it he had to kneel upon the floor, and in this posture he returned the handkerchief to his cousin, who, instead of thanking him, began to laugh anew.

"Why do you laugh?" cried the young prince, hastily springing to his feet.

"O, not at you, Leo,--not at all. I was only thinking how comical your brother would appear in such a position."

"But you will scarcely have the pleasure of seeing him in it. Waldemar will certainly never bend the knee to any lady, and least of all to you."

"Least of all to *me*!" repeated Wanda, in an offended tone. "Ah, yes! you think me such a child that no man would think of falling on his knees to me. I have a great mind to prove the contrary to you."

"How--by making Waldemar kneel to you?" The young girl gave him a defiant glance. "And supposing I really try to bring him to that pass?"

"Try your power over my brother as you like," said Leo, pettishly; "you may learn to duly estimate its extent."

Wanda sprang up with the eagerness of a child delighted with a new plaything.

"It is a bargain," she said; "what shall the wager be?"

"But it must be a genuine falling upon the knees, not a mere act of politeness, like that which just now brought me to your feet."

"Of course. You keep laughing. Do you consider such a thing impossible? I shall win the wager. You will see Waldemar on his knees to me before we leave this place. I make only one condition: you are to give him no hint of this transaction. His bearish nature would be aroused if he should learn that we had presumed to make his formidable self the object of a wager."

"You may rely upon my silence," Leo answered, beginning to enter into the joke, and to share Wanda's confidence in its success. "But he will be furious if you finally reject him and the truth dawns upon him. Or do you intend to say Yes?"

And so these two children of sixteen and eighteen years laughed and jested over the idea of the fine joke they were about to play upon Waldemar. Presumptuous, thoughtless children! They were so accustomed to each other's jests that they felt no compunction at drawing a third party into their sport. They did not at all consider how little the rough, intense nature of Waldemar was adapted to such foolery, and into what terrible earnest he might turn this joke, concocted in their mischievous and frivolous young heads.

CHAPTER VI.

A TRANSFORMATION.

Weeks had passed; the summer was drawing to a close, and the harvest at Altenhof was unusually abundant. Herr Witold, who had been out in the fields the whole forenoon overseeing his workmen, had returned to the house faint and weary, intending to take a much-needed and well-earned rest. While making the needful preparations, his glance fell upon his foster-son, who stood at the window in riding-costume, awaiting the appearance of his horse.

"Are you really going to C---- in the heat of the day?" he asked, in mingled surprise and anger. "You will get sun-struck in that two hours' ride over a shadeless road. You seem unable to exist without visiting your mother at least three or four times a week."

The young man frowned. "I cannot go contrary to my mother's wishes when she asks to see me," he said. "Since we are so near, she has a right to demand frequent visits from me."

"Well, she is making good use of her authority. Still, I should like to know how she has managed to make an obedient son of you. I have been trying it in vain for nearly twenty years; she succeeded in a single day. But she always did understand governing pretty thoroughly."

"Uncle Witold, you know better than any one else that I allow no one to rule me," Waldemar replied, angrily. "My mother has met me with overtures of reconciliation which I can not and will not reject, as you have done ever since I was under your guardianship."

"No doubt they frequently tell you over there that you have attained your majority. You emphasize this fact a great deal of late; but there is no need of it, my boy. You have always had your own way, and often sorely against my will. Your becoming of age is a mere matter of form, so far as I am concerned, but it is a thing of more consequence to your princess-mother. She knows perfectly well what she is about, and this is why she is constantly reminding you that you are your own master."

"Why these everlasting suspicions? Shall I give up all intercourse with my relatives simply because you do not like them?"

"I wish you could put the affection of your clear relatives to the test," rejoined Witold. "They would not make such an ado over you if you were not master of Villica. Now don't fly into a passion! We have disputed so much of late about this matter, that I won't have my noon nap disturbed by it to-day. Your precious relatives will soon leave C----, and then we shall be rid of the whole pack."

Waldemar deigned no reply. He paced up and down the room impatiently. "I'd like to know what they're about there in the stable," he muttered, impatiently. "I gave orders to have Norman saddled, but the groom must have gone to sleep."

"You seem in a prodigious hurry to get away," said Herr Witold. "I actually believe they give you some magic potion over in C----, so that you find peace nowhere else. You are always impatient now when out of the saddle."

Waldemar's only reply was to whistle softly and beat the air with his riding-whip.

"Will the princess return to Paris?" Witold asked, abruptly.

"I do not know; it has not been settled where Leo will finish his studies. My mother will accompany him wherever he goes."

"I wish he would study in Constantinople, and that his princess-mother would go with him to Turkey; then they would be out of the way,--for a time, at least. This young Zulieski must be a prodigy of learning; you are always harping upon his acquirements."

"Leo has learned far more than I, and yet he is nearly four years younger."

"His mother, no doubt, has kept him constantly at his books; but he probably has had but one tutor, while six have run away from you, and the seventh is tempted to remain only for reasons connected with his own scientific researches."

"And why have *I* not been kept at my books?" asked young Nordeck, excitedly and reproachfully.

"I really believe the boy blames me because I have let him have his own way in everything!" exclaimed Witold, in an injured tone.

"O, no. You meant well, uncle, but you don't know how I feel at seeing Leo ahead of me in all his studies, especially when I hear them all speaking of his need of further culture, and I standing there so uncultivated, so-- But, never mind, I may as well tell you at once: I am going to the university."

Herr Witold was so astonished that he let the sofa-cushion he was in the act of arranging, fall to the floor.

"To the *university*?" he repeated.

"Certainly. Doctor Fabian has for months been urging it."

"And for months you have refused."

"I have entirely changed my mind. Leo is going next year; and if he is ready to enter at nineteen, it is high time I were there. I must not remain the inferior of my younger brother. I shall consult Doctor Fabian to-morrow. Now I will go to the stable myself and see that Norman is saddled. I am all out of patience at waiting so long."

With these words he took his hat from the table and rushed out of doors. Herr Witold sat motionless on the sofa, quite forgetting to arrange the cushions for his afternoon siesta. He was too much surprised and excited for repose.

"Doctor, what has happened to the lad? What have you done to my boy?" he angrily cried out to the inoffensive doctor, who was just entering the room.

"I?" echoed the poor doctor, in alarm; "nothing, Herr Witold. Waldemar has just gone out from your presence."

"I do not mean to reproach you," returned Herr Witold, peevishly; "it is those Zulieskis and Morynskis. Since they have had him in hand he has become a changed being, I can do nothing with him. Only think, he wants to go to the university!"

"Ah, indeed!" returned the doctor, with a smile of satisfaction.

The guardian became still more exasperated at the tutor's evident delight. "O, you seem in ecstasies," he said; "you desire nothing more than to get away from here with your pupil, and leave me without a living soul to keep me company."

"You well know that I have always advised a university course for your ward. Unfortunately, I have never been listened to, and if the princess Zulieski has persuaded Waldemar to take this step, I can only consider her influence a salutary one."

"Go to the devil with your salutary influences!" cried the old man, hurling the unoffending sofa-cushion into the middle of the room. "We shall soon see what lies concealed under all this. Something has happened to the lad: he wanders about in broad daylight as if dreaming; he takes no interest in anything around him, and when questioned, gives the most preposterous answers. He returns empty-handed from the chase--he who never missed his aim; and all at once a dogged resolution enters his head to go to the university! I must find out the cause of this transformation, and you, doctor, shall help me. You must accompany him to C----."

"For heaven's sake, don't think of such a thing!" cried Doctor Fabian. "No, and a thousand times no! What should I do there?"

"Keep your eyes open. Something is going on over there, I have no doubt of that. I cannot go myself, for I stand on a war-footing with the princess, and there is always a pitched battle when we meet. I cannot endure her patronizing ways, and she is horrified at my rudeness. But you, doctor, stand on neutral ground; you are just the man."

The doctor still protested. "I am not at all qualified for such a mission," he said; "you know my timidity and helplessness in the presence of strangers, and particularly of ladies. And, besides, Waldemar will never consent to my accompanying him."

"Your protests are of no avail," interrupted Herr Witold, in a dictatorial tone. "You must go to C----, Doctor Fabian; you are the only person in whom I can place confidence. You will not fail me when I most need you." And he stormed the citadel of the doctor's never stubborn will with such an avalanche of entreaties, reproaches, and arguments, that the poor man, half bewildered, yielded, promising to do all that was required of him.

A sound of horse's hoofs was heard outside. Waldemar gave the rein to his fleet Norman, and without even a glance at the window where his guardian sat watching him, galloped away.

"There he goes!" said Witold, half angrily, half admiringly, as his adopted son swept past. "That boy sits his horse as if he and his horse were cast in bronze. And it is no slight matter to manage Norman."

"Waldemar has a peculiar passion for riding wild, young horses," observed the doctor, with a touch of anxiety. "I do not understand why. Norman should be his favorite; he is the most unmanageable beast in the whole stable."

"That is the very reason," said the guardian, laughing. "If the young fellow does not have something to subdue and to break, he cannot be happy. But come now, doctor, we will talk over your mission. You must begin the affair diplomatically."

So saying, he grasped the doctor's arm, and almost forced him to take a seat near him on the sofa. The poor tutor could do nothing but submit patiently; he had all his life yielded to the will of others, and now his only protest was to murmur sadly, yet scarce audibly,--

"*I* a diplomatist, Herr Witold? God help me!"

CHAPTER VII.

STRATEGY AND JEALOUSY.

The princess and her family mingled but very little in the society of C----, and of late they had lived even more retired than usual. Waldemar always found the family alone when he made his visits, which had become very frequent. Count Morynski, after a few days' sojourn, had departed for his estates. It had been his intention to take his daughter along with him, but the princess considered a prolonged stay necessary to Wanda's health, and she knew how to win her brother's consent, which was somewhat reluctantly granted.

In spite of the excessive noonday heat, young Nordeck had ridden in exceeding haste. Upon entering his mother's presence, he found her seated at her writing-desk. If Leo had appeared in such a heated condition, she certainly would have had a word of solicitude or of admonition for him; but Waldemar's appearance, if noticed, called forth no comment. Although this mother and son met very frequently, not the slightest confidence or intimacy had sprung up between them. The princess treated Waldemar with the greatest respect, and he endeavored to restrain his rough impulses in her presence; but there was not the least affection in this mutual effort to maintain a good understanding. They could not cross the invisible chasm that still yawned between them, although an unusual influence had bridged it over for the present. They greeted each other coldly as at their first meeting, but Waldemar's eyes wandered restlessly and inquiringly about the room.

"Are you looking for Leo and Wanda?" asked the princess. "They have gone to the beach, and will meet you there. You have doubtless arranged a sail?"

"Yes; and I will join them at once," said Waldemar, moving hastily toward the door, but his mother laid her hand upon his arm.

"Before you go, I would like to speak with you a few moments. I have something of importance to say to you."

"Will it not answer just as well after our return?" asked Waldemar, impatiently.

"I desire to speak with you alone," the princess replied. "You will still be in time for the sail; it can be postponed for a quarter of an hour."

Young Nordeck showed great annoyance at this request, and accepted his mother's invitation to be seated with evident reluctance. It was impossible to fix his attention, for his eyes constantly turned to the window near which he sat, and which commanded a view of the sea-shore.

"Our sojourn in C---- is drawing to a close," the princess began; "we must soon think of departure."

Waldemar seemed unpleasantly surprised. "So soon?" he said. "September promises to be fine; why not pass it here?"

"I must leave on Wanda's account. I cannot ask my brother to remain much longer separated from his darling. He consented to leave her with me for a short time after his own departure only on condition of my taking her home in person, and the time allotted for her stay is nearly expired."

"His estate lies quite near Villica--does it not?" asked Waldemar, eagerly.

"It is only an hour's drive from there; about half as far as Altenhof is from here."

The young man's face lighted up for a moment; then he gazed uneasily out of the window,--the strand had powerful attractions for him to-day.

"Since we happen to be speaking of Villica," the princess said, with seeming indifference, "may I ask when you think of going there? As you have reached your majority, you will, no doubt, soon assume the management of your estates."

"Arrangements had been made for me to go next spring," Waldemar replied, absently, and still gazing out of the window. "I intended to remain one more winter with my uncle, but that will be impossible, as I am to enter the university."

The mother nodded approvingly. "This is a resolve which has my entire approval," she said. "I have never denied that I consider the education you have received from your guardian far too practical and one-sided. A position like yours demands more thorough culture."

"But I should like to see Villica once more," said Waldemar. "I have not been there since my childhood, and--and you doubtless will remain for some time?"

"I do not know. For the present I certainly shall accept the asylum my brother offers me and my son. It remains to be seen if we are to rely permanently upon his generosity."

Young Nordeck started in amazement. "Asylum--generosity; what does this mean, mother?"

The mother's lips quivered nervously--and this was the sole indication she gave of the inward struggle the step she was taking cost her; otherwise she appeared perfectly unmoved, as she answered,--

"Hitherto I have concealed our family affairs from the world, and I shall continue to do so. I will, however, make no secret of them to you. Yes, I am compelled to seek an asylum with my brother. You are familiar with the public events that occurred during my second marriage. I stood by my husband's side when the storms of the revolution broke around him. I followed him into banishment, and shared with him nearly ten years of exile. Our property was sacrificed to our country's cause; these last years have proved the utter inadequacy of our present means to the requirements of our position. An investigation into our affairs soon after my husband's death showed me that I must abandon the struggle,--our resources are at an end."

Waldemar attempted to speak, but was interrupted by his mother.

"You know what it costs me to make these disclosures, and that I never would have done so if I had been the only one concerned; but as a mother I have to maintain the interests of my son, and here every other consideration sinks into insignificance. Leo is now at the threshold of active life. I care little for the deprivations of poverty, but I greatly fear its humiliations for him; I know that he cannot bear them. Fortune has favored you with wealth, of which hereafter you have full control. Waldemar, I commit your brother's future to your magnanimity."

-To any other woman it would have been a terrible humiliation to plead for help from the son of the man she had deserted with hatred and contempt, but this woman bore the humiliation in a manner that robbed it of all abasement, and which did not in the least compromise her pride. Her attitude was not that of a suppliant; she did not appeal to a filial affection which she knew had no existence. The mother and her rights made no assertion; she appealed to the elder brother's sense of justice in asking him to assist the younger, and the result proved her perfect understanding of Waldemar.

"And do you tell me this for the first time to-day!" he exclaimed, impetuously. "Why did I not know it before?"

The princess met her son's gaze firmly. "What would you have answered me if I had made this disclosure at our first meeting?" she asked, half reproachfully.

Waldemar cast down his eyes. He well recalled the offensive manner in which he had then asked his mother what she wanted of him. "You misunderstood me," he said. "I would never permit you and Leo to seek assistance from any one but me. Could I, the master of Villica, allow my mother and brother to live upon the charity of others? You judge me wrongly, mother; indeed, I have not merited such distrust."

"I did not blame you, my son; I blamed only the influences which had hitherto surrounded you, and which may still in a measure control you. I do not even know whether you will be *allowed* to offer us an asylum."

This was the dart which never failed to take effect, and which the princess always launched at the proper moment.

"I believe I have already proved to you that I know how to assert my independence," cried Waldemar, defiantly. "Now tell me what I am to do; I am ready for anything."

The princess knew that she was running a great risk; still she went firmly and deliberately to her goal. "There is only one form in which we can accept your aid that would be no humiliation to us: you are master of Villica; would it not be a very natural thing for you to receive your mother and brother there as guests?"

Waldemar was startled; at mention of Villica, the old suspicion and animosity broke out afresh. All the warnings of his foster-father as to his mother's plans recurred to him. The princess saw the impending danger, and knew how to ward it off.

"I only desire to reside there in order to be near my brother," she said, "and to still supply in some measure a mother's place to Wanda."

This decided all. The young man replied with beaming eyes and glowing cheeks, "Arrange matters to suit yourself, and I shall be satisfied. I shall not go to Villica to remain long, but I will accompany you thither, and every year I shall pass my vacations with you."

The princess extended her hand. "I thank you, Waldemar, in Leo's name and my own," she said.

There was no warmth, either in the proffered thanks or in Waldemar's answer: "No thanks, mother, I implore; none are needed. The matter is settled. Can I now go to the beach?"

He seemed anxious to avoid further conversation, and his mother did not attempt to detain him. She well knew to whom she owed this victory. She stood at the window and gazed after the young man hurrying through the garden and to the strand. She then resumed her seat at the escritoire, to finish a letter she had begun to her brother.

The letter was finished, and the princess was about to seal it, when Leo entered the room. He appeared flushed and excited, and approached his mother with frowning brow and compressed lips.

"What is the matter, Leo?" she asked, in astonishment. "Why do you come alone? Has Waldemar not joined you and Wanda?"

"O, yes; he came half an hour ago."

"And where is he now?"

"He is taking a sail with Wanda."

"Alone?"

"Yes; entirely alone."

"You know that I trust Wanda alone with no one but you, who have grown up with her as her brother. The sail was arranged for all three; why did you not remain?"

"Because I will not play the rôle of a superfluous third person; because I take no pleasure in seeing Waldemar all the time gazing at Wanda as if she were the only being on earth."

"I have told you my opinion of this petty jealousy," said the princess as she sealed her letter.

"Mamma," cried Leo, with flaming eyes, "do you not, or will you not see that Waldemar loves your niece--that he adores her?"

"And what is that to you, even if it were true? But you only imagine it. Would you have me treat these boyish fancies seriously? You and Waldemar are just at that age when you must have some ideal, and thus far Wanda is the only young girl you have known intimately. She fortunately is enough a child to treat your apparent infatuation as a jest; if this were not so, I should not allow you to be together. If she should ever become in earnest, I should feel in duty bound to interfere, and prescribe limits to your intercourse. But this will never occur. Wanda is only trifling with both of you; so dream about her as much as you like. As to your brother, this practice in gallantry cannot harm him. Unfortunately, he needs it only too much."

The smile that accompanied these words, and also his mother's allusion to his sentiment for Wanda as a boyish passion, offended him. "I wish you would talk to Waldemar about his 'boyish fancies'; he would not bear it as calmly as I do," said Leo.

"I would as soon tell him as you that I consider this infatuation a mere juvenile folly; if you or Waldemar, four or five years hence, tell me of your love for Wanda, I will pay due respect to your feelings; but for the present you may both play the cavalier to your cousin, and no disputes need arise between you."

"I have just had a dispute with Waldemar, and given up the sail of my own accord. I will not allow him to monopolize Wanda's company and conversation, and I will not any longer put up with his domineering manner; I shall let him understand that."

"You will do no such thing," returned the mother. "A good understanding between you is more needful than ever, for we shall accompany Waldemar to Villica."

"To Villica! And must I be his guest there, his subordinate? Never! no, never! I will be under no obligations to him; even though my whole future is at stake, I will accept nothing from his hands."

The princess remained calm, but her voice was proud and stern, as she said, "Even if you are foolish enough to imperil your whole future for a mere whim, I am at your side, and I shall not permit it. You know that I shall never ask anything humiliating of you, but I am not at all inclined to allow my plans to be frustrated by your jealousy. I am accustomed to have my wishes treated with respect. Other considerations higher than merely personal ones, urge me to make Villica my home. We are going there, and you will treat your brother with the same respect I show him. I demand obedience from you, Leo."

Leo understood this tone, and knew that when his mother assumed it, she would carry out her plans at any sacrifice; but an influence mightier than he had ever known before spurred him on to resistance. He ventured no reply, but rebellion was written in his face.

"I shall take care that no such disputes arise between you and your brother in the future," said the princess. "We leave within a week, and when Wanda is at her father's house, you will see her less frequently. To-day's solitary sail with Waldemar will be her last."

She rang the bell for Paul, and sent him to post her letter. It announced to Count Morynski the speedy return of Wanda under the Princess Zulieski's protection, and also informed him that the princess and her son would not require his kindly proffered hospitality; that the former mistress of Villica would soon be reinstated in her old position.

CHAPTER VIII.

THE OLD "WONDER-CITY."

The boat which bore the two young pleasure-seekers sped along under full sail. The sea was rough; the waves broke into foam, scattering showers of spray around them; but Waldemar held the helm with a steady hand, and Wanda, who sat opposite him, evidently took delight even in the danger and discomfort of the passage.

"Leo will complain of us to his mother," she said, gazing toward the shore, which was already receding in the distance. "He was very angry when he left us; you were not courteous to him, Waldemar."

"I do not like to have another steer when I am in the boat," replied Waldemar, imperiously.

"And what if *I* wanted to steer?"

His only reply was to rise hastily, and offer the young girl the helm. She burst out laughing. "O, no, thank you. I only asked the question to see how you would answer it. I should not enjoy the sail if I had to give my whole attention to steering the boat."

Without a word Waldemar again took the rudder which had occasioned the dispute between himself and Leo, although its real cause had been a very different matter, which neither would own.

"Where shall we sail?" asked Wanda, after a brief silence.

"Shall we not go to the beech-holm, as we intended?"

"Is it not too far?"

"With this favorable breeze we shall be there in half an hour. You wanted to see the sunset from that spot."

Wanda offered no opposition, although a restless, anxious feeling came over her. Hitherto Leo had been her constant companion in all out-door excursions; to-day, for the first time, she found herself alone with another. Young as she was, her womanly penetration taught her the reason of Waldemar's timidity and embarrassment at his first visit. He was incapable of dissimulation, and although he had not betrayed himself by a single word, his eyes spoke only too plain a language; he was less demonstrative towards her than towards others, but yet she was fully conscious of her power over him and knew how to use it. She certainly, at times, misused this power, for the whole affair was only a jest to her. She was pleased with the idea of controlling this obstinate, ungovernable nature by a word or a glance. Her vanity was flattered at this mute and strange yet passionate adoration, and it amused her prodigiously to see Leo so jealous of Waldemar. She did not intend to give the preference to the elder brother; his exterior repelled her, while his uncouthness horrified and his conversation bored her. Love made him no more agreeable. He never showed that gallantry and politeness of which Leo, although so young, was already master. He seemed to yield reluctantly to the spell the young girl threw around him, to resign himself to a passion from which he could not break away--a passion that had made him its unwilling slave.

The beech-holm might once have been a small island; it was now a densely wooded peninsula connected with the mainland by an isthmus, across which it could be easily reached on foot. Beautiful as it was, the place was seldom visited; it was too solitary and remote for the pleasure-seekers at C----, whose favorite excursions were to the neighboring villages lying along the coast. To-day, there was no one at the holm when the boat landed. Waldemar stepped out, and Wanda, without waiting for his help, sprang lightly upon the white sand and hurried up the hill.

The beech-holm was rightly named. Primeval beeches spread their mighty branches far and wide, casting their sombre shadows over the verdant turf and weather-beaten boulders which lay scattered here and there, marking, so tradition said, the site of an old pagan place of sacrifice. On both sides of the landing-place the trees receded, forming a sort of frame to the open sea, which a deep, blue, unmeasurable expanse stretched out into the distance. No shore, no island bounded the vision; no sail appeared on the horizon's verge; there was nothing but the sea in its vastness and beauty and grandeur; and the beech-holm lay there as lonely and forsaken as if it were a small island in mid-ocean.

Wanda removed her straw hat, whose only trimming was a simple band of black ribbon, and sat down on one of the moss-covered stones. She still wore light mourning for her aunt's husband. Her white dress was trimmed with black, and a black sash with long ends encircled her waist. This white and black apparel gave a sombreness to the young girl's appearance which did not properly belong to her. She sat there radiant in youth, health, and beauty, with beaming eyes and clasped hands, gazing out upon the water.

Waldemar, who had seated himself on the trunk of a beech, was lost in admiration of the beautiful young girl. No other object, far or near, possessed the slightest interest for him, and he started as if from a dream when Wanda jestingly asked, pointing to her seat,--

"Is this one of your old Runic stones?"

Waldemar shrugged his shoulders. "You must ask my tutor, Doctor Fabian, about that. He is more at home in the first centuries of our era than in the present. He would give you a very learned and exhaustive lecture upon ancient graves, Runic stones, and all that sort of thing; and nothing would afford him greater pleasure."

"Spare me that, for heaven's sake! But if Doctor Fabian has such an enthusiasm for past ages, I wonder he has not instilled a similar taste into you. You seem very indifferent to the past."

"What do I care for all this old-time nonsense? The fields and forests of to-day interest me only on account of the game they offer."

"How prosaic! Then here upon this beautiful beech-holm you were doubtless thinking only of the deer and rabbits possibly lurking in the thickets."

"No," replied Waldemar, emphatically, "not *here*."

"Such thoughts would be unpardonable amid this scenery," said Wanda. "Just look at that sunset illumination! The waves give forth rays just as dazzling as those of the sky above them."

Waldemar gazed indifferently. "Ah, yes!" he said; "Vineta must have sunken right there."

"What must have sunken there?" Wanda asked, eagerly.

"Have you never heard about Vineta? It is one of our sea-shore traditions. I thought everybody knew it."

"I do not; tell me all about it."

"I am a poor story-teller. Ask any old sailor along the coast to relate it to you; he can do it far better than I."

"But I will hear it from your lips; so tell it."

Waldemar's brow grew dark. The young lady was too imperious.

"You *will*!" he returned, rather sharply.

"Yes, I *will*," she repeated, with the same obstinacy as before. She evidently knew her power, and meant to use it.

The frown on the young man's brow deepened. He felt like rebelling against the spell that fettered him, but when he met the dark eyes whose glance seemed to change from command to entreaty, his defiance vanished, his brow cleared, and he smiled.

"Well, then, I must tell the story in my own abrupt, *prosaic* way," he said, emphasizing the last adjective. "According to the legend, Vineta was an old, fortified city by the sea, the metropolis of a people who ruled land and water far and near, who surpassed all the world in pomp and grandeur, and into whose lap the wealth and treasure of all lands were poured. But the inhabitants of Vineta became so haughty, so overbearing, and so wicked, that their pride and sin called down the vengeance of Heaven upon their city, and it was swallowed up by the waves. Our sailors swear that yonder, where the shore recedes, the great city rests to-day in all its olden splendor. They declare that they frequently catch glimpses of its towers and domes glistening fathoms deep below the waters; that occasionally the city in its olden magnificence rises from the sea, and that certain favored ones are allowed to behold the enchanting sight. Indeed, there are mirages enough along this coast, and we have here in the North a sort of *fata morgana* whose cause I cannot explain, although my tutor has told me all about it--"

"Never mind the explanation," interrupted Wanda. "Who cares for that, if the legend is only beautiful? And it is delightful--don't you think so?"

"Well, really, I have never given its beauty a thought," replied Waldemar.

"Have you, then, no feeling for the poetic? That is deplorable."

"Do you really think so?" he asked, in surprise.

"Indeed I do."

"No one has ever taught me to know or to appreciate what you call the poetic," the young man said, in a tone of apology. "The poetic plays no part in my uncle's house, and my tutors have given me only dry lessons in practical things. I now begin to comprehend for the first time that there is such a thing as poetry."

As Waldemar said this, his face had an unusually dreamy expression. He threw back the hair which usually hung low over his forehead, and leaned his head against the trunk of the tree. Wanda now for the first time made the discovery that a remarkably high and finely shaped forehead lay concealed under that mass of blonde hair. It was a forehead that dignified and ennobled the plain, irregular features. Over the left temple ran a peculiarly marked blue vein, clearly and sharply defined even in calm, untroubled moments. Wanda had often ridiculed that "tawny lion's mane," little dreaming of the clear, high brow that lay beneath.

"Do you know, Waldemar, that I have just made a discovery?" she said.

"Ah! what is it?" he answered, abstractedly.

"That singular blue vein on your forehead; my aunt has one just like it, only not so strongly defined."

"Indeed! Then this is the only point of resemblance between my mother and me."

"That is true; you resemble her only in this one respect; but Leo is her exact image."

"Leo!" echoed Waldemar, with a peculiar intonation. "Ah, yes! that is very natural."

"And why ought the younger brother to have the advantage of the elder?"

"Why not in all else, since he has the first place in his mother's love?"

"But, Waldemar--"

"Is this news to you?" interrupted the young man, almost sadly. "I thought my relations toward my mother were known to every one. She forces herself to treat me kindly and courteously, and effort enough it costs her. But she cannot overcome her inward aversion--neither can I; so we stand on the same footing."

Wanda made no reply. The turn the conversation had taken surprised her greatly. Waldemar did not seem to notice her astonishment; he went on in a tone of great bitterness. "The Princess Zulieski is a stranger to me and must remain so. I do not belong to her or to her son; I have no part in their life. I feel this more and more at every meeting. You have no idea, Wanda, what it costs me to cross their threshold. It is a torture I have imposed upon myself, and I would never have believed I could endure it so patiently."

"Why do you endure it? No one forces you to come," exclaimed Wanda, thoughtlessly.

He gazed at her intently, and his whole soul was in that gaze. The answer beamed so plainly from his eyes that the young girl blushed deeply. That ardent, reproachful look spoke only too plainly.

"You do my aunt injustice," she said, excitedly, trying to conceal her embarrassment. "She must surely love her own son."

"O, most assuredly!" returned Waldemar, impetuously. "I have no doubt that she loves Leo very much, although she treats him harshly; but why should she love me or I her? I was only a year old when I lost both my father and my mother. I was torn from my home to grow up in a stranger's house. When I learned to reflect and to ask questions, I was told that the marriage of my parents had been unfortunate for both, and that they had parted in bitter hatred. I have since experienced the disastrous effects of this hatred upon my own life. I was early taught that my mother was solely to blame, but I heard such hints thrown out in regard to my father's character that I could not hold him guiltless. And so I grew up to dislike and suspect my parents--

those two beings a child should hold in the highest love and reverence. I cannot now rid myself of these early impressions. My uncle--I call him uncle, although he is only a distant relative of my father--has been very good to me, but he could offer me nothing different from the life he himself led. You doubtless know what that life has been; my mother's family are all well informed on that point. And yet, knowing all this, Wanda, do you demand from me a knowledge of æsthetics and of poetry?"

These last words had a tone of indignant reproach, but beneath them lurked a melancholy regret. Wanda gazed with wide-open eyes at her companion whom she did not at all understand to-day. This was her first serious conversation with him; he had never before broken his silent reserve toward her. The peculiarly distant relations between this mother and son had not escaped her notice, but she had not believed Waldemar at all sensitive upon this point. Hitherto not a syllable on the subject had fallen from his lips, and now all at once he showed a depth of feeling which was almost passionate lamentation. At this moment, for the first time, the young girl realized how lonely, and empty, and neglected Waldemar's childhood must have been, and how forsaken and friendless was this young heir of whose wealth she had heard so much.

"You wished to see the sunset," Waldemar said, abruptly, and with an entire change of voice and manner. "I think it will be one of uncommon splendor to-night."

The layer of clouds which skirted the horizon was all aflame with warmth and glow, and the sea, flooded with light and reflecting from its clear depths all the splendor of the illuminated sky, gave back the farewell greeting of the departing day. From both sky and land streamed a flood of radiance, diffusing itself far and near. But above the spot where the wondrous city Vineta rested upon the ocean's floor, the waves burned with a scarlet glow, and rose and fell in undulations of liquid gold, while thousands of fiery sparks danced upon the waters.

There is in old traditions something that outlives superstition, and however versed we may be in modern lore, there come moments when these tales and legends loom up before our minds, and receive at least a transient recognition. The everlasting riddles of these old legends, like their eternal truths, even to-day lie deep in the human heart. True, this mysterious fairy kingdom is now accessible only to favored mortals, to poets and to those who live close to the great heart of nature; but these two on the beech-holm must have belonged to the favored ones, for they plainly felt the magical influence which gently but irresistibly drew them within its circle, and neither had heart or courage to flee from it.

Over their heads the tree-tops swayed to and fro in the wind, while the sea surged ever more loudly at their feet. Wave upon wave came rolling to the shore, each bearing a white crest upon its forehead, leaping up in its giant strength for a moment, only to be dashed in pieces on the strand. It was the grand, old melody of the ocean, a melody made up of the whistling wind and the roaring waves, that grand, eternal diapason which awes, yet enthralls the heart. It sings of dreamy, sun-kissed ocean calms, of raging storms bearing terror and destruction in their path, of restless, tumultuous billows; and from every wave comes a tone, from every breeze an accord.

Waldemar and the young girl at his side must have understood this language well, for they listened to it in breathless silence; and these were not the only strains they heard. Up from the water's depths, from the turrets of the sunken city, came a sound as of silver bells; they listened, and their hearts felt an aching and a yearning, and at last the premonition of a great and enduring happiness. From the gold and purple waves rose a gleaming apparition. It hovered over the sea, bathed in the evening sunlight; it stood in mid-air, with its roofs, and spires, and battlements lighted up by gold and opal and sapphire hues; the phantom-apparition, the theme of so many a song and story--the old "wonder-city"--VINETA!

The descending sun now touched the gleaming waters with its radiant disc, and sinking lower and lower, soon passed from sight. But the dissolving hues gathered new brightness; once again the western horizon was illuminated as by fire; then the light slowly paled, and the fairy vision vanished.

Wanda sighed half audibly, and passed her hand over her forehead. Then she said, softly, "The sun has set; it is time for us to think of returning."

"Of *returning*?" echoed Waldemar, as in a dream. "Why so soon?"

The young girl rose quickly as if to flee from some painful emotion. "We must reach home before dusk," she said, "or my aunt will never forgive me for this excursion."

"I will be responsible to my mother; still, if you wish to return immediately--"

"O, yes; please let us go!"

The young man started for the boat, and then paused suddenly:--

"Wanda, you intend to leave in a few days, do you not?"

He asked this question in a strangely excited tone, and Wanda's voice lacked its usual composure, as she replied,--

"I must go to my father, we have been so long separated."

"My mother and Leo are going to Villica--" Here Waldemar hesitated and gasped for breath. "There is some talk of my accompanying them. *May* I?"

"Why do you ask me?" replied Wanda, with an embarrassment very unusual to her. "It is for you to decide whether you will visit your estates."

The young man paid no heed to her reply. He bent over her, his voice trembled, he was deeply moved.

"But I ask *you*, Wanda, you alone. May I come to Villica?"

"*Yes*," replied Wanda, involuntarily; but she was startled when Waldemar seized her hand with a violent gesture, and held it clasped tightly as if he would never let it go. She now felt what he understood by this *yes*, and the idea terrified her. She flushed deeply like one in a burning fever. Waldemar perceived her emotion.

"Am I too violent with you?" he asked, gently. "You must not be angry with me, Wanda, at least not to-day. I could not bear the thought of your departure. But now that I am sure of seeing you again, I will wait patiently until we reach Villica."

Wanda made no reply. They walked in silence to the boat. Waldemar set the sails, and grasped the oars. A few powerful strokes sent the tiny bark far out upon the water. The waves were still tinged with roseate reflections as the boat shot over them. Neither spoke during the passage; but the sea rose and fell with a hollow murmur, while the last flush in the sky faded away, and the first evening shadows settled down upon the beech-holm, receding farther and farther into the distance. The sunset vision had ended; but the ancient legend declares that the mortal who has once seen the submerged Vineta, who has once listened to the chiming of its bells, can never more know peace until the magical city again rises to greet him, or draws him downward to its depths.

CHAPTER IX.

DOCTOR FABIAN'S DIPLOMATIC MISSION.

The diplomatic mission about to be intrusted to Doctor Fabian did not seem half so difficult to Herr Witold in its execution as in its preliminary arrangements. In order to gain reliable information of what was going on at C----, the doctor must have access to the house of the Princess Zulieski, and this could be obtained only through Waldemar. But how could the old man broach this matter to his foster-son without receiving a decided refusal? Chance came very unexpectedly to his aid. At Waldemar's last visit the princess had expressed a desire to become personally acquainted with her son's tutor. Herr Witold admitted, for the first time in his life, that the princess had expressed a very proper and reasonable wish. The doctor had indulged a secret hope that the proposed mission would be thwarted by the obstinacy of his pupil, but he found himself held inexorably to his promise, and was obliged to accompany Waldemar to C----.

Waldemar went on horseback; riding was a passion with him, and he disliked slow driving over the stony road, when he could ride at full gallop. It did not occur to him that he ought to take a seat in the carriage with his tutor; but Doctor Fabian was accustomed to such slights, and being naturally timid and yielding, he neither had the courage to resent uncourteous treatment, nor to resign his position. Besides, he possessed no fortune, and a situation was a vital question with him. Life at Altenhof did not please him, and he took little part in it: he appeared in the family circle only at meals and when he passed an occasional hour with Herr Witold. His pupil engrossed none too much of his attention; Waldemar was always glad when study hours were over, and his tutor was still more so. The rest of the time was at the tutor's disposal, and he could freely devote himself to his hobby--ancient German history. Thanks to this favorite study, Doctor Fabian had not followed the example of his six predecessors, and run away. Knowing that Altenhof offered him ample opportunities and abundant leisure for historical research, he patiently endured all the discomforts of his lot. He did not think of complaining to-day when Waldemar galloped on ahead of him, promising to await him at the entrance of the town, where he would arrive toward noon.

Upon their arrival they found Wanda alone in the drawing-room. Doctor Fabian, although very much embarrassed, went through the introduction passably well; but, unfortunately, his evident and somewhat comical anxiety to please provoked the young girl to set about teasing him at once.

"And so you are my cousin Waldemar's tutor?" she said; "I offer you my sincere condolence, and pity you with all my heart."

Fabian was alarmed and astonished. He gazed, now at the ceiling, and now at his pupil, who seemed not to have heard the mocking words, for his manner did not betray the slightest indication of anger.

"I--I do not quite understand you, countess," stammered the doctor.

"I mean that, in educating Waldemar Nordeck, you have no enviable task," replied Wanda, saucily, and evidently very much amused at the tutor's embarrassment.

Doctor Fabian, knowing the extreme sensitiveness of his pupil, gazed at him in alarm. Often enough far less offensive words from Herr Witold had roused him to fury; but now, for some unaccountable reason, there was not the slightest token of a storm. The young man leaned calmly against Wanda's chair, and even smiled as, bending over her, he asked,--

"Do you really think me so bad?"

"Of course I do. Didn't I see you in a rage day before yesterday about a rudder?"

"But I was not angry with you," said Waldemar.

The doctor dropped the hat which he had thus far held in both hands. What sort of a tone was this, and what meant the glance that accompanied it? The conversation went on in the same strain. Wanda, inclined to mischief as usual, teased Waldemar most unmercifully; but he submitted with inexhaustible patience. It seemed that nothing from this source could irritate or offend him. He smiled at all the young girl's sallies; he seemed completely transformed when in her presence.

"Doctor Fabian is listening to us with the greatest interest," she said, laughing. "He is, no doubt, delighted with our good-humor."

Poor Doctor Fabian! He was not at all delighted, he was only bewildered. Small as was his experience in love affairs, the truth, little by little, dawned upon him; he began to see what was going on. This explained Waldemar's sudden reconciliation, his eagerness to ride to C---- in sun and storm, his complete transformation. It would be a terrible blow to Herr Witold, who cherished such a deeply-rooted hatred of the whole "Polish party." The diplomatic mission was even at the outset an entire success, but its result so surprised the ambassador that he would have very likely forgotten his instructions and betrayed his amazement, if the princess had not appeared at that moment.

The princess had more than one reason for desiring a personal acquaintance with her son's tutor, who would also accompany his pupil to the university. Now that she and Waldemar had become reconciled, his immediate surroundings could not be a matter of indifference to her. A ten minutes' acquaintance with Fabian convinced her that no opposition need be feared from him; that, on the contrary, he would be a passive instrument in her hands. From this constant companion much could be learned in the future which could not be obtained from the inaccessible Waldemar. She did Fabian the honor to regard him as a suitable instrument for her plans; she lavished the most condescending attentions upon him, and the humility with which he received her condescensions pleased her greatly. She forgave his timidity and embarrassment; or rather, she thought them quite proper in her presence, and she was graciously pleased to enter into a prolonged conversation with him.

Upon his mother's entrance into the room Waldemar became reserved as usual. He took little part in the conversation, but he finally said a few words to the princess in an undertone. She rose and walked with him to the balcony.

"Do you wish to speak with me alone?" she asked.

"Only a moment. I merely wished to say that it will be impossible for me to accompany you and Leo to Villica, as we had proposed."

"Why?" asked the mother, anxiously. "Have difficulties been placed in your way?"

"Yes; there are certain formalities to be complied with on my arriving at my majority,--certain legal transactions at which I must be present. My father's will has specifications in this respect of which neither I nor my uncle Witold dreamed; and just now, when I wish to go away, the notice comes. For the present I must remain at Altenhof."

"Well, then, we too shall postpone our departure, and I must send Wanda alone to her father."

"By no means," returned Waldemar, vehemently. "I have written to Villica that you will arrive there in a few days, and have ordered the preparations necessary for your reception. I shall follow you as soon as I am at liberty to do so; in any event, I shall pass a few weeks with you before I leave for the university."

"Does your guardian know of this, Waldemar?"

"No; I have only spoken to him of my intention to visit Villica."

"Then you will have to explain our sojourn there to him?"

"I shall do so; for the rest, I have directed the superintendent of the estate to place himself at your disposal until I come myself. You have only to give your orders; they will be obeyed."

The princess would fain have expressed her thanks, but the words died on her lips. She well knew that this generosity was not for her sake, and the peculiarly cold manner in which it was tendered compelled her to accept it just as coldly, if she would not humiliate herself.

"We shall certainly expect you. As for Leo--"

"Leo is still sulking over our quarrel of day before yesterday. On my arrival, he went down to the strand to avoid meeting me."

The mother frowned. Leo had received an especial command to meet his brother kindly, and this defiance came at a most inopportune moment.

"Leo is often hasty and indiscreet; I will see that he asks your pardon."

"O, no; don't give yourself that trouble," said Waldemar, indifferently; "we will arrange matters ourselves."

They re-entered the drawing-room, where Wanda had been amusing herself by throwing Doctor Fabian from one embarrassment into another. The princess now came to his relief: she wished to speak with him privately about her son's course of study, and begged him to accompany her into the next room.

"Poor doctor," remarked Wanda, gazing after him. "It seems to me, Waldemar, that you and your tutor have changed rôles; you have not the least respect for him, but he is mortally afraid of you."

Waldemar did not contradict this assertion, which was only too true. He merely replied, "Do you consider Doctor Fabian a person calculated to inspire respect?"

"O, no, not at all; but he seems very good-tempered and forbearing."

"That maybe; but these are qualities I do not at all appreciate," replied Waldemar, contemptuously.

"Must one tyrannize over you in order to gain your respect?" asked Wanda, archly.

Waldemar drew up his chair, and sat down near her. "That depends upon who the tyrant is," he said. "I should not advise any one at Altenhof to try this game, and here I allow it to only one individual."

"*I* should not dare attempt such a thing," said Wanda, in a low tone.

He made no reply; his thoughts seemed to flow in another channel.

"Did you not think it very beautiful at the beech-holm day before yesterday?" he asked, abruptly.

The young countess blushed, but assuming a contradictory tone, she answered, "The place seemed dismal in spite of its beauty, and as for those sea legends of yours, I shall not listen to them at sunset again. Ere long I might come to believe in the old traditions."

"Yes, that is true. You reproached me for not being able to comprehend the poetry of the legend; what should *I* know about poetry?"

Wanda was silent; that strange embarrassment she every now and then felt in the presence of this young man, again came over her. She had attempted to banish it by laughing and jesting, and in the presence of others she succeeded; but as soon as they were alone, the feeling returned with new power, and she could not assume her usual unconstrained manner. That eventful sojourn at the beech-holm had given a peculiar gravity to an affair which ought to be a jest and nothing more.

Waldemar waited in vain for an answer, and felt hurt at not receiving it. "I have informed my mother that I cannot go to Villica just now," he said; "I shall come in three or four weeks."

"Well, that is a very short time," Wanda observed.

"A short time! It is an eternity! You have no idea of what it costs me to remain here and allow you to depart alone."

"Say no more, I entreat you," interrupted Wanda, with perceptible emotion. But Waldemar went on in the same impassioned strain:--

"I promised you to wait until we were in Villica, but then I hoped to accompany you. Now a month perhaps will pass ere we meet again, and I cannot remain silent all this time. I cannot endure the thought of your being with Leo so long, and not knowing that you are mine, and mine only."

The declaration came so suddenly, so impetuously, that Wanda had no time to avert it; and if time had been given her, the effort would have been fruitless. He had again seized her hand, and held it firmly as at the beech-holm.

"Do not shrink from me, Wanda; you must long have known what chains me here. I could not conceal it; you have allowed me to come; you have not repelled me, and so I have been encouraged to speak. I know that I am not like others, that I am deficient in much, perhaps in everything that would please you; but I can and will learn. It is solely for your sake that I impose upon myself these years of study at the university. What do I care for learning or for society? They have no charm for me; but because I lack these advantages, I have seen you shrink from me and make sport of me. The time will come when you cannot do this. Let me only know that you will one day be mine, that I may come back to claim you, and I will shrink from no effort that would make me worthy of you. Wanda, I have been lonely and forsaken from my infancy. If I appear, rough and uncultivated, you must remember that I have had no mother's care, no mother's love. Do not wonder that I am not like Leo, who has enjoyed all of which I have been deprived. But my nature is more intense than his; I can love more warmly and deeply than he. You are the only being I have ever loved, and a single word from you will atone for all the past. Speak this word to me, Wanda; or at least give me the hope that I may one day hear it from you. But do not say *No*, for I will not bear it."

He had literally fallen on his knees before her; but Wanda had no thought of exultation in the triumph she in her girlish arrogance had sought. A dim premonition had now and then come over her that the sport might have a more serious ending than she had anticipated, that its *finale* would not be a mere joke: but she had banished the apprehension with all the levity of her sixteen years. Now the decisive moment had come, and she must speak. She must face an ardent proposal, which inexorably demanded acceptance or refusal. True, this was no chivalrous, attractive wooing; it had nothing of that romance and tenderness a young girl craves. Even in the declaration of his love, Waldemar's rude, impetuous nature was apparent, but every word expressed violent and long pent-up emotion, and was full of the ardor of intense passion. For the first time Wanda comprehended the deep earnestness of Waldemar's love for her, and her conscience uttered this burning reproach: "What hast thou done?" Her voice trembled with anguish as she said,--

"Rise, Waldemar, I entreat you!"

"When I hear Yes from your lips, and not until then."

"I cannot answer you--not now; rise, I beg you!"

He would not listen. He still remained on his knees, when the door unexpectedly opened, and Leo entered. For a moment he stood in the middle of the room like one petrified. Then an exclamation of anger passed his lips,--

"*You have won, after all!*"

Waldemar sprang to his feet, his eyes flashing with rage.

"What do you want here?" he cried.

Leo had been white with passion, but the tone of his brother's question sent the blood mounting to his forehead. In an instant he stood before Waldemar.

"You think my presence superfluous and intrusive, and yet I could give you the best possible explanation of the scene that just met my eyes."

"Silence, Leo!" exclaimed Wanda, half entreatingly, half imperiously; but jealousy made Leo forget all discretion and forbearance.

"I will not be silent; my promise extended only to the decision of the wager, and I have now seen with my own eyes how it is decided. I have often entreated you to stop this sport. You knew that it vexed me--that it drove me to despair; and yet you pushed it to the last extremity. And shall I now humbly submit to be shown the door as an intruder by Waldemar, who exults in his supposed triumph? Shall I bear all this in silence,--I, who have heard you boast that you would bring him as suitor to your feet? You have accomplished your purpose, but he shall at least know the truth."

Waldemar, thunderstruck at that word *wager*, stood motionless, his right hand clutching the back of his chair, while his eyes were fixed upon Wanda with a bewildered, inquiring expression.

"What does this mean?" he asked, in a scarce audible voice.

Wanda hung her head in conscious guilt. Anger against Leo struggled in her breast with her own sense of shame. Leo did not reply to his brother's question; the sudden change in Waldemar's face silenced him. Moreover, he began to realize the critical position in which he had placed Wanda, and he dared not seek to rescue her.

"What does this mean?" Waldemar repeated, starting from his momentary stupor, and confronting Wanda. "Leo speaks of a wager, of a game of which I am the victim. Answer me, Wanda; I can believe you, and you only. Tell me that it is false--"

"And so you think me a liar!" broke out Leo. But his brother did not hear him. Wanda's silence told him enough; he required no further confirmation. As the truth was laid bare to him, the whole ferocity of his nature broke forth; the spell that had held him so long was broken, and passion carried him beyond all bounds.

"I *will* have an answer," he said. "Have I been a mere plaything for you, nothing but an object of ridicule? Have you been laughing at me and deriding me, while I-- Wanda, you shall answer me on the spot, or--"

He did not end the menace, but his look and tone were so threatening that Leo stepped before Wanda to protect her. She, too, stood erect and defiant; the half-uttered threat had exasperated her and restored her self-control.

"I will not be called to account in this way!" she began, excitedly; then her eye met Waldemar's, and she stopped short. Although his features were livid with rage, his eyes betrayed the unspeakable torture of the man who sees his love betrayed and mocked, and his adored idol ruthlessly torn from him. Wanda's voice seemed to have brought him back to his senses; the clenched hands relaxed, but the lips closed firmly as if no sound must escape them. The chest rose and fell in a violent struggle to repress its pent-up fury; but the effort was too great, the young man staggered and sank into a chair.

"What is the matter, Waldemar?" Leo asked, becoming alarmed, and repenting of his inconsiderate action. "If I had known that you would take the affair so seriously, I should have remained silent."

Waldemar rose with blanched face and trembling limbs, and, with a defiant gesture at his brother, turned to go without uttering a word.

At this juncture the princess appeared, accompanied by Doctor Fabian. The loud talking had penetrated her apartment, and she knew that something unusual was going on in the drawing-room. She entered softly, and remained for a moment unobserved. Wanda still stood in her place, oscillating between fear and defiance; but fear at length gained the mastery, and in the tone of an offending child begging pardon, she called the young man back.

"*Waldemar!*"

He paused. "Do you wish to speak with me, Countess Morynski?"

The young girl trembled. It was the first time such an icy, cutting, contemptuous tone had met her ear, and the deep glow that suddenly overspread her face showed how intensely she felt it. The princess now confronted her son.

"What has happened? Where are you going, Waldemar?"

"Away from *here*!" he replied, morosely, without meeting her gaze.

"But tell me the reason--"

"I can not-- Let me go. I will not remain;" and pressing past her, he hurried away.

"Explain this strange scene to me," said the princess, imperiously, turning to Wanda and Leo. "Remain, doctor," she added, as Doctor Fabian, who had stood nervously in the doorway, made a movement to follow his pupil. "In any event here is some misunderstanding, and I wish you to bear an explanation of it to my son Waldemar. I cannot do this, his abrupt departure has rendered it impossible. What has happened? I must and will know."

Wanda, instead of answering, threw herself upon the sofa, and began to sob violently; but Leo followed his mother to a remote part of the room, and told her the whole affair. At every word the lady's brow grew darker; it evidently cost her an effort to maintain her composure, but she at length turned to the doctor, and said, with apparent calmness,--

"It is just as I supposed; a misunderstanding--nothing more. A foolish wager between my niece and younger son has given Waldemar cause for offence; I beg of you to tell him that I sincerely regret this occurrence, but I hope he will attach as little importance to the folly of these presumptuous children as it deserves."

"I had perhaps best seek my pupil immediately."

"Yes, certainly," replied the lady, glad to have the innocent yet unwelcome witness of this family quarrel take his departure. "*Au revoir*, doctor. I depend upon your speedy return in Waldemar's company."

She spoke these words very graciously, and answered the tutor's farewell greeting with a smile.

But as soon as the door closed behind him, she turned to Wanda and Leo with a face and gestures that indicated, before she had spoken a word, the violent storm that was raging in her breast.

Meanwhile Doctor Fabian learned from Paul that Waldemar had ridden away. No alternative was left him but to follow immediately to Altenhof, and he started at once. Upon his arrival he learned that Waldemar had not been there, and he could not help feeling alarmed at an absence which ordinarily he would not have noticed. The conclusion of the excited scene he had witnessed allowed him to divine the truth; he felt sure that something more weighty than a mere jest or a slight misunderstanding had caused Waldemar's fit of passion and abrupt departure. The young man who had just before borne so patiently Wanda's whims and caprices, would not have allowed a slight matter to move him so deeply. That whole afternoon the doctor awaited Waldemar's return to Altenhof, but he did not appear. Herr Witold had gone to the city and was not expected home until evening, and so the doctor was not harassed by questions from the guardian, which he could not have answered.

Hour after hour glided away; the evening shadows began to fall, but Waldemar was neither seen nor heard of by any one connected with the household. Anxiety drove the doctor out of doors. He walked along the carriage road leading to the estate, over which every visitor must pass. A short distance from the highway lay a very wide and deep ditch, usually full of water, but now the summer's heat rendered it perfectly dry, and the huge stones at its bottom were exposed to view. The bridge crossing it afforded a splendid view of the surrounding landscape. It was still broad day in the open fields, but twilight already enveloped the forest. As the doctor stood on the bridge considering whether he had better go on or turn back, the figure of a horseman advancing on the gallop appeared in the distance. The doctor heaved a sigh of relief. He had not really known what to fear, but he now felt that his anxiety had been groundless, and full of delight he hastened along the edge of the ditch to meet the rider.

"Thank God, you have come, Waldemar! I have been so anxious on your account."

Upon seeing his tutor, Waldemar reined up his horse. "Why have you been anxious?" he asked. "Am I a child who cannot be trusted out of your sight?"

In spite of this forced composure there was a strange ring in the young man's voice, which again aroused the doctor's misgivings. He now for the first time noticed that the horse was panting with fatigue, that his nostrils were covered with foam and his breast heaved violently. The animal had no doubt been mercilessly ridden, but the rider showed no signs of fatigue. He sat erect in the saddle, holding the reins with an iron grip, and instead of turning aside in the direction of the fields, it was his evident intention to leap the ditch.

"For heaven's sake, stop!" cried Fabian. "You will not be guilty of such rashness! You know that Norman has never leaped this ditch."

"But he will now!" replied Waldemar, plunging his spurs into the horse's flanks. Norman sprang forward, but bolted at the margin and refused to take the leap.

"Listen to me!" cried the doctor, imploringly, as he approached the frantic beast. "You require an impossibility; the leap cannot be made, and you will be dashed in pieces on the rocks below."

Without deigning a reply, Waldemar again urged Norman on. "Get out of my way," he cried; "I shall make the leap. Get out of the way, I tell you!"

That wild, anguished tone showed the tutor the mental condition of his pupil, who really would as soon have been dashed in pieces as to make the leap in safety. In his intense fear of impending calamity, the doctor conquered his usual timidity and seized the bridle, determined to dissuade the young man from his foolhardy attempt. But Waldemar gave a terrific stroke of the whip to the refractory animal, which reared and beat wildly with his fore-feet in the air, but refused to take the leap. At this moment a faint cry of distress reached the rider's ear. He was startled, paused, and, quick as lightning, reined back his horse; but it was too late! As Waldemar, the next instant, sprang to the ground, he saw his tutor lying before him motionless and bleeding.

CHAPTER X.

LEO'S VISIT TO ALTENHOF.

A week of anxiety and sorrow passed over Altenhof. Upon Herr Witold's return on that ill-fated evening, he found the whole house in commotion. Doctor Fabian lay senseless and bleeding in his room, while Waldemar, with a face that startled his foster-father quite as much as that of the tutor, was endeavoring to stanch the wound. Nothing could be drawn from him excepting that he alone was to blame for the accident, and his uncle was, consequently, obliged to seek an explanation from the servants. He learned from them that young Nordeck had come home at twilight bearing the wounded man in his arms, and had at once dispatched a messenger for the nearest physician. A quarter of an hour afterward, the horse had appeared panting and exhausted. On finding himself deserted by his master, Norman had followed the well-known road home. The servants knew nothing more.

The physician, who soon arrived and saw the state of the wounded man, looked grave and anxious. The wound in the head, evidently caused by a blow from the horse's hoof, seemed a serious one, while the tutor's frail constitution and the great loss of blood rendered his case very critical. The sufferer for a long time hovered between life and death. Herr Witold, whose own health like that of his ward was perfect, and who had never known what pain and illness really were, after these mournful days were over, often declared that he would not pass through them again for all the world. To-day, for the first time, the old gentleman's face assumed its usual placid and unconcerned expression, as he sat down by the sick man's bed.

"The worst is over," he said; "and now, Doctor Fabian, have the goodness to set Waldemar's head right again. I have not the slightest influence over him, but you can do anything you like with him, so bring the lad back to reason, or this unfortunate affair will prove his ruin."

Waldemar stood at a window pressing his forehead against the panes, and gazing vacantly out into the yard. Doctor Fabian, who still wore a broad white bandage around his head, looked pale and exhausted. He, however, sat upright, supported by pillows, and although his voice was weak, it had no tremor of illness as he asked,--

"What would you have Waldemar do?"

"I want him to be rational," said Herr Witold, emphatically, "and to thank God that this affair has turned out no worse, instead of going about silent and downcast as if he had a murder on his conscience. I suffered enough, heaven knows, during those first few days when your life hung by a thread;

but now that the physician has pronounced you out of danger, I again breathe freely. By-gones are by-gones, and I cannot endure to have my boy go around with such a face, never speaking a word for hours at a time."

"I have often enough assured Waldemar that I alone am to blame for the accident. His attention was entirely absorbed in managing the horse, and he could not see that I was standing near. I was so imprudent as to seize Norman by the bridle, and he dragged me down."

"Did you take Norman by the bit--you who never venture within ten paces of any horse?" exclaimed Herr Witold, in surprise. "What in the world possessed you to do such a foolhardy thing?"

Fabian glanced over at his pupil, and replied, mildly, "I was fearful of an accident."

"Which would doubtless have occurred," added the old gentleman. "Waldemar must have been out of his senses to think of leaping the ditch at nightfall, and with a horse half dead from fatigue. I have always told him that some accident would happen to him for being so venturesome. He has now learned a lesson, but he lays it too much at heart. Doctor, give him a good talking to, and persuade him to be reasonable."

The guardian then rose and left the room. Teacher and pupil remained for some moments silent, and then Fabian said,--

"Waldemar, did you hear my instructions?"

The young man, who until now had stood at the window silent and indifferent, as if the conversation in no way concerned him, turned and approached the bed. He appeared the same as usual, except that he was somewhat pale; at the first glance one felt that Witold's solicitude was excessive, but closer scrutiny revealed a great change. The face had assumed an expression of indifference and rigidity which excluded the play of any other emotion. Perhaps this was only a mask with which Waldemar sought to hide from the world a deeply wounded sensibility. The voice no longer had its usually powerful ringing tone; it was hollow and expressionless, as he replied,--

"Do not heed my uncle's words; nothing is the matter with me."

Doctor Fabian grasped his pupil's right hand in both of his, the young man offering no resistance. "Herr Witold thinks you are still censuring yourself for the accident which occurred to me. This, you must know, is wholly unnecessary, now that all danger is past. I fear that the cause of your sadness lies in quite another direction."

Waldemar's hands trembled; he turned his face away.

"Hitherto I have not ventured to allude to this subject," Fabian went on, hesitatingly. "I see that it still pains you; shall I keep silent?"

Waldemar sighed deeply. "No," he answered; "say what you please; but first let me thank you for not telling my uncle. He has tortured me nearly to death with his questions, but I could not answer them. My mood that evening nearly cost you your life. I can not and will not deny what you already know."

"I know nothing; I only have my conjectures in regard to the scene I witnessed. For heaven's sake, Waldemar, what happened?"

"A childish folly, nothing more," Waldemar replied, with bitter irony; "a mere stupid whim not worth noticing,--at least so my mother wrote me day before yesterday. But I was in earnest, so terribly in earnest that nothing the future has in store for me can atone for my disappointment."

"Do you love the Countess Morynski?" asked Doctor Fabian, timidly.

"I *have* loved her--but that love is a thing of the past. She did her best to fascinate me; I now know that she was only playing a heartless game. The wound was deep, but it will heal. I shall conquer this weakness. I shall learn to forget and despise the girl who trifled with the holiest sentiment of my heart. But do me this favor: never mention the matter to my uncle, never speak of it again to me. I cannot talk about it, not even with you. Leave me to fight out the battle alone, and it will end all the sooner."

His quivering lips betrayed the anguish he suffered from any probing of the wound that was still so recent. Fabian saw that he must desist.

"I will obey your wish and be silent," he said. "You shall never hear an allusion to this subject from my lips in future."

"In future!" echoed Waldemar; "and will you then remain with me? I took it for granted that you would leave us immediately upon your recovery. I would like to have you stay, but I cannot ask it when I have made so poor a return for your kindness, and so nearly caused your death."

Doctor Fabian again grasped his pupil's hand. "I know that you have suffered far more than I," he said; "and one good thing has resulted from my illness. It has proved--you will pardon me for saying it--that you really have a heart."

Waldemar did not seem to hear the words, he was lost in thought. At length he said, "Why did you save my life at the risk of your own? I thought no one cared for me."

"No one? Not even your foster-father?"

"Ah, yes! Uncle Witold, perhaps--but I thought him the only one."

"I have proved to you that he is not the only one," replied the tutor, gravely.

"I deserved this of you least of all," said Waldemar. "But I have learned a severe lesson, so severe that I shall not forget it as long as I live. When I brought you home bleeding on that ill-fated night, when the doctor gave you up for lost, I knew how a murderer feels. If you are really willing to remain with me, you shall not regret it. I have sworn by your couch of pain to overcome that ungovernable fury which has all my life made me deaf to reason, blind to my own good and the good of others. You will have no further cause to complain of me."

"I wish you would promise me this with another look and tone," said Doctor Fabian. "I have no idea of leaving you, but in our future intercourse I would rather contend with your old impetuous nature, than endure this forced, hopeless resignation. Your manner does not please me."

Waldemar rose with a quick, repellent movement, as if to avoid further scrutiny. "I wish you would make your conversation less personal," he said; "the room is close, shall I raise the window?"

The doctor sighed, feeling that he could not win his pupil's confidence. But all further conversation was here interrupted by the entrance of Herr Witold.

"Waldemar," he said, "Prince Zulieski is downstairs, and wishes to see you."

"*Leo*?" asked Waldemar, in astonishment.

"Yes, Leo. Go down at once, and I will remain with Doctor Fabian."

Waldemar left the room, and Herr Witold took his place at the bedside.

"The Zulieskis are in a great hurry to get Waldemar back again," he said. "Three days ago a letter came from her Highness the princess-mother. I am very sure that Waldemar has not answered it; the mother could not induce him to leave your side, and now comes the brother in person; and a very handsome lad the young Polish stripling is! But he is too much like his mother to suit my taste. Speaking of the princess and her son reminds me that I have not yet asked about your discoveries at C---. In my anxiety for you, I entirely forgot the fact of my sending you there on a sort of voyage of discovery."

Doctor Fabian cast down his eyes, and in his embarrassment pulled nervously at the coverlet. "Unfortunately, I have nothing to communicate, Herr Witold," he said; "my visit at C---- was very short, and I told you before I went that I had no skill as a diplomatist."

"Then you learned nothing? That is unfortunate. But how is it with Waldemar? Have you given him a good talking to?"

"He has promised me that he will endeavor to forget the past."

"God be praised! I knew that you could do anything with him you liked. We have both done the lad wrong in thinking he had no feeling. I had no idea he would lay the affair so to heart."

"Neither had I," said the doctor, with a sigh whose import Herr Witold did not understand.

Waldemar found his brother awaiting him. The young prince, who upon his arrival had been greatly surprised at sight of the old, low-roofed house and dilapidated outbuildings of Altenhof, was still more astonished at the plainness and bareness of the room into which he was shown. He had all his life been accustomed to lofty and elegant apartments, and could not understand why his brother, while possessed of such vast wealth, could be content to live in so humble a manner. The parlor of that hired villa at C----, which seemed so inferior to himself and his mother, was luxurious in comparison with the reception-room at Altenhof.

He was musing over these strange discrepancies of fortune, and asking himself why luxurious tastes were given to him without means to gratify them, while his brother, who was possessed of unbounded wealth, cared little for those advantages wealth offers, when Waldemar entered the room. Leo advanced to meet him, and said hastily, as if he would discharge an unpleasant duty as quickly as possible,--

"You are surprised at my coming; but as you have neither visited us nor answered my mother's letter, no alternative remained but for me to come to you."

It was easy to see that the young man did not make the visit of his own accord. His greeting and manner were evidently forced; he seemed to feel in duty bound to offer his hand, but failed in the attempt to do so.

Waldemar did not or would not notice his embarrassment. "Do you come at your mother's bidding?" he asked.

Leo flushed deeply at the thought of his aversion to an interview, which his mother had secured only by the exercise of her whole maternal authority.

"I do," he finally replied.

"I am sorry, Leo, that you have been compelled to do what you must feel to be a humiliation. I certainly would have spared you this visit if I had been consulted."

"Mamma thinks that you have been insulted in our house, insulted by me, and that I ought to take the first step toward reconciliation. I admit that she is right; and, believe me, Waldemar, if it had not been for this conviction, I would not have come--*never*!"

"I fully believe you," returned Waldemar.

"Pray don't make it so difficult for me to apologize!" Leo exclaimed, extending his hand, but Waldemar refused to take it.

"I can accept no apology from my mother or from you; neither of you were to blame for the insult I received in your house; and, besides, it is already forgotten. Let us drop the subject."

Leo's surprise increased every moment; he could not reconcile himself to this unexpected indifference, so far removed from Waldemar's terrible excitement scarce a week ago.

"I did not think you could forget so quickly," he replied, in undisguised perplexity.

"Where I despise, I forget easily."

"Waldemar, this is too severe!" exclaimed Leo. "You do Wanda wrong; she has herself requested me to say to you--"

"Spare me the message, I implore you! My idea of the affair differs entirely from yours; but let us say no more about it. Under the circumstances, my mother cannot expect me to bid her good-by in person; for the present I must avoid her house. I shall not go to Villica this fall as we had arranged; I may visit it next year."

The young prince frowned. "Do you think that after this icy message I am compelled to take home from you, we can still become your guests?"

Waldemar crossed his arms and leaned against the mantel. "You mistake; you and my mother are not at all concerned in this affair; it has nothing whatever to do with your stay at Villica. But you have opposed going there from the first; may I know the reason?"

"Because to live there humiliates me. Mamma may decide upon what she thinks best for herself, but, as for me, I shall never set foot--"

Waldemar laid his hand soothingly upon his brother's arm. "Do not say that, Leo; the hasty promise might prove a restraint to you. I have offered my mother a home at Villica, and she has accepted it. This was simply my duty; it would disgrace me to have her dependent on any other person than myself. You need have no sensitiveness in the matter; you are going to the university, and will only pass your vacations at Villica. A mother need feel no humiliation in accepting a home and support from her eldest son; and what her pride can tolerate you certainly will be able to endure."

"I know that we are both entirely dependent upon you, and I also know that I have insulted you, although not intentionally and deliberately. How can I accept everything from your hands?"

"You have not insulted me," said Waldemar, gravely. "On the contrary, you are the only one who has been true to me. I thank you for opening my eyes to Wanda's real character, and to the plot she laid for me. All enmity between us is at an end."

Leo was overwhelmed with mortification; he well knew that jealousy alone had driven him to the step which called forth his brother's thanks. He had come prepared for a violent scene with Waldemar, and this apparent indifference and self-control quite unmanned him. He was still too superficial a judge of human nature to see or to suspect what lay concealed beneath Waldemar's strange composure, and what it cost him. He accepted it for genuine; but he did perceive clearly that his brother was resolved to allow him and his mother no reparation for the past, and that he still insisted upon giving them a home at Villica. He knew that he himself would be incapable of such magnanimity, and on this very account he felt it more deeply.

"Waldemar, I sincerely regret the wrong we have done you in the past," he said, extending his hand. This time the movement was not forced; it came from his whole heart, and his brother accepted it.

"Promise me that you will accompany our mother to Villica," said Waldemar; "if you really think you have wronged me, this shall be your reparation."

Leo bowed assent, and his opposition was at an end.

"Will you not bid our mother good-bye?" Leo asked, after a slight pause. "Your neglect to do so will pain her deeply."

Waldemar's lips curled in a derisive smile as he answered, "She will endure it. Good-bye, Leo, I am very glad to have seen you once more."

The young prince gazed for a moment into his brother's face, and then yielding to a sudden impulse, threw his arms around his neck. Waldemar submitted to the embrace in silence, but did not return it, although it was the first between them.

"Farewell," Leo said, distantly, unclasping his arms.

A few moments after, the carriage which had brought the unexpected visitor rolled out of the gate, and Waldemar entered the house. Whoever now saw him with his quivering lips, drawn features, and fixed melancholy glance, must have understood the nature of the composure he had maintained during this whole interview. His wounded pride had asserted itself; Leo must not see that he suffered, and least of all tell it in C----. But now that self-control was no longer needful, the wound bled anew. Waldemar's love had been violent and impetuous like his whole nature; it had been the first tender emotion aroused in the heart of this isolated, uncultured youth. He had adored Wanda with all the ardor of a first passion, and the sudden annihilation of his cherished ideal had wrought a radical change in his whole being.

CHAPTER XI.

THE NEW RÉGIME AT VILLICA.

Villica Castle, which gave name to the broad territory surrounding it, formed the central point of a large number of estates lying very near the Polish border. So extensive a landed property is seldom found in the possession of one individual, and seldom does a proprietor have so little care of his broad acres as the elder Herr Nordeck had for Villica. During his lifetime the estates had no organized, judicious management. He had acquired his property in the way of speculation, and remained a speculator to the end. He had been fitted neither socially nor practically for the position of a wealthy landlord. He had leased all his farms and estates with the exception of Villica, his own place of residence, and this was given over to the care of a superintendent. The chief revenue of the estates came from the extensive forests which covered nearly two thirds of the land, and required the assistance of a whole army of foresters, who formed a sort of society by themselves.

Herr Witold, who, at Nordeck's death, was left guardian of the infant heir and manager of the property, did not change the existing order of affairs. Although well fitted to control a small estate like Altenhof, every detail of which passed through his hands, he was not qualified for the far more difficult task of superintending the vast concerns of Villica; he was a poor manager, and a worse disciplinarian. Having a profound faith in human nature, and believing most persons honest as himself, he accepted the bills and receipts handed him without question, and conscientiously invested all returns in the interest of his ward. While he flattered himself that his duties were thoroughly discharged, he really allowed the officials to do as they pleased. Such management would have brought ruin to a less valuable estate, but it could not irretrievably injure Nordeck's property; for if thousands were lost, hundreds of thousands still remained; the immense income of the property not only covered any chance deficiency, but went to swell the original amount. This income, under proper management, might have been far greater, but neither Witold nor the young heir cared to increase it. Very soon after attaining his majority, Waldemar went to the university, and as he passed his vacations in travelling, he had not visited Villica for several years.

Villica Castle formed a striking contrast to most of the residences of the neighboring gentry, which scarce deserved the name of castle, and whose gradual dilapidation and decay could be concealed by no attempts at outward splendor. Villica bore its honors proudly as an old princely and seigniorial residence, dating back for nearly two centuries, from that brilliant epoch of Poland when the power of the nobility equaled their wealth, and when their residences were scenes of a splendor and luxury seldom known in our day. The palace could not really be called beautiful; it would scarce have found favor in an artist's eye. In its plan and construction it bore evidences of uncultivated, almost barbaric tastes, but the massiveness of its proportions and the grandeur of its location made its general effect very imposing. In spite of all the changes and alterations more modern ideas had given it, Castle Villica still retained its original character; the solid walls, with their long rows of windows, rose grandly and picturesquely from the extensive park encircled by primeval forests.

For many years after Herr Nordeck's death the castle had remained uninhabited. The young heir came seldom; he was always accompanied by his guardian, and his visits were very brief; but when the former mistress of Villica, the now widowed Princess Zulieski, again took up her abode there, the old place wore a different aspect. The long-closed apartments were reopened, and their original splendor was fully restored. Waldemar had made over to his mother all the revenues of the estate immediately belonging to the castle; these revenues, although forming only a small portion of his income, were ample for the princess and her younger son, allowing the lady even that large sum which she required to live "conformably to her position." She saved nothing of the liberal amount placed at her disposal, and her surroundings and style of living were as elegant as they had been when she came a young bride to Villica, and when her husband still took delight in displaying his wealth to her and to her relatives.

It was the beginning of October. The autumn wind blew chill over the forests, whose foliage had begun to put on those hues so beautiful and yet so sad, which tell of speedy decay and dissolution. The sun vainly struggled to pierce the dense mists that enveloped the landscape, and it was high noon today ere his rays illumined the state parlor of Villica, and the room adjoining, which the princess called her study, and where most of her time was spent. It was a large apartment, with high walls and vaulted ceilings, deep window recesses, and a huge fireplace in which a wood-fire was now burning.

The heavy, green velvet curtains were thrown back, admitting the full sunlight, which revealed the massive splendor of the furniture, green being the prevailing color in the carpet and upholstery. The princess and her brother, Count Morynski, sat there alone. The count and his daughter often came from their estate to pass days and even weeks at Villica; and they had come to-day, intending to make a long visit. The prince was looking much older than at our first meeting with him: his hair was gray, his brow more furrowed; but otherwise his grave, expressive face had not changed. The princess did not look a day older; the features of the still handsome woman were as cold and proud, her manner as haughty and distant, as ever. She had laid aside deep mourning, but still wore black of a very rich material, which was exceedingly becoming to her. She was engaged in earnest conversation with her brother.

"I do not understand how this news can surprise you," she said; "we should have been prepared for it long ago. I have always wondered how Waldemar could remain so long away from his estates."

"It is this very circumstance that makes me surprised at his coming now," returned the count. "When he has so long avoided Villica, why does he come so suddenly, and without any previous intimation. What is the object of his visit?"

"O, merely to hunt," said the princess; "he inherits his father's passion for the chase. I am convinced that he chose the university of J---- solely from its nearness to a forest, and that, instead of attending the lectures, he has been roaming about all day long with his rifle and game-bag. He probably passed his time in the same way on his travels, he really understands nothing thoroughly but the chase."

"He could not come at a worse time for us. Just now everything depends upon your remaining absolute mistress here. My estate lies too far distant from the frontier; there we are watched on all sides, and meet with obstacles at every turn. We *must* retain control of Villica."

"I know it, and I shall take care that it remains in our hands. You are right: Waldemar's visit comes most inopportunely, but I cannot prevent his visiting his own estates. We must exercise all the greater precaution."

"Precaution alone will not answer," returned the count, impatiently. "As matters stand, we must give up all our plans while Waldemar is in the house; and delays are dangerous."

"This will not be needful; he will be within doors very little, unless I mistake the attraction our forests will have for his Nimrod nature. Hunting was his father's mania, making him indifferent to all else; Waldemar resembles him perfectly in this respect. We shall seldom have sight of him; he will remain in the woods all day, and will not pay the slightest attention to what is going on within doors. The only thing here that can possibly interest him is his father's large collection of weapons, which we will gladly make over to him."

The princess said this with a sort of compassionate irony; but the count answered, doubtfully and hesitatingly,--

"You have not seen Waldemar for four years; then he obeyed you in all things. I hope you can as easily influence him now."

"I think I can; he is not so hard to manage as you suppose. If you yield for the moment to his rude impetuosity, and make him believe that he will have his own way in any event, you have him completely in your power. If we remind him daily that he is absolute master of Villica, he will never think of becoming so in reality. I do not consider him intelligent enough to make a thorough examination into affairs here. We need have no concern."

"As I have met Waldemar only twice, I must depend entirely upon your judgment. When did you receive his letter?"

"This morning, an hour before your arrival. We may expect him very soon. He writes in his usual laconic style, avoiding all details."

"Is he coming alone?" asked the count, gravely.

"His former tutor, who is his constant companion, will be with him. I thought I might gain some definite information from this man in regard to my son's studies at the university; but I was deceived in him. In answer to my inquiries, I obtained nothing but some learned disquisitions upon special studies,--not a word of what I desired to know. This Doctor Fabian is one of the most unobtrusive and harmless of men. You need fear nothing from his presence nor his influence, for he really has no influence."

"Waldemar is the one with whom we have to do; if you think we need fear no strict observation from him--"

"No close observation, at all events; nothing like that to which we have been subjected for months," interrupted the princess. "I thought the superintendent had taught us precaution."

"Yes, this man Frank and his whole household are playing the spy upon us," exclaimed Count Morynski, vehemently. "I cannot understand, Maryna, why you do not rid yourself of such an intrusive person."

The princess smiled in conscious superiority.

"Give yourself no further uneasiness, Bronislaw," she said; "the man will leave in a few days. I could not dismiss him; he has held his position for twenty years, and has managed excellently. I preferred to treat him in such a manner as to induce him to resign. He has done so orally; the formal notice will not be long deferred. I preferred that it should come from his side, as Waldemar's arrival is so near."

"It was high time," returned the count, with a smile of intense satisfaction. "He was beginning to be dangerous to us. Unfortunately, we shall be obliged to tolerate his presence a while longer; his contract doubtless specifies some months' notice."

"Certainly; but I think he will prefer to leave at once. He has for a long time been above his position; it is said that he proposes buying an estate for himself; he in fact possesses a very independent spirit. If I can only manage to bring about a scene in which he feels his pride wounded, he will leave at once. This will not be difficult, now that he has resolved to go.--What, Leo, are you already back from your walk?"

These last words were addressed to the young prince, who now entered the room.

"Wanda did not wish to remain longer in the park," he said. "I hope I do not intrude upon your conversation."

"Not at all," said the count, rising. "We have just been notified of Waldemar's speedy return, and were discussing its unavoidable results. One of them will be that Wanda and I must shorten our visit; but we shall remain and take part in the festivities arranged for to-morrow evening, and then return home the next day. I do not think he will be here before that time; in any event, we cannot stay in the house as his guests."

"Why not?" asked the princess. "Is it because of that childish affair? Wanda has certainly forgotten it, and you will not find Waldemar, after the lapse of four years, still brooding over that fancied insult. His heart was never deeply enlisted, for only a week after he told Leo, with the utmost composure, that he had forgotten all about the affair. Our remaining at Villica is conclusive proof that he cherishes no resentment. The best course for us all is to entirely ignore the whole occurrence. If Wanda meets him cordially as his cousin, he will scarcely recollect that he ever had a boyish fancy for her."

"I quite approve of your idea," said the count, turning to leave the room, "and I shall mention it to Wanda."

Leo had taken no part in the conversation, but after his uncle's departure he flung himself angrily into the vacant chair.

"Your walk ended suddenly," said the princess; "where is Wanda?"

"In her room--I suppose."

"You have had another quarrel; do not attempt to deny it, Leo. Your face tells it plainly enough, and you would never leave Wanda if she did not drive you from her."

"She takes a peculiar delight in driving me away," said Leo, bitterly.

"You constantly annoy her with your unfounded jealousy of every one who approaches her," replied the princess.

Leo was silent, and his mother went on,--

"It is an old proverb that if love has no thorns, it will itself create them. You and Wanda have no obstacles to encounter; you may follow the bent of your affections with the full approval of your parents, and yet you are often wretched. I do not hold Wanda blameless; I am not blind to her talents, her accomplishments and her beauty; but her father has spoiled her with his unreasoning indulgence. She knows no will but her own, and even you dare not rebel against her."

"I assure you, mamma, I did rebel to-day," replied Leo, in a resentful tone.

"Yes, perhaps you asserted yourself to-day, but to-morrow you will be at her feet, begging forgiveness. She has many a time brought you there. Can I never convince you that this is not the way to gain from a proud, headstrong girl like Wanda the respect which is due her future husband?"

"I am incapable of coolly deliberating as to what will prove for my future advantage when I adore with all the ardor of my soul," replied Leo, passionately.

"Then do not complain if your passion does not meet with the desired response. My knowledge of Wanda convinces me that she will never love a man who yields unconditionally to her control. A nature like hers needs to be forced to love; you do not understand her."

"I have no right to Wanda's love," replied Leo, angrily. "I am not allowed to call her my betrothed, and the time of our marriage is indefinitely postponed."

"Because the present moment, when your country's welfare is at stake, is no time to think of betrothal or of marriage; because you have now other and more serious duties to perform than to worship and adore a young wife. You need not say that the marriage is postponed indefinitely, when the delay will not be more than a year, at the longest. Show yourself worthy of Wanda; earn the hand of your bride; opportunity will not be wanting. But, Leo, I have something to say to you which must not longer be deferred; your uncle is displeased with you."

"Has he been complaining of me?" the young man asked, morosely.

"Unfortunately, he has been obliged to do so. Need I remind you that you owe deference and obedience to your uncle under all circumstances? And yet you have placed yourself at the head of several young men of your own age, and openly oppose his political plans and wishes."

"We are no longer children who must submit to be led as if we had no will of our own," replied Leo, defiantly. "Even though we are young, we have a right to our own opinions, and we cannot much longer endure this everlasting hesitation and delay."

"Do you suppose that my brother will allow your youthful, fiery ardor to lead him and his cause on to certain ruin? He finds it very difficult to reconcile and restrain the opposing elements, and it cuts him to the heart to see his own nephew setting an example of disobedience?"

"I have opposed him in words only, never in deeds. I honor and love Count Morynski as your brother and as Wanda's father, but I must be allowed some independence of thought and action. You have often enough told me that my name and ancestry entitle me to a leading position, and yet my uncle requires me to be content with a subordinate one."

"He does not dare intrust momentous interests to a fiery head of twenty-two years; you entirely misunderstand your uncle. An heir has been denied him, and although Wanda is his idol, the hopes that can be realized only through a son rest solely upon you, who are allied to him in blood, and will soon be called his son. Although he considers it necessary to restrain you for the present, you are his main dependence in the future; he looks to you to carry out the plans his years and failing health will not permit him to realize. I have his word that when the decisive moment comes, Prince Leo Zulieski will assume the position which is his due. We both hope that you may prove yourself worthy."

"Can you doubt it?" asked Leo, with glowing cheeks and flashing eyes.

The mother laid her hand soothingly upon his arm. "We do not doubt your courage, but we question your discretion. You have your father's temperament; in his fiery zeal and ardor he had little thought for consequences, and his yielding to generous but misguided impulses brought untold sorrow upon both him and me. But you are also my son, Leo, and I think you must have inherited some traits from your mother. I have told my brother that I would answer to him for your loyalty and obedience; it is for you to redeem the pledge."

So much maternal pride was expressed in these words, that Leo threw his arms around his mother's neck, and assured her of his entire devotion to her wishes. The princess smiled, and all a mother's tenderness lay in her look and tone, as, returning her son's embrace, she said,--

"I need not repeat to you, Leo, the hopes I have so often expressed in regard to your future. You have always been my only one, my all."

"Your *only* one!" returned Leo. "Have I not a brother Waldemar?"

The princess started. At mention of this name all the tenderness vanished from her voice and features. Her face resumed its usual severe expression, and her voice was icy-cold, as she said,--

"Ah, yes! I had quite forgotten him. Fate has made him master of Villica--we must endure him!"

CHAPTER XII.

THE NEW CONSPIRATORS.

Not far from the manor-house of Villica stood the dwelling of Superintendent Frank. The castle was quite aloof from the other houses. Whether occupied or not, it had always an air of aristocratic seclusion. Villica itself was in charge of an official whose stately residence, with the tenant-houses around it, nearly all of them new, formed a striking contrast to those of the neighboring estates, and were regarded throughout that region as unique and admirable models. The position of superintendent of Villica was one that many a proprietor might have craved, both for the income and the style of living.

It was growing dark. The whole row of windows on the second floor of the castle began to be illuminated; the princess was giving a large party. There were as yet no lights in the superintendent's sitting-room, the two gentlemen who sat there being so absorbed in conversation that they did not heed the gathering darkness.

The elder gentleman, who was in the full vigor of middle life, had a fine face, an imposing figure, and a complexion bronzed by exposure to sun and weather. The younger man was of a pale, delicate complexion, which bore no trace of the life and surroundings of the country. Although below the medium height, he might still be called a handsome man. His carefully curled hair and fashionable apparel gave him a somewhat foppish appearance, but he was really devoid of affectation. His speech and manner indicated a vast amount of dignity and importance, which formed a ludicrous contrast to his diminutive stature.

"My mind is fully made up, I shall go," the elder man said. "I told the princess that I would do her the favor of leaving Villica, as her man[oe]uvres had for some time past tended in that direction. I got no further, for her Majesty interrupted me with, 'My dear Frank, I sincerely regret your determination, but I cannot oppose it. Be assured that my son and I can never forget your long and faithful service at Villica.' And she said this to me--to one, whom she has systematically driven away! Her look and tone awed me into silence. I had resolved to free my mind, and tell her the unvarnished truth, and--I made a bow, and left."

"The princess is a remarkable woman," said the younger gentleman, "but a very dangerous one. We who belong to the government have proofs of this fact. I tell you, Herr Frank, she is a menace to the whole province."

"I cannot see that her influence extends beyond Villica. She has done much harm here. She has succeeded in bringing everything under her control. I was the last stumbling-block, and she is now to be rid of me. Believe me, Herr Assessor, I have endured this state of things as long as possible, not for the sake of retaining my position,--God knows I can stand upon my own feet any day,--but because it pained me to know that all I have done in twenty years would be in vain if the old Polish troubles should revive. I came here two years after Nordeck's death. His son was at Altenhof with his guardian, and tenants, foresters, and overseers were having a jolly time. Here at Villica affairs were managed worst of all. My predecessor had stolen so openly and so shamelessly that even Herr Witold became alarmed and suddenly discharged him. The castle, of whose splendor wonderful tales were told far and near, was closed, and I can give you no idea of the aspect of things in the village and around the estate. The dwellings of the tenants were wretched, dilapidated wood and day huts; all was chaos and disorder. The servants were fawning, hypocritical, and full of national hatred of the Germans; the fields were in a condition appalling to a good farmer. It was six months before I could have my wife and children with me, for there was not a decent place for them to live in. How could things be otherwise? The deceased Nordeck had done nothing but hunt and quarrel with his wife, and Herr Witold did simply nothing at all. If the accounts were only laid before him in black and white, and balanced the expenditures, he was satisfied, and did not ask whether the pretended outlay had really been made.

"What prodigious sums I was obliged to ask for in the beginning! They were granted unhesitatingly, and the fact that I did not pocket them, as my predecessors had done, was quite contrary to the usual order of proceedings. The old gentleman must have considered me the only honest man among the whole pack, for after the first year he so increased my salary that I realized more from my honesty than the others had realized from their pilferings. If he were living now, I should not leave Villica. The princess would know that her chicaneries must cease--that if I wrote to Altenhof and told the whole truth, there would be an explosion. During Herr Witold's lifetime I had peace, but at his death two years ago, all concord was at an end. I have endured the persecution and the interference of this woman long enough, and I am going to leave."

"But your leaving is a great misfortune," said the assessor; "you are the only one who can in any way thwart the princess. Your argus-eyes impose a wholesome restraint upon her. We who belong to the *government*" (he used this phrase often, and always emphasized it), "we better than any other class know what the result will be if Nordeck's estates, with their immense size and nearness to the Polish frontier, are under the rule of a Zulieski."

"The princess has accomplished a great deal in these four years," resumed the superintendent, in a bitter tone. "She began her intrigues the first day she came here, and she has gone on, step by step, with an energy and persistency that, displayed in a better cause, would be truly admirable. As the leases expired, she has managed to have the farms fall into the hands of her countrymen. Every German element has been gradually eliminated from the management of the forests, all the servants are obsequious tools of the princess, and I have been obliged to exert my utmost influence to keep my German inspectors and overseers in their places. Of late they have resigned voluntarily, being no longer able to endure the insolence of their subordinates, I think that my successor is already appointed. He is a drinking man, who knows almost nothing about the management of an estate, and who will ruin Villica, as Nordeck's other estates are being ruined; but he is a Pole, and that explains his selection for the place."

"Could you not induce young Herr Nordeck to come here?" asked the assessor; "he can have no idea of the condition of affairs."

"Our young landlord cares nothing for Villica. He has not set foot on the estate for ten years. There was some talk of his coming here to live when he should reach his majority, but he chose to send his mother in his stead. Not one of his subordinates is in direct correspondence with him; we are ordered to render our accounts to his attorney at L----. I however ventured to write to him four weeks ago, informing him of the exact state of affairs. I have received no answer; nothing is to be hoped from him. But I beg your pardon, sir, for keeping you so long in total darkness. I cannot imagine why Gretchen does not bring in the lamps as usual; she probably does not know that you are here."

"O, yes, she does," replied the assessor, in an aggrieved tone. "Fräulein Margaret was standing in the hall-door as I came up the walk; she gave me no opportunity to greet her, but ran up stairs to the garret as fast as she could."

"I think you must be mistaken," returned Gretchen's father.

"She ran up two flights of stairs to the garret," reiterated the small gentleman, emphatically, and with a look of great displeasure.

"I am sorry," said the superintendent, "but I cannot help it; I have to let the child do about as she pleases."

"Ah, but you *can* help it!" exclaimed the assessor. "You have only to assert your paternal authority. You can say to your daughter that it is your desire and command--"

"Nothing could induce me to say any such thing," interrupted the superintendent. "I place no hindrance in the way of your suit. I believe that you have a sincere affection for my daughter, and I have nothing against you or your position and prospects. But you must win the girl's consent; I shall not interfere. If she voluntarily accepts you, I shall not object to you as a son-in-law; but, honestly, I do not think your prospects are very flattering."

"There you are in an error, Herr Frank,--most decidedly so. I know that your daughter often treats me coldly and indifferently, but I understand all this; it is nothing but the prudery usual to young girls. They want to be wooed long and ardently; they strive by their reserve and coyness to make the prize more desirable. I have made these matters a profound study. The young lady's indifference is only seeming; I am sure of success."

"I am happy to hear it," returned Herr Frank, as the object of the conversation entered the room bringing a lamp.

Margaret Frank--or Gretchen, as every one called her excepting the formal assessor--was about twenty years old. She was a beauty of no delicate, ideal type, but a perfect picture of youth and health. Her form was stately and robust like her father's, and her fresh, rosy face, clear blue eyes, and the blonde braids arranged in a coronet above her smooth, white forehead, made her so altogether lovely, that we may well understand the assessor's forgetfulness of that offensive flight up the garret-stairs, and his eagerness to salute his chosen one.

"Good evening, Herr Assessor," Gretchen said, coldly, in response to the gentleman's warm greeting. "Then it was you who drove through the gate a little while ago? I did not imagine it could be you again, for you were here only last Sunday."

The assessor thought proper not to answer these last words. "I come here to-day upon official business," he said. "An affair of great importance has been intrusted to me, and will detain me some days in this neighborhood; I have therefore taken the liberty of accepting your father's hospitality. We who are connected with the government are having serious times now, Fräulein Margaret. We find everywhere secret intrigues and revolutionary movements; the whole province seems involved in one great conspiracy, and Villica is in fact the headquarters of all sorts of intrigue."

"And the most favorable place for operations," added Frank. "The Nordeck estates are surrounded by forests, and all the foresters and their satellites are at the beck of the princess who rules here. Strictly as the boundary is watched, people pass too and fro every night, and whoever comes finds the doors of Villica Castle wide open."

"We know all that, Herr Frank," returned the assessor, with a gesture that indicated nothing short of omniscience; "but we can do nothing, for we do not possess the slightest proof, and we can discover none, for at our approach all operations are at once suspended. My mission is to ferret out this affair, and since you have charge of police regulations here, I am ordered to solicit your aid."

"I will aid you if I must, but I dislike engaging in any secret service. They even now, at the castle, consider me a spy and an intermeddler, because I will not voluntarily close my eyes, and because I severely punish the disobedience of my subordinates."

"I am to-day upon the track of two very dangerous characters, who are roaming about this neighborhood under all sorts of pretexts," said the assessor, "and who must be secured as soon as possible. In coming here I met two very suspicious-looking individuals, who in all probability are the ones I am seeking. They were on foot."

Gretchen laughed. "Is that a ground for suspicion? They doubtless had no money to pay coach-hire."

"I beg your pardon; they had money enough to hire an extra-post-chaise, for they passed me in one; but at the last station they left the carriage, and made many inquiries about Villica. They declined to take a guide, and proceeded on foot, avoiding the highway, and cutting across lots. They would not answer the postmaster's questions. Unfortunately I did not arrive in time to make investigations to-day, but I shall carry them on to-morrow with all possible vigor. Doubtless both men are in the neighborhood."

"Perhaps they are up there," said Gretchen, pointing to the castle, whose illuminated windows gleamed through the darkness. "The princess is holding a great meeting of conspirators to-night."

The assessor sprang from his chair. "A meeting of conspirators! How? What? Do you positively know this? I will surprise them. I will--"

"Don't make a fool of yourself," said the superintendent, laughing; "this is only a girl's jesting--nothing more."

"But, papa, you said there were secret reasons for these frequent festivities at the castle," interposed Gretchen.

"That is my opinion. Fond as the princess is of pomp and show, I do not believe she would indulge in mere merry-making in times like these. Her large balls and hunting-parties are convenient pretexts for bringing all sorts of people to Villica, without attracting particular attention. True, there is dancing and dining,--appearances must be kept up,--but the greater portion of the guests remain over night, and what occurs after the ballroom-lights are extinguished may not be of so harmless a nature."

The assessor listened eagerly to these disclosures. Unfortunately the superintendent was called out at this moment, and left the two young people alone.

Gretchen's displeasure was as boundless as the assessor's delight at this unexpected *tête-à-tête*. He twirled his moustache with an air of satisfaction, stroked his glossy hair, and resolved to make the best use of so favorable an opportunity.

"Your father informs me that he intends to resign his position," he began. "The idea of seeing him and his daughter no more at Villica would be a heavy blow, indeed a thunderbolt to me, were it not for the fact that I do not purpose remaining much longer in L---- myself."

"Are you, too, going away?" asked Gretchen, in surprise.

The assessor smiled--and it was a smile of great significance. "You are aware, Fräulein Margaret, that with us government officials, promotion usually involves a change of residence, and I hope soon to be promoted."

"Ah, indeed!"

"There is no doubt of it. I am already government assessor, and in a State like ours, that means everything. It is the first round of the great ladder that leads directly to the minister's chair."

"You have some distance to travel before you reach that elevation," remarked Gretchen, incredulously.

The small gentleman leaned back with as much dignity as if the simple cane-bottomed chair upon which he sat were really the longed-for chair of the prime minister.

"True, such a position cannot be reached at one stride; but the future is full of grand possibilities. Fräulein Margaret, a public man ought always to have great things in view, and to aim for the highest. Ambition is the official's noblest incentive. I am in daily expectation of being appointed government counsellor."

"You have been expecting that a long time."

"Yes, and the realization of my hope has been deferred because envy and malice assail me on every side. We younger officials are kept down as long as possible by our superiors. Hitherto I have had no opportunity to distinguish myself, but now I have been selected as the man best fitted to discharge the duties of a very important mission. His Excellency, the governor of the province, has himself given me the requisite instructions, and ordered me to report to him personally the result of my investigations. If my efforts prove successful, I am sure of the counsellorship."

As he said this, he gave the young lady a look so significant that she could not possibly be in doubt as to what person he had chosen to be the wife of the future counsellor; but she maintained an obstinate silence.

"Then a change of residence would follow as a matter of course," continued the assessor. "I should probably be called to the capital. You are not acquainted in the capital, Fräulein Margaret?" he asked, as he went on depicting life at the Residence, its advantages and amusements, discoursing largely upon his influential connections there, and making all these things add vastly to his own personal importance. Margaret listened with mingled curiosity and incredulity. The brilliant pictures unrolled before her had something very enticing to a young girl reared in the solitude of the country. She rested her blonde head in her hand, and gazed thoughtfully at the table-cover. Her sole objection to such a life evidently lay in the fact that the present assessor and future minister must share it. He however marked his advantage, and was resolved to profit by it. He felt that the decisive moment had come.

"But amid all the gayety and splendor of the capital I shall feel sad and desolate," he said, pathetically; "my heart will remain with you, Fräulein Margaret--"

Margaret was startled. She saw that the assessor, who had made a long, momentous pause after her name, had now risen with the unmistakable intention of falling on his knees before her. But the solemnity and ceremoniousness with which he was arranging the preliminaries of his declaration proved fatal to its success; they gave the young girl time to deliberate, and she too sprang to her feet.

"Please excuse me, Herr Assessor; I think--I believe that the hall-door just closed. It has a spring lock, and papa will not be able to get in when he returns. I will run down and open it;" and so saying, she ran out of the room.

The assessor stood there with his dramatic pose and half-bended knees, looking very much bewildered. For the second time to-day his chosen one had fled from him, and her prudery began to be very annoying. It never once occurred to him that Gretchen's opposition was serious. It was obstinacy, coquetry, and perhaps--so the suitor thought with a smile--fear of those fascinations and advantages which rendered him irresistible. The girl certainly had no idea of refusing him, and in her charming timidity she had run away from an immediate decision. This thought greatly comforted the young gentleman, and although he regretted the fact that no decision had been reached, he had not the slightest doubt of ultimate triumph. He had made such matters a study, and knew all about the coyness and playful obstinacy of young girls.

The pretext of which Gretchen had availed herself was not pure invention. She had actually heard the front door close with a loud bang. Although she knew that her father had only to ring, and a servant would let him in, she ran down to the door and opened it violently at the very moment when a hand from without was laid upon the knob. The visitor staggered, and would have fallen if his companion had not caught him.

"Good heavens, what has happened?" cried the young lady.

"I sincerely beg your pardon," replied a timid voice, in a tone of unusual politeness. Before Gretchen had time to reply, the other visitor advanced and accosted her.

"We wish to see the superintendent; is he at home?"

"Papa is not in at this moment, but he will be presently," answered Gretchen, delighted that this late and unexpected visit relieved her from the alternative of leaving the assessor alone or keeping him company until her father's return. Instead of ushering the visitors into her father's office, she conducted them to the sitting-room.

"Two gentlemen who desire to speak with papa," she said, while the wondering assessor rose and greeted the strangers. Gretchen left the room to send a servant in search of her father. As she was about to re-enter, the assessor met her in the hall and asked, excitedly, if she had sent for the superintendent; then he whispered in her ear, "Fräulein Margaret, these are the men!"

"What men?"

"The two suspicious characters I was speaking of; I have them fast in my trap."

"But how do you know, Herr Assessor?"

"They are the two individuals who passed me in the extra-post-chaise," he said. "I shall examine them, and arrest them if necessary."

"But must this be done in our house?" asked the young girl, indignantly.

"My official duty requires it," he answered loftily. "First of all, egress from the house must be prevented. I will lock the door." He double-locked the front door, and placed the key in his pocket.

"But what need is there of all these precautions?" asked Gretchen. "How do you know they are suspicious characters?"

"Fräulein Frank, you have not the sagacity of a professional detective," the assessor answered, patronizingly. "I know how to read faces, and I tell you these two physiognomies bear the unmistakable stamp of conspirators. They are Poles; they cannot deceive me even though they speak the purest German. I shall question them sharply until your father appears, and then we two will consult together concerning what had best be done. I know that I risk my life by remaining alone with such desperate men when they know that I see into their designs, but duty requires it, and I do not flinch."

"I will go with you," said Gretchen, courageously.

"I thank you," replied the assessor, solemnly, as if Gretchen had promised to accompany him to the scaffold. "The moment for action has come."

He returned to the reception-room, followed by the young girl, who was naturally very courageous, and awaited the development of the affair with quite as much curiosity as anxiety. The two strangers evidently had no suspicion of the storm about to burst over their defenceless heads; on the contrary, they seemed entirely unsuspicious of danger, and very much at their ease. The younger man, who was of a remarkably fine figure and a head taller than his companion, walked to and fro with folded arms; while the elder, who had a slender form and agreeable features, accepted the proffered seat, and sat in the superintendent's large easy-chair, an apparently perfectly harmless individual.

The assessor put on his most authoritative air. A conviction of the importance of the occasion, and a consciousness of acting in the presence of his future bride, had an inspiring effect upon him. He appeared like a personification of the day of judgment as he confronted the two "individuals."

"I have not yet introduced myself to you," he began, politely, and yet with a very consequential air, "I am Government Assessor Hubert, of L----."

The two strangers could not have been novices in conspiracy, for they did not even turn pale at this announcement of official dignity. The elder gentleman rose, bowed very politely, and then sat down again. The younger merely nodded, and said indifferently,--

"Happy to meet you."

"May I ask your names?" continued Hubert.

"What for?" asked the younger, abruptly.

"I wish to know them."

"But, unfortunately, we do not care to tell you."

The assessor nodded as if to say, "I thought as much." "I am connected with the police department of L----," he added, emphatically.

"A very unenviable position," returned the younger, glancing from the assessor to Gretchen, who was standing at the window.

Hubert was nonplussed for a moment. These must be hardened conspirators, for they were not frightened even at mention of the police department, and yet the words must give them a premonition of their fate. This obduracy must be broken; the examination went on.

"You drove past me in an extra-post-chaise some two hours ago?"

The younger deigned no answer; he seemed bored beyond measure; but the elder man replied politely,--

"Yes; and we also observed you in your carriage."

"You left the chaise at the last station, and proceeded on foot. According to your own admission, you wished to go to Villica; you avoided the highway and took a path across the fields." The assessor again wore his doomsday face as he hurled these accusations one after another at the heads of the two conspirators. They did not fail of their effect. The elder conspirator began to grow uneasy; but the younger, whom the piercing glance of the government official had singled out as the most dangerous, hastily approached and placed his hand upon the arm of his companion's chair.

"In addition to all this, we wrapped our cloaks around us when it began to grow cold; and we accidentally left a pair of gloves in the post-office," he said, with undisguised irony. "Do you wish to add these two facts to your minute observations upon our proceedings?"

"Sir, a representative of the government does not allow himself to be addressed in this disrespectful manner," exclaimed Hubert, passionately.

The young man deigned no answer; he shrugged his shoulders and turned toward the window where Gretchen was standing.

"Fräulein Frank, you keep entirely aloof from us. Will you not by your presence deliver us from the intolerable inquisitiveness of this man?"

The assessor chafed in righteous anger; this impudence was more than he could bear, and as the superintendent was every moment expected, he abandoned his wary manner, and broke out in an overbearing tone,--

"I fear that something more intolerable yet is in store for you. First of all, you will give me your names, and produce your papers: I demand it--I insist upon it! In a word, you are under suspicion."

The elder of the two gentlemen started up pale with terror, and ejaculated, "For heaven's sake!"

"Ha, ha! your sense of guilt is aroused at last," said Hubert, triumphantly. "And you, too, writhe," he added, turning to the younger, and giving him a withering glance. "Do not deny it! I see a twitching in your face."

There was indeed a peculiar play of the muscles around the young man's mouth; it became still more marked as his companion said, in an imploring tone, "Why do you not put an end to this nonsense?"

"Because it amuses me," he answered.

"No whispering allowed here," interposed the assessor. "Do not dare hatch any new plots in my presence. Once again, your names? Will you answer me?"

"And so you take us for conspirators?" said the young man, drawing himself up and gazing contemptuously down upon his accuser.

"And for traitors also," added Hubert.

"And for traitors also? Yes, the two vocations are usually united."

The assessor was dumbfounded at such insolence. "I command you for the last time to give me your names and to hand me your papers," he said. "Do you dare refuse?"

The younger visitor sat down in a very unconcerned manner upon the arm of his companion's chair, and said, coolly,--

"Yes, we *dare*!"

"Sir, I believe you presume to make sport of me," shrieked the assessor, his face glowing with anger. "Do you not know that this will make your case all the more serious? The police department of L----"

"Must be in a very deplorable condition to choose you for its representative," added the young man, with entire composure.

This was more than mortal man could bear. The insulted official was beside himself with rage.

"Monstrous!" cried he. "Your insolence has reached such a point that you openly defy and insult the officers of the law. You shall pay dear for this. You have derided and attacked the government in my person. I arrest you; I shall have you bound and taken in fetters to L----."

He darted like a game-cock at his adversary, who quietly allowed him to come on, and then unceremoniously thrust him back. This required but one movement of his powerful arm, and the assessor bounded like a ball against the sofa, which fortunately was near and arrested his course.

"Force has been used!" he gasped; "an attack has been made upon my person! Fräulein Margaret, go for your father."

"The young lady had better go for a glass of water, and pour it over this fellow's head; he needs it," interrupted the younger man.

Margaret had no time to respond to either of these very dissimilar requests, for hasty steps were heard in the ante-room, and the superintendent entered.

The assessor still lay upon the sofa, struggling with might and main to get once more upon his legs; but, owing to the height of the one and the shortness of the other, the task was quite difficult.

"Herr Frank," he exclaimed, "guard the door! Call the servants. You have police authority in Villica; you must help me arrest these scoundrels, in the name--"

Here his voice failed him; he beat the air despairingly with his hands, and by a powerful effort regained a sitting posture.

The younger man had meantime risen and approached the superintendent.

"Herr Frank," he said, "inasmuch as your police authority in Villica is derived from me, you will doubtless hesitate about delivering over your own landlord."

"My landlord!" exclaimed the superintendent, starting back.

The stranger drew a paper from his pocket, and handed it to him. "I come very unexpectedly, and after the lapse of ten years you will scarce recognize me. This letter may serve to identify me; I received it from you nearly a month ago."

Herr Frank scanned the sheet hastily, and then gazed intently upon the gentleman standing before him. "Are you Herr Nordeck?" he asked.

"Yes, I am Waldemar Nordeck, and immediately upon my return to my estates I am arrested as a villain. This is a very agreeable welcome!"

He glanced over at the sofa where the assessor sat, stiff and motionless as a statue. His mouth was wide open, his arms hung powerless at his side, and he stared at the young landlord as if bereft of his senses.

"This is a very unpleasant misunderstanding," said the superintendent, in extreme embarrassment. "It grieves me deeply, Herr Nordeck, that it should occur in my house. The assessor will regret infinitely--"

The poor assessor! He was so completely overwhelmed that strength was not left him to apologize. He had threatened to put into irons and transport as a criminal to L---- the lord and master of Villica, the millionnaire, the man whom the governor had charged him to treat with peculiar respect if he should happen to return!

Fortunately, Waldemar seemed to have forgotten that the assessor still existed. He introduced his companion to the superintendent and his daughter.

"This is Doctor Fabian, my friend and tutor. We saw the castle illuminated, and heard that a large party was in progress there. As I have no acquaintance with my mother's guests, and as my sudden arrival might interrupt the festivities, I preferred to call here and await the breaking up of the company. And, besides, I wished to speak with you, Herr Frank, in regard to your letter, which reached me only a few days ago. I was travelling, and it was sent after me from place to place. Can we be alone for half an hour?"

Frank opened the study-door, and invited his landlord to enter.

Waldemar turned at the threshold, and said, "Please wait for me, Doctor Fabian; I shall soon return." Then bowing to Margaret, but ignoring the assessor, he entered the study with the superintendent.

"Herr Assessor," said Margaret, in a low voice, approaching the unfortunate representative of the public police, "I congratulate you upon your success; it must pave the way to your appointment as government counsellor."

"O, Fräulein Frank!" groaned the assessor.

"You will doubtless report to his Excellency, the Governor, the result of your investigations?"

"How can you be so cruel, Fräulein Margaret?"

"It is very true I have not the sagacity of an official detective," continued the young girl, unmercifully; "and besides, who but an expert could have seen at a glance that our landlord has a face which clearly stamps him as a conspirator?"

The assessor could endure no more. Derision from these lips was harder than all else he had to bear. He stammered an apology to Doctor Fabian, and pleading indisposition, hastened away.

"Fräulein Frank," observed Doctor Fabian, in his usual timid manner, and yet in a compassionate tone, "that young gentleman seems to be of a somewhat eccentric nature. Is he--" He touched his forehead significantly.

Margaret laughed. "O, no, doctor. He is not idiotic; he is only ambitious of promotion, and he thought to attain his end by the arrest of a pair of conspirators, whom he imagined he had found in you and Herr Nordeck."

The doctor shook his head gravely. "Poor man!" he said; "there must be something morbid in his nature. I do not believe he will be promoted."

"Of course he will not!" said Margaret, with great positiveness; "the government has too much good sense to promote *him*."

CHAPTER XIII.

THE YOUNG LANDLORD'S RETURN.

It was noonday. The festivities at the castle had been continued until a late hour, and the greater number of the guests had remained over night. Count Morynski and his daughter tarried after all the others had left, as politeness required that they should stay to welcome the young landlord. The count's acquaintance with his nephew was so slight that he cut short his first greetings and congratulations, and Wanda felt that she had no right to assert the claims of relationship with one whom she had so deeply and so justly offended.

The princess was alone with her two sons; she sat upon a sofa in the green drawing-room; Waldemar occupied a seat opposite her, and Leo stood leaning over the back of his brother's chair. They seemed an affectionate, harmonious family group.

"No, Waldemar, I cannot forgive you," said the mother, in a half reproachful tone; "it was unpardonable in you to go first to the superintendent's house, as if your own castle was not at any moment open to you; as if it would not have given me pleasure to introduce you to my guests! I cannot accept the pretext that your sudden intrusion might have disconcerted me or the company."

"Then let my disinclination to enter a circle of strangers be a sufficient reason."

"Do you still indulge your old antipathy for society? We must then see less company at Villica."

"Do not change your mode of life on my account, I implore you. But you must excuse me if I do not often appear in your drawing-room. I have in some measure learned to adapt myself to social requirements, but I am never at my ease in large companies."

The princess smiled. Waldemar's unsocial disposition harmonized perfectly with her wishes. She saw that, in spite of the outward improvement these years of culture and travel had made in her eldest son, his nature remained fundamentally the same, and that his exterior had undergone no great transformation. His tall figure, towering above that of Leo, who was also above the average height, was no longer awkward and ungainly; the immaturity of boyhood had given place to a ripe, vigorous manhood. The plain, irregular features had won a grave, self-contained expression; the sudden bursts of passion which had once disfigured them were no longer visible. The blonde hair--"that tawny, yellow mane," as Wanda had been wont to call it--no longer fell in disordered masses over the forehead; it was always carefully arranged, and parted back from the handsome, commanding brow that arched over the deep-blue eyes, whose usual glance was sombre, but which, when lighted up by some momentary excitement or enthusiasm, glowed with a strange lustre, and transfigured the whole face. This broad, high forehead, these deep, earnest eyes, were the only beauty nature had bestowed upon this rugged face, and they had come to the young man through his Polish lineage. But although Waldemar Nordeck had seen much of the world, although the old diffidence and uncouthness had vanished, although his mind was enlarged and improved by years of study and travel, he was no drawing-room knight, no man to win hearts by grace of person or fascination of manner. There was a reserve and distance in his bearing which repelled intimate acquaintance, and forbade anything like familiarity.

The contrast between the two brothers was more marked than ever. Leo was no longer the boy of eighteen years, whom Herr Witold, much as he disliked his mother and his race, had declared "handsome as a picture;" he was a rare type of that Polish beauty which, although exceptional in men of the Slavonic race, appears in rare perfection when it exists at all. He possessed every endowment of grace and fascination of person and manner which had been denied his elder brother. He inherited his mother's refined features, her splendid hazel eyes, which flamed up at the least excitement, and her dark, wavy hair, which in its rich luxuriance formed so pleasing a contrast to the fair, open forehead.

A halo of romance and poetry seemed to encircle his princely form, which united the elegance of the high-born gentleman with the graces of culture and society. Leo Zulieski realized the highest ideal of manly beauty and chivalry.

"And so you have really brought your former tutor along with you," said the young prince. "I wonder at your taste, Waldemar. I was glad enough to be rid of mine, and I would not for the world have taken him with me to the university or upon my travels."

Waldemar's face lighted up, as it always did when he spoke of his tutor, for whom he cherished a profound respect and admiration.

"You must not look upon Doctor Fabian as a mere teacher, Leo; he now devotes himself exclusively to historical researches. Poverty alone made him a tutor; he has always been a scholar in heart and soul, but teaching was the only means he had of turning his knowledge to practical account."

"His manners have all the dryness and pedantry of a book-worm," interposed the princess.

"You do not know him," returned Waldemar, almost angrily. "He has a future before him of which you little dream."

The princess thought best to turn the conversation. "Leo takes great pleasure in the prospect of being your guide and companion in the chase," she said. "The forests around Villica offer such attractions that I cannot expect to have you in the house a great deal for the next few weeks."

Waldemar glanced up at Leo, who stood leaning against his chair. "I only fear, Leo," he said, "that our manner of hunting may prove very different; even as a huntsman you will still remain an elegant gentleman, who can come directly from the forest to the parlor; but I must follow my game through almost impenetrable thickets, and often enough through swamp and moor. Perhaps this will not suit you."

The young prince laughed. "It will prove a more serious matter here in our Polish forests than in your peaceful hunting-grounds at Altenhof. You will soon be able to judge for yourself if a hunter can come off from a conflict with wolves in a suitable condition for the *salon.* I have had plenty of adventures; and as Wanda is a passionate huntress--But do you know that she is here in Villica?"

"The Countess Morynski? Ah, yes! I have heard so."

"Countess Morynski!" echoed the princess, reproachfully. "She is your cousin, Waldemar, and she will soon stand in a nearer relationship to you. Leo, I think you have no desire to conceal from your brother a fact which is still kept secret from strangers?

"Certainly not," replied the young prince, eagerly. "You must know, Waldemar, that I am betrothed to Wanda?"

"Betrothed--indeed!" replied Waldemar, without the slightest emotion, and with no change in his half-recumbent posture.

"You do not seem at all surprised," said Leo, somewhat hurt by his brother's indifference.

"O, not at all!" returned Waldemar, carelessly. "I think you always loved your cousin, and I imagine that you have met no opposition either from our mother or from Wanda's father. I wish you happiness, Leo," he added, extending his hand.

Leo grasped the proffered hand with genuine cordiality. He had feared to broach the subject, knowing that he and Wanda had wantonly trifled with Waldemar's feelings; but the composure with which his brother learned of his engagement reassured him and his mother.

"You will see Wanda and her father to-day," said the princess, turning to Waldemar. "Their estate lies so near us that our intercourse is quite frequent; you must accompany us there very soon. But how do you like Villica? You have remained away from it a long time. When we were at C---- that summer, you promised to come the next spring, and four years have passed since then."

"It was my intention to come sooner," said Waldemar, as he rose and walked to the large bay-window. "But you are right; I am almost a stranger here. I shall have to wander over the whole estate before I feel at all at home."

"The whole estate?" returned the princess, gravely. "I hardly think you will find much to interest you excepting the forests. The superintendent will report to you upon the condition of the estate. He has no doubt informed you of his intention to resign?" She asked the question with apparent unconcern, and in no way betrayed the anxiety with which she awaited the answer.

"Yes," said Waldemar, gazing absently out of the window, "he is going about New Year's."

"I regret his departure on your account, and all the more from the fact that I am its indirect cause. Frank's excellent management is conceded by all, and it will be difficult to fill his place. His services, however, involve the continual absence of the landlord, for he will submit to no dictation. His subordinates complain bitterly of his imperiousness. I myself have felt aggrieved by it, and have been forced to remind him that Villica Castle and its mistress were not subject to his absolute control. This has led to his resignation. The question now arises, Whose part will you take? I think the superintendent will willingly remain, if you allow him to continue sole master. I, of course, shall submit to your decision."

"I came only last night," returned Waldemar, "and it is impossible for me to fully understand the state of affairs so soon. If Frank wants to leave, I shall not hinder him, and if a misunderstanding with you is the cause of his resignation, I hope that you do not harbor a thought that I would allow the superintendent to prevail against my mother."

The princess felt greatly relieved. She had feared that during Waldemar's brief stay at the superintendent's, some disclosures had been made prejudicial to her interests. The young landlord's manner indicated nothing of the kind. It was evidently a matter of small importance to him whether the superintendent went or stayed, and his native sense of propriety would urge him to take his mother's part without investigation.

"I knew that I could depend upon you, Waldemar," she said, graciously. All was turning out according to her wishes. "But why should we at the outset fall to discussing dry business details, as if there were nothing better at our command? I wished to say-- Ah, come in, Bronislaw," she added, turning to her brother, who stood in the doorway with his daughter.

At these words, Waldemar also turned around. His first emotion in glancing at the young girl who stood opposite him, was profound astonishment. He had known Wanda as a girl of sixteen years,--as a charming child, rather than a woman. This form was new to him; the early promise of uncommon beauty had been more than fulfilled. Wanda's beauty did not lie in regularity of features, which were of the Slavonic rather than of the Greek or Roman type; but the fresh, rosy countenance possessed an indefinable charm that did not consist in perfection of outline, but in expression.

The deep-black hair, not arranged after the reigning mode, but in a fashion of Wanda's own, which displayed its wonderful beauty and luxuriance, set off more strikingly the exceeding fairness of the complexion; but the great charm of this unique face lay, after all, in the eyes,--large, dark, and lustrous, now veiled by their long, silken lashes, now opening wide and full, with an expression changing with every new and varied emotion. These eyes now revealed something more than childish arrogance and mischief. Whether veiled in dreamy repose, or lighted up by glowing enthusiasm, they remained unfathomable and dangerous. They had a spell which could irresistibly ensnare and steadfastly retain, and the young Countess Morynski had often tried this power, of which she was fully conscious.

"Your sudden arrival has surprised us all," the count remarked to Waldemar; "and you found your house full of guests. We intended to leave early this morning, but being informed of your presence here, we remained to greet you."

"Welcome home, Cousin Waldemar!" added Wanda, extending her hand with a charming smile, and with the most graceful ingenuousness.

Waldemar bowed very formally and coldly to his beautiful cousin. He seemed neither to have seen the extended hand nor to have heard the courteous words, for, without making the slightest answer, he turned to Count Morynski.

"I sincerely hope I do not hasten your departure, Herr Count. I as well as you am my mother's guest, and both are equally welcome to remain."

The count was agreeably surprised by these gracious words; he had not thought Waldemar could be so courteous. He replied politely. Wanda stood opposite the young landlord like one stricken dumb with astonishment. She had thought proper to meet her cousin with the graceful ease of a lady well versed in the ways of good society, and to spare him all painful recollections; and now she saw that her urbanity was not accepted, that her magnanimity was repelled. The look of icy indifference Waldemar gave her showed that he must have forgotten the old affection, but that he had not forgiven the old insult, and that he was now taking his revenge.

The conversation soon became general. There was no lack of subjects. They talked of Waldemar's travels, of his return, of Villica and its environs. But there was no familiarity; it was like talking to a stranger. This scion of a plebeian race did not belong to the Zulieski and Morynski circle; all felt this, and the remarks assumed a corresponding tone. The count could not bring himself to accost his sister's elder son with the familiar "thou" which he naturally used in addressing the younger, and Waldemar invariably saluted his uncle as "Herr Count." He was rather silent and reserved, but all trace of his former diffidence and embarrassment had vanished.

As it was autumn, the conversation naturally turned upon the chase, which was the chief amusement in that region. The ladies were not strangers to this sport, and eagerly joined in its discussion. Leo having highly extolled several rifles found in the deceased Nordeck's large collection of weapons, the gentlemen at length left the room to examine them.

"The same Waldemar as of old," the princess remarked, gazing after them. "He does not manifest the least emotion, excepting when matters connected with the chase are discussed. Nothing else seems to interest him. Do you find him changed, Wanda?"

"Yes; he has acquired great self-control."

"Heaven be praised! His manners, too, are wonderfully improved. I can now introduce him to my friends without fear of incurring their ridicule, and without dreading an outburst of rage from him at every harmless observation. He doubtless keeps his explosions of temper for his subordinates."

Wanda made no reply; she had thrown herself into an easy-chair, and was toying with its silken tassels.

"His manner of arrival was a genuine Nordeck trick," continued the princess, in an annoyed tone. "He left the post-chaise at the last station, and came on foot like some penniless adventurer. On seeing the castle illuminated, and hearing that we had company, he went to the superintendent's house for fear that we might inveigle him into taking part in our festivities. Late at night he came here with the doctor, made himself known to Paul, and was conducted at once to his apartments. His orders were that I should not be disturbed, but I was informed of his arrival five minutes afterwards; my servants are better trained than he imagines. As his commands were positive, the only alternative left me was to ignore his presence and allow myself to appear greatly surprised the next morning."

"And the surprise made it necessary for us to remain," said Wanda, impatiently. "I hope that papa will soon return, and that we may leave immediately."

"But will you not stay to dinner?"

"No, aunt; I wish to go at once. Do you think it is pleasant for me to remain here and be ignored by Waldemar Nordeck, as I have been for the last half hour? He never spoke to me once; he did not even answer me."

The princess smiled. "Well, you can afford him this petty revenge at your first meeting; the old grudge still remains, but it will wear away upon longer acquaintance. What do you think of his personal appearance? I consider him very much improved."

"He is just as repulsive as ever!" exclaimed Wanda, passionately, "and even more so, for now he studies to repel. But, in spite of everything, for some undefined reason, perhaps it is on account of his really fine eyes and forehead, he no longer suffers from comparison with Leo."

The same observation had forced itself upon the mother, as her two sons stood side by side. Although the beauty of the younger son was unquestionable, and the elder had very slight claims to good looks, still there was in Waldemar a certain something which usurped the place of every mere personal advantage, and the mother was compelled to admit the fact.

"Such tall, well-developed figures always possess an advantage," she said. "They make a favorable impression at first, but that is all. Mind and character are never associated with them."

"*Never?*" asked Wanda, with a peculiar emphasis. "Are you perfectly sure?"

The princess looked at her niece in surprise, and Wanda continued,--

"We both know the designs now on foot at Villica, and how inconvenient and dangerous to our purposes it would be to have Waldemar give evidence of the possession of mind and character. Let us be cautious! This outward composure, and above all this forehead, do not please me."

"Will you allow my ability to read my son's true character?" replied the princess, in a tone of self-conscious superiority; "or do you credit your twenty years with a greater discernment than mine, which more than double them, can claim? Waldemar is a *Nordech*--that tells the whole story."

"And you have always judged him from this standpoint. In other respects he may be the living image of his father, but he has inherited that forehead from his mother. Do you consider it impossible for him to have inherited some of your mental traits?"

"*I do!*" replied the princess, emphatically. "Leo inherits all that could be transmitted of my nature. I am at a loss to comprehend how you can infer intellect and character in Waldemar from his stubborn persistence in an old rancor; to me it proves just the reverse. Any other young man would have thanked you for seeking to help him avoid a painful recollection, and would have met his brother's affianced bride with at least an attempt at courtesy--"

"Does Waldemar already know?" interrupted the young girl.

"Certainly; Leo himself informed him."

"And how did he receive the news?"

"With the most perfect indifference. He has entirely overcome his boyish fancy for you, but the old resentment for an imagined injury still remains. And you wish me to accept this obstinate, revengeful feeling as a token of character?"

"Certainly not!" replied Wanda, starting up impatiently; "but I will no longer expose myself to his studied neglect; you must excuse us, dear aunt. *I*, at least, shall not remain here any longer, and papa will hardly allow me to depart alone. We shall go within an hour."

In vain the princess protested. She once more had evidence that her niece, as well as herself, knew how to carry out her wishes, and that Count Morynski was inexcusably weak in all attempts at opposition to his daughter's plans.

Leo's wishes and entreaties, joined to those of his mother, were alike unavailing; neither could his evident displeasure move Wanda in the least. Ere the expiration of the hour the young lady had named as the term of her visit, the Morynski carriage bore the father and daughter back to Radowicz.

CHAPTER XIV.

THE HUNTING-PARTY.

Weeks rolled away, but the arrival of the young landlord had produced little change in Villica. His old passion for the chase seemed to have again taken full possession of him: he was seldom found in the castle, his days being mostly passed in roaming about the forests. He did not appear regularly at meals, his jaunts often taking him so far from home that he was obliged to lunch at some forester's place or farm-house. He usually returned late, and spent the evening in his own apartments with Doctor Fabian, the only person whose society he sought. He entered his mother's drawing-room only at rare intervals, and always reluctantly.

Leo had ceased accompanying his brother to the chase; the two could not hunt together, their manner of engaging in the sport was so different. In hunting, as in everything else, the young prince was fiery and venturesome, but not persistent; he shot whatever came in his way, he was deterred by no obstacle, and danger lent new zest to his enjoyment. Waldemar, on the other hand, followed the game with tireless energy, never thinking of food or rest, and imposing hardships upon himself which only an iron frame could endure. Leo thought such persistence wearisome and useless, and when he found that his brother preferred to hunt alone, he only too gladly allowed him that privilege.

Although Waldemar saw and conversed daily with his mother and brother, he could not be regarded as one of the family. His unconquerable reserve and his aversion to familiar intercourse increased rather than diminished. After a stay of several weeks at Villica, he was not one step nearer the princess or Leo than on the day of his arrival. This state of things was highly gratifying to the Princess Zulieski; Waldemar's daily absence perfectly coincided with her hopes and plans, and he was far more affable than she had expected. He even carried his courtesy so far as to call occasionally at his uncle's castle, and intercourse between the two estates became more frequent than ever. The count and his daughter often drove over to Villica, although they seldom met its master.

One thing only marred these very pleasant and satisfactory relations: this was the coldness and evident hostility between Waldemar and Wanda. The princess, after many fruitless attempts to act as mediator, concluded to let "the two obstinate children" have their own way, so long at least as there was no open quarrel between them. Waldemar evidently made an effort to be gracious and amiable to his uncle, and he gratified all his relatives in one particular, if in no other,--he kept away from them as much as possible.

The princess had made arrangements for another of her large hunting-parties, which brought together the Polish gentry of that region far and near. The invitations had all been accepted, and the party would be larger than usual. Waldemar having been consulted in regard to the arrangements and invitations, had begged his mother to assume the entire responsibility, his acquaintance in the neighborhood being limited, and his tastes being averse to these large social gatherings. The princess, although full of polite regrets at the loss of his assistance, was really in her element; she dearly loved to rule in all matters both great and small, and wanted no rival near her throne.

The morning of the eventful day dawned cloudy and threatening; when the sky at length cleared, so that the hunt could be safely decided upon, the hour was unusually late. The princess and Leo stood in the centre of the large reception-room to receive the farewell greetings of the party, and as the young prince assisted his mother in doing the honors of the house, a stranger would have taken him for the master of Villica. Waldemar meanwhile remained unnoticed at a window, in earnest conversation with Doctor Fabian. He seemed to regard himself as merely his mother's guest, and as he claimed no deference for his real position, he received none. He was sure of a respectful greeting as he came and went, and was listened to attentively whenever he chose to take part in the conversation; but he was landlord of Villica only in name. None attempted to approach him familiarly, or to pierce the mail of his obstinate reserve. There seemed to be a mutual understanding; the visitors took no more notice of him than he of them.

"Pray do not ride in your usual reckless manner, Leo," said the princess, as she took leave of her younger son with a fond embrace. "You and Wanda rival each other in adventurous daring; be cautious, I beseech you." She then turned to her elder son, and offering him her hand as a mere friend might do, she added, "Good-bye, Waldemar; you are no doubt in your element to-day."

"Indeed I am not," he replied, abruptly; "large, fashionable hunting-parties are not to my taste. The hunters and beaters go before these fine ladies and gentlemen, and run down the game for them, so that neither effort nor skill is required."

"Waldemar is happy only when alone with his beloved rifle," said Leo, laughing. "I really believe he dragged me through swamps and underbrush, and exposed me to hunger and thirst and all sorts of disagreeable things, merely to get rid of me as soon as possible. I am no novice at hunting, but I soon tire of the hardships Waldemar calls pleasure."

"I told you beforehand that my mode of hunting would not suit you," replied Waldemar indifferently, as the party left the room.

A portion of the hunters had already assembled upon the broad lawn in front of the castle; among them were Count Morynski and his daughter. The gentlemen were in raptures over Herr Nordeck's fine saddle-horse, which had arrived two days before. All agreed that the young landlord had shown great taste and judgment in its selection.

"A splendid animal!" said the count, as he patted the slender neck of the horse, which stood patient under his caresses. "Waldemar, is this really the wild Norman you used to ride in C----? He was then so dangerous that your groom was always in mortal terror when holding him by the bit."

"Norman was very young then," replied Waldemar, coming up with his brother; "he had just begun to wear the saddle. He has since become accustomed to control, and I myself am not so adventurous a rider as at that time. You can ask Leo about the animal's docility; he attempted to mount Norman yesterday."

"He is a demon of a horse!" exclaimed Leo, excitedly. "I believe you have trained him to act like a mad creature whenever any one else sets foot in the stirrup. But I will conquer him yet!"

"You had better not try it; Norman will obey no one but me."

Leo's face glowed as he met Wanda's eyes, which imperiously commanded him to refute this assertion. The glance stung him, and he said, impetuously,--

"Norman's obstinacy is the result of your own training, Waldemar. I have not taught my Vaillant any such tricks," he added, pointing to a handsome sorrel nag, held by his groom, "but you might succeed no better with him than I did with Norman. You have never cared to make the attempt; will you do so to-day?"

"No," replied Waldemar, coolly. "Your horse is very unruly at times; you indulge him in all sorts of antics, and in a stubbornness which I could not endure. I should be obliged to misuse him, and I would not like to treat an animal you are fond of in such a manner."

"You had better make the experiment, Herr Nordeck," said Wanda. She had never said "Cousin Waldemar" but once. "Indeed, I believe you ride *nearly* as well as Leo."

"I thank you for the compliment, Countess Morynski," he replied, bowing profoundly.

"The Germans are very fair riders," she added, in a still more irritating tone; "but in this accomplishment, as in most others, they are far behind our Polish gentlemen."

Nordeck's only answer was to say to his brother, "Will you resign your Vaillant to me for this one day, Leo? Are you willing to expose him to hardship, perhaps to danger?"

"To *danger*!" reiterated Leo, with flaming eyes.

"Do not insist upon it, Herr Nordeck," interposed the count; "the horse is wild and unmanageable, and Leo has accustomed him to all sorts of mad freaks and rash ventures, which a strange rider, even though the most expert, cannot understand. He will be sure to throw you."

"But if Herr Nordeck is willing to run the risk, let him do so!" said Wanda, obstinately.

The count gave his daughter a reproving glance, but Waldemar took no seeming notice of her words. "Have no fear, Count Morynski," he said; "I shall ride the horse. Your daughter wishes to see me thrown: I *may* allow her that pleasure. Come, Leo."

"I entreat you to desist, Wanda," whispered the count. "Waldemar hates you bitterly enough already, and still you go on irritating him at every opportunity."

The young countess stroked the folds of her velvet riding-dress with her whip. "You mistake, papa," she said; "Herr Nordeck does not allow himself to be irritated,--least of all by *me*."

"Then why do you continually attempt it?"

Wanda made no reply. Her father was right; she neglected no opportunity of taunting the young man, who had once flown into a passion at every trifling word, but whose stolid composure she could not now ruffle in the least.

The other gentlemen had become deeply interested in the venture; they knew Nordeck as a daring, skilful rider, but they had no idea that he could rival Prince Zulieski, and, less thoughtful than Count Morynski, they coolly resigned this "foreign plebeian" to certain discomfiture. The brothers stood near the splendid steed. The slim, fiery animal pawed the ground impatiently, and threatened every moment to break away from his groom. Leo took the bridle and held the horse while his brother mounted. His eyes beamed with satisfaction; he knew his Vaillant, and he was confident which would win the victory.

Vaillant scarcely felt the strange hand on the bridle, when he began to manifest his native obstinacy. He reared and plunged, and made the most violent efforts to rid himself of the burden; but the rider sat firmly in the saddle, and resisted the horse's frantic opposition so coolly and yet so energetically, that the animal soon grew quiet. But when Waldemar was ready to start, he refused to obey; the rider's whole skill and energy could not move him, he positively refused to stir, and at length became furious and decidedly dangerous. Thus far, Waldemar had remained perfectly composed, but now his brow grew dark, his lips compressed; his patience was exhausted. He raised his whip, and a merciless blow fell upon the refractory animal.

This unusual severity maddened the obstinate and spoiled Vaillant; he made a leap which caused the bystanders to scatter right and left, and shot like an arrow across the lawn into the broad avenue leading to the castle. There the ride became an infuriated combat between man and beast. Vaillant seemed determined to throw his rider. Waldemar retained his place, but it was at the risk of his life.

"End this mad conflict, Leo," said Count Morynski to his nephew. "Vaillant will grow quiet if you approach him; persuade your brother to dismount, or he may be killed."

Leo stood before his uncle with folded arms, and made no movement at interference. "I did not conceal from Waldemar the danger of riding my horse," he said, coldly. "If he purposely exasperates Vaillant, he must take the consequences; he knows that the animal will not endure harsh treatment."

Waldemar returned to the place whence he had started. He had forced Vaillant into the direction he wished to take, but had not conquered him. The horse still resisted his rider's iron will, and tried to throw him. Nordeck showed that the passion of his boyhood, so long repressed, had again revived; his face glowed, his eyes flashed, his teeth were set; he used the whip and spur in so unsparing a manner that Leo was beside himself. He had calmly contemplated his brother's danger, but he could not endure this ill-treatment of his favorite Vaillant.

"Stop, Waldemar!" he cried, angrily; "you will ruin my horse; you have proved that you can force Vaillant to carry you, now give him up to me."

"I shall first teach him obedience," said Waldemar, in a voice that betrayed the wildest excitement. He paid no heed to Leo's protests--their only result was the harsher treatment of the horse in a second course around the lawn. On the third round, Vaillant ceased his opposition, kept straight on in the road, and, at a single pressure of the bit, halted before the castle, but in a state of entire exhaustion.

Nordeck dismounted; the gentlemen thronged around him and complimented him, although somewhat reluctantly, upon his horsemanship. Leo had not a word to say. He patted his trembling, panting Vaillant in sullen silence, and his ill-humor was not at all improved when he saw that his favorite's glossy, brown coat bore blood-stains here and there from the merciless use of Waldemar's spurs.

"An unparalleled test of endurance!" said Count Morynski, gravely; "Vaillant will not soon forget this ride."

Waldemar had regained his self-control; but his flushed face and the swollen blue vein on his temple still bore evidence of his inward perturbation, as he replied,--

"It was my duty to prove that I in some measure deserved the Countess Morynski's flattering testimony, that I could ride *nearly* as well as my brother."

Wanda stood near Leo, her face wearing an expression which indicated that she too had suffered a defeat which must be avenged. Her dark eyes flashed ominously.

"I regret that my thoughtless remark has subjected poor Vaillant to this cruel treatment," she answered, struggling for breath. "The noble animal is accustomed only to kindness."

"Neither am I accustomed to such opposition," sharply retorted Waldemar. "It is not my fault that Vaillant will submit only to whip and spur,--for submit he must."

Leo forestalled the angry reply already upon Wanda's lips, by ordering his groom in a loud voice to take Vaillant to the stable, to care for him in the kindest manner, and to bring him another horse. Seeing his nephew's excitement and resentment, Count Morynski took him aside and implored him to control his anger. "Do you wish to have a quarrel with your brother, here in presence of all these guests?" he asked.

"I don't care if I do," hotly replied the young prince, in a low sullen tone. "Has he not declared before them all that I cannot manage his Norman? Has he not ridden my Vaillant nearly to death, and all for a paltry bit of braggadocio?"

"But consider! You proposed the test, and he at first declined to accept it."

"He wanted to display his superiority in mere physical force. As if any one ever disputed that point which is his one great merit! I tell you, uncle, that my patience will never bear the like of this again, even were he tenfold master of Villica."

"Do show some discretion," said the count. "You and Wanda subordinate everything to your personal feelings. Nothing delights my daughter more than to exasperate Waldemar."

"Wanda can openly show her dislike," muttered Leo. "But I--There he stands by his Norman, as if they both were peace and tranquillity incarnate; but just let any one interfere with them."

The new horse was brought, and the hunting-party rode away. It was fortunate that the chase kept the brothers apart, for Leo's anger might have broken out into open hostility. Both brothers entered eagerly into the sport, and their quarrel was for the time forgotten.

Waldemar was wrong in despising those large, fashionable hunting-parties which were carried out in a style of princely magnificence at Villica. All the foresters and their assistants were required to appear in gala dress, the entire forest was in commotion, and swarmed with woodsmen and game-beaters, while the large, elegant, and exciting hunting-party sweeping past, formed an imposing pageant. The gentlemen, mostly distinguished by splendid figures, and wearing rich hunting-costumes, were mounted on spirited and gayly caparisoned horses, while the ladies at their side, in their beautiful riding-dresses and waving plumes, were equally well mounted, and the servants brought up the rear. The sounding of horns, the yelping of dogs, the shouts of the game-beaters, all combined to form a spectacle full of life and animation, which became even more lively and excited when the fleeing game and the whizzing shots awaking echoes through the forest, announced that the sport had actually begun.

The weather was everything that could be desired; it was a cool and hazy, but yet a fine November day. The Villica hunting-grounds boasted a matchless stock of deer, and excellent arrangements for securing a large booty had been made. The hunt was the more animated from the lateness of the hour; amends must be made for the morning's delay, and the autumn afternoon was already drawing to a close.

A few thousand yards distant from the forester's place, which to-day served as a rendezvous, lay a wooded meadow, lonely and almost lost in the midst of the foliage. During the summer season it was concealed from view by thick underbrush and stately trees, but now it was in full sight, the trees and bushes being nearly dismantled of their foliage. In the centre of the clearing there was a body of water, a small, transparent lake such as the forest often conceals in its depths. In summer, waving swamp-grasses and dreamy water-lilies threw a peculiar charm about the place which was now sombre and colorless, its withered leaves and faded turf being in unison with the autumnal aspect of the surrounding landscape.

Under one of these stately, wide-branching trees the Countess Morynski stood alone. Her seclusion was voluntary; she could not have been left behind by the hunting-party, which was distinctly heard at a short distance, and the forest-keeper's house where she had left her horse was also near. She leaned against the tree and gazed intently into the water, but her thoughts were evidently far away. Her beautiful eyes had a lowering glance, and the deep frown that furrowed her fair brow showed that she was under the influence of some angry emotion. The noisy hunting party drew nearer and then turned suddenly toward the river which flowed at some distance, very remote from the place Wanda had chosen as her retreat. The wild, confused sounds died away in the distance, only the far-off report of a rifle was heard at intervals, and soon death-like silence reigned.

As Wanda stood there seemingly lost in thought, the sound of a footstep and a rustling of branches startled her. Somewhat vexed at the disturbance, she looked around to discover its cause; the bushes parted, and Waldemar Nordeck appeared before her.

His surprise fully equalled her own. This unexpected meeting seemed as unpleasant to him as to her; but retreat was impossible, recognition had been mutual. Waldemar bowed stiffly, and said,--

"I was not aware, Countess Morynski, that you had left the chase; I did not suppose that so indefatigable a huntress would give up the pursuit until the last moment."

"And you too are an ardent hunter. Why did you leave the party so soon?" asked Wanda.

"I have had enough of it," returned Waldemar, shrugging his shoulders. "Such a crowd and tumult spoil all my pleasure. I prefer to hunt alone."

Wanda also had grown weary of the rush and noise, and had come here in quest of silence and solitude, but she would not confess it. "Do you come from the rendezvous?" she asked.

"No; but I have sent my horse there. The day's sport is nearly over; the hunting-party will pass here on its return, and I propose to await it."

As he said this, he set down his fowling-piece and the cock he had shot.

Wanda frowned. What business had he to be waiting here in the place she had chosen as her own retreat? Her first impulse was to leave; but was it not his duty to withdraw? She resolved to remain, even at the cost of being forced to tolerate the presence of this detestable man.

He did not manifest the slightest intention of leaving; he stood near her with folded arms, gazing upon the surrounding scene. The sun had been all day hidden behind a dense veil of clouds, but now a golden radiance broke through the fog, lighting up the western horizon and shimmering through the tree-tops. Ere long misty shadows, the harbingers of approaching night, began to rise from the meadows. The forest with its half dismantled trees and the withered leaves strewing the ground, lent the scene a bleak, autumnal aspect. There was no trace of that fresh, invigorating breath which pulsates through the woods in spring and summer; no token of that potent, life-giving power which at those seasons throbs through the veins and arteries of nature. Waning existence, slow, irresistible decay, were impressed upon all around.

Wanda's eyes rested as if in gloomy meditation upon the face of her companion; she seemed anxious to decipher his hidden thoughts. Although his face was half averted, he must have been conscious of her gaze, for he turned abruptly, and said indifferently,--

"There is something really comfortless in an autumnal landscape at an hour like this."

"And yet it has its own melancholy, poetic charm," returned Wanda; "do you not think so?"

"I?" he said, coldly; "I have had very little to do with poetry; you know that, Countess Morynski."

"And yet there are moments when the most prosaic natures must feel its spell."

"That may be, and to romantic natures such moments very often come. One like me must get through the world as best he can without romance or poetry. Such an existence, although not enviable, is at least endurable."

"How calmly you say this. And yet endurance was never your distinguishing virtue."

"Would you expect me to remain my whole life long a passionate, impetuous boy? Do you not think me capable of outgrowing juvenile follies?"

Wanda bit her lips; he had already proved the contrary.

"I certainly do," she said. "Indeed, I think you capable of a great deal more than you think proper to admit."

Waldemar scanned the young lady's face very closely. "Then you differ from all others in Villica; it is the general belief here that my abilities are of no high order."

"Because you choose to have them think so. I perhaps have deeper insight than the others."

"You flatter me," returned Waldemar, ironically; "but although you mean this kindly, it is cruel in you to deprive me of the only merit I possess in the eyes of my mother and brother--that of being harmless and insignificant."

"If my aunt could only hear the tone in which you say this, she would change her mind," returned Wanda, irritated by his sarcasm. "At present, I am alone in my opinion."

"And will remain so," added Waldemar. "It is conceded that I am an expert hunter, and after to-day's test, I may, perhaps, have the credit of being a skilful rider--but that is all."

"Are you really hunting, Herr Nordeck, when you roam about all day with your rifle and game-bag?"

"What else can I be doing?"

"I do not know, but I imagine that you are making a very thorough inspection of Villica. There is not a village, a forester's hut, or a farmhouse far or near upon your estates, that you have not visited. In all these places, as well as in your mother's salon, where you appear seldom and play a very indifferent part, you are constantly in search of information. You seem to take no notice of your mother's guests, but there is not a single one of them who has not been submitted to your scrutiny, upon whom you have not passed judgment. Not a word or glance escapes you."

She hurled all this at him blow after blow, with a precision and a determination which were well calculated to embarrass him, and for a moment he could not reply. He stood there with knit brows and compressed lips, evidently struggling to keep down his anger. But it was not so easy to disconcert Waldemar Nordeck. When he looked up at Wanda, a frown still rested upon his forehead, but his voice was sarcastic rather than angry.

"Your ladyship really embarrasses me. It seems that from the first day of my sojourn here I have been the object of your minute and almost exclusive observation. This is an honor which I really do not deserve."

Wanda was furious. Her cheeks glowed with rage as she met the glance of the audacious man who had dared to parry her blow with her own weapons.

"I do not deny this minute observation; but you yourself will admit, Herr Nordeck, that I have not made it from the slightest personal interest in you."

His lips curled in a bitter smile. "You are perfectly right; I had no idea that you could take the slightest personal interest in me; the indifference is perhaps mutual."

"But you will at least allow that I have been frank with you: it only remains for you to admit or deny the truth of my conclusions."

"But what if I choose to do neither?"

"Then my opinion will be confirmed, and I shall earnestly endeavor to convince my aunt that her son is more dangerous than she supposes."

Waldemar's voice had a tone of cutting irony as he replied,--

"You may have very excellent judgment, Countess Morynski, but you are not a diplomatist; if you were, you would be more guarded in your expressions. *Dangerous?* That is a significant word."

The young girl gave an involuntary start. "I merely repeated your own expression," she said, regaining her self-control.

"Ah! I began to think that something was going on in Villica, the success of which might be endangered by my presence."

Wanda made no reply. She began to see how indiscreet she had been. Her adversary had parried every thrust, returned every blow, and entrapped her in her own words. He had also possessed the advantage of remaining cool and collected, while she had lost her temper. She saw that she must attempt to rescue herself from the net which her own indiscretion had woven around her.

"Will you desist from this mockery?" she said, fixing her large, defiant eyes full upon his face. "I know that it is directed solely against me. You at last force me to allude to a subject which I recall very much against my will. I once wronged, perhaps insulted you, and you have never forgotten it. I was entirely to blame--I confess it--will you forgive me?"

The apology was made in a tone which expressed all the pride of a woman who realizes that it is no humiliation to ask forgiveness of the man with whom she has trifled. Its effect was entirely different from what she had expected.

Waldemar approached a step nearer, and his eyes rested with a penetrating glance upon her face. "Indeed," he said, slowly, and strongly emphasizing every word,--"indeed, I was not aware that Villica was of so much consequence to your party."

"Do you believe--" Wanda began.

"I believe that one day I shall have to pay dear for being master of these estates," interrupted he. "Four years ago the main point was to induce me to open Villica to my mother and her interests; now the main point is to retain it in her interests at any price; but they forget that I am no longer an inexperienced boy. You yourself have opened my eyes, countess, and I shall keep them open even at the risk of incurring your resentment."

Wanda turned deathly pale; her right hand clenched involuntarily the folds of her velvet riding-dress.

"Enough!" she said, making a powerful effort to regain her self-control, "I see that you spurn all reconciliation, and try to offend me so as to render an understanding impossible. Well and good! I accept the proffered enmity."

"You mistake!" rejoined Waldemar, calmly. "I do not proffer you enmity: that would be very ungallant toward--"

"Toward whom?" exclaimed Wanda, with flashing eyes, as he hesitated.

"Toward my brother's affianced bride."

Wanda's whole frame was convulsed. Strange as it may appear, that word stabbed her to the heart. Her eyes involuntarily sought the ground.

"I have hitherto neglected to offer you my congratulations," continued Waldemar; "will you accept them to-day?"

She bowed her thanks in silence. She herself did not know what sealed her lips, but she could not answer at this moment. For the first time the betrothal had been alluded to between them, and the mere mention of it seemed sufficient, for even Waldemar did not add a syllable to his congratulations.

The golden lustre of the western sky had long since faded into a pale, sombre gray; the light evening wind rustled the underbrush and swayed gently the tree-tops now half dismantled of their foliage, which hung in mottled shreds from the branches, or had fallen, leaf by leaf, strewing the forest-floor and the unruffled surface of the lake. Other withered, dying leaves, swayed to and fro by the breeze, seemed sighing a low wail for all that life and beauty which had known its brief hour of bloom and brightness, and was now passing to its grave. Ever deepening shadows wrapt the forest; vapory clouds from the damp meadows, growing denser as they rose, ere long hung in threatening masses above the water. Now, floating in mid-air, appeared a ghostly apparition, stretching out its humid, nebulous arms to these two beings standing on the edge of the lake, as if it would draw them to itself,--anon it dissolved into thousands of phantom forms and pictures, each succeeding the other in endless variation.

No sound was heard save the low, sad, monotone of the winds and the gentle dropping of the leaves; but through the ever-changing mists above the water appeared a sort of *fata morgana*, the picture of a forest knoll with primeval beeches, and of a heaving sea stretching out to the horizon's verge, the whole illuminated by the golden light of a summer sunset. The sun sank slowly beneath the waters, and amid a flood of radiance rose again the old wonder-city of tradition,--that city which has been the theme of so many a story, the inspiration of so many a song. Fairy-land again opened to mortal gaze, and from the depths was heard a musical chime, the chime of the bells of Vineta, the sunken city beneath the wave.

The fairy vision had not kept its word to these two who had seen it that day upon the beech-holm. They had parted in estrangement and hostility, they met again upon the same footing. The youth had become a man who was passing through life unloving and solitary; the young girl had become a woman blessed with beauty, love, and fortune: but they had never again found what that one hour at the beech-holm had brought them, never until this autumnal evening, when the old vision reappeared before their eyes. And now, as they stood there together, the intervening years vanished, hatred, strife and bitterness were at an end, and nothing remained in their hearts save a deep, inexpressible yearning for a happiness they might never know, a happiness whose first premonitions had come to them with that vision of Vineta--that mirage at sunset.

Waldemar was first to speak. "The atmospheric effects in this North-sea region are very wonderful," he said. "This mirage, this *fata morgana* which is so often seen here, has given rise to one of the most beautiful of our North-German legends. So clearly defined are the outlines of the city which seemingly rises from the waters, that we cannot wonder at the old traditionary belief in Vineta, a city like the island of Atalantis sunken beneath the waves, and remaining in its pristine splendor at the ocean's depths; but unlike its prototype, our submerged city often revisits the upper air, and appears beautiful as of old to mortal eyes."

"We have seen it twice," said Wanda, "and both times I have fancied I heard the chiming of its bells."

"The reflection of city roofs and spires was real, the sounds were purely imaginary."

"I never heard the legend of Vineta until you told it to me four years ago," observed Wanda. "Since then I find that it has been a favorite theme of our poets."

"Yes, I am aware of that. During these years of study and travel I too have learned something of poetry, and I have in mind several little ballads founded upon this legend."

"Will you not recite one of them?" asked Wanda, eagerly.

"O, no! I never recite poetry, and I only recall a stanza here and there."

"But, please, repeat what you know," pleaded Wanda, in her most irresistible tone.

"There was a time when your wish was my law, but now--"

"Now I no longer command; I beg and entreat."

"I may yield to your entreaties if you will first recite one of your favorite poems to me," replied Waldemar.

"I know a ballad upon Vineta by Finelius. I will repeat a few stanzas." And Wanda recited, with fine expression and deep feeling, these lines from a well-known ballad:

"On Easter-morn, when the jubilant bells
Ring out 'Our Lord is risen!'
They call forth an echo loud and long
From church-spires which the waves imprison.

"Then she rises slow from the ocean's breast,
Awed to rest are the waves around her,
As Vineta, the ancient, proud, and great,
Breaks the spell that long has bound her.

"She comes forth the Queen of the Northern Sea,
Fair as in her olden seeming;
Her church-spires cleaving the upper sky,
Her roofs in the sunlight gleaming.

*   *   *   *   *

"But all is silent. No host, no guest,
No priest in her holy places;
Her ships lie anchored with drooping sails,
In her streets are no living faces!"

"Thank you; the lines are very beautiful," said Waldemar. "Now, when we read these poet fancies, we may know that they are not all fancy, for have not we too seen the enchanted, enchanting old Wonder-city? I can repeat no poem to you, but these lines of Wilhelm Müller haunt my memory to-day:

"From the sea's deep, deep abysses,
Evening bells chime sweet and low,
Of that olden city telling,
Lost and sunken long ago.

"From the heart's deep, deep abysses
Sounds come like those bells of even,
Telling of the loves it cherished
In the days when earth was heaven."

Wanda blushed painfully and was silent. Waldemar passed his hand over his forehead as if to dispel these romantic fancies. "Perhaps we had better return to the rendezvous and await our party," he said, hastily. "Twilight is falling, and there is something very oppressive in this heavy atmosphere."

Wanda eagerly assented. She too longed to end the interview, to break away from the spell that was enthralling her. Just as he had shouldered his rifle and they were on the point of going, Waldemar paused suddenly.

"My suspicions have offended you deeply," he said, "and perhaps they were unjust; but tell me, candidly, was the half-apology you deigned to make really addressed to Waldemar Nordeck? Was it not made rather to the master of Villica, with whom a reconciliation is desirable, so that he may tolerate, or at least overlook what is taking place on his estates?"

"Do you really know--" began Wanda, in surprise.

"Enough to remove your apprehension that you were indiscreet a few moments ago. Did you truly think me so short-sighted as not to observe what is town-talk in L----, that Villica is the focus of party schemes of which my mother is the heart and soul? You may safely confess to me what the whole neighborhood already knows. I knew it before I came here."

Wanda was silent. She tried to read from his features if he really meant what he said, but they were a sealed book to her.

"That, however, is not the point," he resumed; "I asked an answer to my question. Was that magnanimous apology of yours a voluntary one, or was it only a commission you were bound to execute? Do not be angry; I ask merely for information, and you must pardon me, Wanda, if I question an act of friendliness coming from you."

Wanda would certainly have taken these words as a fresh insult and answered them accordingly, if Waldemar's mode of saying them had not disarmed her against her will. His attitude had changed, the icy, hostile manner had vanished; his voice also had another tone; it was softer and deeper, and the young girl trembled as he called her Wanda for the first time in years.

"If my aunt has made me an unwilling instrument of her plans, you must settle with her and not with me," she said, in a low tone, and there was no sting in her words. "I suspected nothing, I was only a child following every momentary whim; but, now,"--she raised her head proudly,--"now I am responsible for my conduct, and I make confession to you of my own free will. You are right; the apology was not to Waldemar Nordeck. Since our meeting, after long years of absence, he has given me no cause to seek or to desire a reconciliation. I wanted to force the master of Villica to open his closed visor. That is no longer necessary. I have just learned from you what I had hitherto only suspected, that in you we have a bitter, merciless enemy, who will use his power at the decisive moment, even if he must tread underfoot all ties of family and of nature."

"And to whom should these ties bind me?" asked Waldemar, excitedly. "To my mother? You know our mutual relations, and that she is now less than ever inclined to forgive me for being the heir of the Nordeck wealth in place of her younger son. To Leo? Possibly there may be a feeling of brotherly love between us, but I do not believe it will survive when our ways cross--at least not on his side."

"Leo would gladly have met you as a brother if you had not made it impossible for him," returned Wanda. "You were always inaccessible even to him, but there have been moments when he might have approached you fraternally. He is too proud to seek to break through the icy reserve you maintain toward him and all around you. Any manifestation of affection from him or from your mother would be shattered against a hardness that cares nothing for them, or perhaps for any one in the wide world."

She stopped suddenly as her eyes met Waldemar's searching gaze. "Your judgment is correct, although merciless," he said, gravely. "Have you ever asked yourself what made me hard? There was a time when I was not so--at least not toward you,--when a word or a glance of yours ruled me, when I patiently submitted to your every whim. Wanda, you could then have made much, perhaps everything of me. You did not wish to do so. My handsome, chivalrous brother was your favorite. This was but natural, I cannot blame you. I was not at all suited to you then. But that was the turning-point of my existence, and a man like myself, who is resolved not to allow his life to be blighted by disappointment, will become hard and suspicious. I now consider it very fortunate that my youthful passion was spurned and derided. If it had been otherwise, my mother would have insisted upon our repeating the drama which was played here twenty-five years ago, when a Nordeck led home a young countess for his bride. You perhaps, with your sixteen years, might have yielded to the will of your family, and have married a fortune, while I should have shared my father's fate. We have both escaped such a calamity, and that foolish past is now buried and forgotten. I only wished to remind you that you have no right to upbraid me with hardness, or to complain when this hardness is manifested toward you and yours. Shall I now accompany you to the rendezvous?"

Wanda complied in silence. Although she had at first been irritated and combative, the turn taken by the conversation had finally wrested the weapons from her hands. To-day they again parted as enemies, but both felt that from this hour the conflict between them was of another character, although perhaps none the less bitter.

The whole landscape was wrapped in twilight shadows that grew deeper every moment, and misty vapors rose from field and forest. White clouds, a now shapeless, dissolving mass, still hovered over the lake. The vision that had risen above the waters had sunk beneath their depths, but it would never be forgotten by this strong, earnest, reticent man and this dreamy young girl, who walked so silently side by side.

Here in the desolate autumnal forest, at the ghostly twilight hour, the breath of that old ocean fable of the distant North again floated around them, and whispered anew its ancient prophecy:--"Whoever has once seen Vineta and listened to the chiming of its bells, must be consumed by regret and longing until the fairy vision again appears to bring him peace, or until the old phantom-city draws him downward into its ocean depths."

CHAPTER XV.

THE "HISTORY OF ANCIENT GERMANY."

The two rooms in the castle assigned to Doctor Fabian faced the park. The princess, while having the suit of rooms which had been occupied by her first husband put in readiness for his son, had set apart an adjoining one for his tutor, which, although small and noisy from its nearness to the main stairway, was supposed to be ample for a dependant who had been obliged to put up with all sorts of discomforts at Altenhof, and was not likely to be either fastidious or exacting. This arrangement did not suit Waldemar; immediately upon his arrival he ordered that two of the guest-chambers on the other side of the castle should be assigned to Doctor Fabian. These happened to be the apartments occupied by Count Morynski and his daughter on their frequent visits to Villica; but Waldemar, who was not aware of the fact, chose these rooms as the best and most pleasant, and had the corridor leading past them closed up, so that Doctor Fabian might not be disturbed in his studies.

The princess, when informed of this proceeding, made no protest; she was resolved never to oppose her son in minor matters. She had other rooms arranged for her brother and his daughter, but she felt some natural resentment against Doctor Fabian, the innocent cause of Waldemar's mistake. She, however, gave no expression to her displeasure, for she and all the inmates of the castle soon learned that, although the young master required but little attention for himself, he resented keenly any neglect shown his former tutor. And so it happened that all in the castle, from the princess down to the humblest servant, treated the shy, unobtrusive student with the greatest consideration.

This was no difficult task, for the doctor was a polite, unassuming man, who required few services, and returned thanks for every slight attention. He appeared only at meals, his days being passed with his books and his evenings with Waldemar. Master and pupil were on terms of the greatest intimacy.

"Doctor Fabian is the only person for whom Waldemar has any regard," said the princess to her brother, as she informed him of the change of apartments. "The young landlord's whims must be humored," she added, "although I cannot see what he finds to admire in this tiresome pedagogue whom he once slighted, but now treats with such marked respect and affection."

The complete change of relations between himself and his pupil had exerted a favorable influence over Doctor Fabian. He still retained his old modesty and diffidence, but that subdued, anxious look he had once worn disappeared with the humility and dependence of his former position. He had become almost healthy and vigorous in appearance; those four years passed at the university in congenial pursuits and varied by extensive travel, had done much toward making a man of the once sickly, timid, and oppressed tutor. His pale, but agreeable face, his soft, well-modulated voice, made a very favorable impression, and it was his own fault that his natural shyness and reserve prevented his asserting his claim to the position his worth and talent merited.

Doctor Fabian had a visitor--a very unusual occurrence. Near him, upon the sofa, sat no less a personage than Assessor Hubert; but the great man's intentions were now entirely pacific, he had no idea of arresting any one at present. That unfortunate blunder had paved his way to an acquaintance with Doctor Fabian. When the affair became known (which was only too soon), the doctor was the assessor's sole friend and comforter. Margaret Frank had been so heartless as to relate the full details to her friends in L----. The story of the attempted arrest of the young master of Villica was told and laughed at throughout the city, and when it reached the ears of the chief of police, he sharply admonished his over-zealous official, advising him to use more caution in future, and in his pursuit of suspicious Polish emissaries to beware how he attacked wealthy German proprietors, whose attitude, in the present state of affairs, was of the most vital importance. At L----, in Villica, wherever the poor assessor went, he was subject to annoying allusions to this matter, and to open ridicule.

The day after his unfortunate blunder he had come to apologize to Herr Nordeck, but not finding that gentleman at home, he had applied to the doctor, who, although one of the aggrieved persons, acted very magnanimously, comforting the contrite assessor to the best of his ability, and proposing to act as mediator with the young landlord. The assessor's contrition, however, was neither of great depth nor of long duration; his overweening self-conceit enabled him to bound back to his former position, like a steel spring when the pressure is removed. The derision he everywhere met exasperated and wounded him without depriving him of a particle of self-confidence. After such an occurrence, any other person would have remained quiet as possible so that the matter might be forgotten, instead of rushing into similar undertakings with the feverish ardor which now characterized Hubert. He felt that he must redeem himself at all hazards, and show his official colleagues and all his acquaintances that he really possessed a master-mind. He must by some means lay hold of a brace of conspirators, or ferret out a plot, it was immaterial where or how, so that he could win the renown he coveted and the promotion he had long and vainly sought.

Villica remained the chief goal of his efforts, for its loyalty, under the present rule, was exceedingly doubtful. Young Nordeck's return gave little hope of a change for the better, as he was supposed to be entirely under the influence of his Polish relatives. He must, it was thought, be their aider and abetter, or else indifferent to what occurred on his estates. The young landlord was severely criticised in L----, and Assessor Hubert was his sternest judge. If Hubert had but possessed the required authority, he would at once have crushed all revolutionary movements, and have won the applause of his country and the world. Unfortunately, as he was neither master of Villica, nor a high government official, he could do nothing but ferret out the conspiracy which was no doubt brewing. His whole energy and ambition were directed to this one end.

The two gentlemen in their conversation alluded to none of these things. The good-natured Fabian must not suspect that this visit had been prompted by an irresistible desire to gain entrance to the castle, and the wary assessor made another pretext for coming.

"I have a favor to ask of you, Doctor Fabian," he began, after the first greetings were over; "not a favor to myself, personally, but to the family of Superintendent Frank, where I am a frequent visitor. You doubtless are master of the French language?"

"O, yes; I read and speak it," answered the doctor, "but I have not had much practice for the last few years. Herr Nordeck does not like French, and here in Villica they do us the favor to speak only German in our presence."

"Practice is also what Fräulein Frank lacks," said the assessor. "When she returned from school two years ago, she spoke French very fluently, but she has no opportunities for conversation here in the country. As you have such abundant leisure, would you not be willing occasionally to read and speak French with the young lady? By so doing, you would, confer the greatest possible favor upon me."

"Upon *you*, Herr Hubert? I must confess my surprise that this proposition comes from you rather than from the young lady's father."

"There are certain reasons for my asking this favor," replied Hubert, in a dignified tone. "You doubtless have observed--indeed, I make no secret of it--that I cherish certain wishes and intentions which may be realized at no distant day. In short, I regard Margaret Frank as my future wife."

The doctor stooped to pick up a piece of paper from the floor, and seemed deeply engrossed in deciphering its contents, although not a word was written on the blank surface. "I congratulate you," he said at length, in a constrained voice.

"O, I cannot just yet accept your congratulations," replied the assessor, with a smile of indescribable self-satisfaction. "We are not really engaged, but I am certain of being accepted. To tell the truth, I wish to obtain promotion before urging my suit (I expect soon to become government counsellor), and then my position will plead powerfully for me. You must know that this young lady is a very excellent match."

"Ah, indeed!"

"A very excellent match; her father is a wealthy man. He is about to resign his present position in order to become himself a proprietor, and he has a large sum of money to invest in an estate of his own. He has only two children, this daughter, and a son who is now in the agricultural college. I can rely upon a handsome dowry and upon quite a large inheritance at some future day. And besides, Fräulein Margaret is a charming, amiable girl, whom I adore."

"*Besides!*" echoed the doctor, in a low tone, and with a bitterness quite unusual to him. The assessor did not hear the half-suppressed exclamation; he went on in a very consequential tone:

"Superintendent Frank has spared no expense in the education of his children; his daughter for a long time attended one of the first young ladies' seminaries in P----, and I am entirely satisfied with her proficiency. You can easily understand, Doctor Fabian, that in the position I shall one day occupy, I must have a wife of fine culture and elegant manners. As a high officer of the government I shall be obliged to go much into society, and to entertain a great deal at my own house, and I am particularly anxious that my future wife should be a proficient in piano-music and French. In regard to the latter, if you will have the kindness--"

"If the superintendent and his daughter desire my assistance, it will be given with great pleasure," returned Doctor Fabian, with forced composure.

"Most certainly they desire it, but the idea of presuming upon your obliging disposition is solely my own," said Hubert, exceedingly proud of this brilliant piece of strategy. "The young lady having recently complained that she was forgetting her French, the superintendent proposed to have a master come from the city and give her lessons; but I could not consent to that! Why, this master would no doubt be some young Frenchman who would make love to his pupil at the very first lesson. Frank is so much absorbed in business that he would not be on his guard, but I am more cautious. I would not for the world allow a youthful, susceptible French master to be so frequently in the society of this young girl, while an elderly gentleman like you--"

"I am thirty-seven years old," interrupted the doctor.

"Ah, is that all?" replied Hubert; "I really thought you older; your sedentary habits and absorption in books give you a gravity beyond your years. In any event, I have no fear of *you*," he added, with a patronizing smile. "But, speaking of books, tell me, doctor, why have you brought along all these books that I see lying around everywhere? What are you studying? The best modes of teaching, probably. May I examine them?"

He rose and moved toward the writing-table, but Doctor Fabian was quicker than he. With a hasty movement he threw a newspaper over some unbound volumes that were lying there, and took his station in front of them. "I am at present engaged in some historical studies," he said, blushing deeply; "this is a favorite amusement of mine."

"Ah, historical studies!" repeated the assessor. "May I ask if you are acquainted with the great authority on this subject, Professor Schwarz? He is my uncle. Of course you know him; he is connected with the university of J----, where young Nordeck studied."

"I have that pleasure," replied Fabian, mechanically, casting a timid glance at a newspaper which lay upon the table.

"O, yes, everybody knows him; he is a celebrated man, and is endowed with talents of the highest order. Although my family can boast of many renowned names, we have every reason to be proud of this relationship. I hope also to do honor to our name and lineage."

The doctor stood anxiously guarding his writing-table from an attack on the part of the assessor, but that young gentleman was too much absorbed in the importance of his family in general, and that of his celebrated uncle in particular, to pay any regard to the productions of a mere private tutor. Nevertheless, he felt constrained to show him some courtesy.

"It is very commendable in non-professional men to interest themselves in such studies," he observed, condescendingly. "I only fear that you have not the requisite leisure; it must be very noisy in the castle. Is there not a constant coming and going of all kinds of people?"

"There may be," replied Fabian, ingenuously, and without the least suspicion of his visitor's aim, "but I hear nothing of it. My former pupil, knowing my studious inclinations, has had the kindness to give me the most quiet and secluded rooms in the castle."

"O, certainly, certainly!" replied Hubert, who now took his stand at a window and endeavored to obtain a broad outlook from that point. "I should think such an ancient structure as this Villica, with its historical associations, must deeply interest you; there are so many rooms, halls, and stairways; and what vast cellars the castle must contain! Have you been in the cellars yet?"

"In the cellars!" echoed the doctor, in astonishment. "No, sir; what business have I there?"

"I would like to visit them; I have a fancy for such old vaults, as I have for all ancient and curious things. By the way, is the large collection of arms that was left by the late Herr Nordeck still intact? That hobby of his must have cost large sums of money, as it resulted in the accumulation of hundreds of the finest weapons. Are they all here yet?"

Doctor Fabian shrugged his shoulders. "You must ask his son," he said; "I confess that I have not been in the armory."

"It is doubtless on the other side of the castle," observed Hubert, with an omniscient glance. "According to Superintendent Frank's description, it is a dark, ghostly-looking hall, in keeping with the general character of Villica. Have you never heard that there are mysterious manifestations around here? Have you never observed anything remarkable or unusual at night?"

"I sleep all night long," replied the doctor, smiling at his visitor's belief in ghosts.

The assessor raised his eyes to heaven, and mentally ejaculated, "This man, whom chance has placed within Villica Castle, sees and hears nothing of what is transpiring around him; he has not visited the cellars, he has not even entered the armory, and, most astounding thing of all, he sleeps at night! There is nothing to be learned from such a harmless book-worm."

After a few polite commonplaces, Hubert took his leave.

He passed slowly along the corridor. Upon his arrival, a servant had conducted him to the doctor's rooms, but now he was alone--alone in a "nest of conspirators," which this bright forenoon, with its carpeted halls and stairways, looked as quiet and elegant and harmless as the most loyal castle of the most loyal citizen. But the assessor was not to be deceived by appearances; right and left he scented the conspiracy which he could not openly attack. At length he espied a door which he thought had a suspicious aspect. It stood in the shadow of a huge pillar, and was set deep in the wall. This door, he thought, must lead to a side stairway, perhaps to a secret passage, and possibly down to the cellars which his vivid imagination at once filled with concealed weapons and bands of traitors. He would at least turn the knob; perhaps here lay the key to the whole mystery. In case of discovery, he might pretend to have made a mistake, or to have become lost in the winding passages of the castle. The little man's cogitations were cut short and his further investigations prevented by the sudden opening of the door and the appearance of Waldemar Nordeck. A single glance through the open portal showed him that it led to no nest of treason, stratagem, and spoils, but simply to the sleeping-apartment of the master of Villica. Waldemar nodded indifferently to the assessor, and passed on to Doctor Fabian's rooms. Hubert saw that, in spite of his apologies, the recent insult had not been forgiven, and that his best course would be to relinquish for the present all attempts at further discoveries, and to leave immediately.

Waldemar found Doctor Fabian at his writing-desk, re-arranging the books and papers he had screened from the assessor's inquisitive gaze. "Well, what news?" asked the young landlord. "I noticed, when I sent in your mail, that you had received letters and papers from J----."

The doctor replied, almost bitterly, "O Waldemar, why did you force me to give the public the results of my quiet studies and labors? I opposed it from the first, but you entreated and insisted, and so I published the book."

"Of course I did! Of what benefit was it to you and to the world, locked up in your writing-desk? Your 'History of Ancient Germany' has been received with unexpected favor. In truth, the first recognition of its merits came from Professor Weber, of J----, and I should think that his name and judgment ought to be of sufficient weight."

"I think so too," replied Fabian, dejectedly. "I was only too proud and happy in receiving praise from such a source; but this very circumstance has provoked Professor Schwarz to make an exceedingly severe attack upon me and upon my book. Just read what he says."

Waldemar took the newspaper, and read the criticism. "This is most detestable malice," he said. "Why, the article really ends with a personal attack upon you and me:--'We are told that this learned and literary celebrity, lately discovered by Professor Weber, was for a long time tutor to the son of one of our first landed proprietors; but the young man's culture reflects little credit upon his teacher. The influence of this wealthy pupil may, however, have had its share in eliciting such boundless over-estimation of a work through which an amateur seeks to intrude into the ranks of men of science.'"

Waldemar flung the paper upon the table. "Poor Doctor Fabian," he exclaimed, "how often you have to atone for having educated such an unruly, uncultivated being as I am! True, you are in no way responsible for my unworthiness, and I have not in the least influenced Professor Weber's panegyric of your book; but in those exclusive circles where this Schwarz moves, you can never be forgiven for having been a tutor, even though you one day win a professorship."

"Good heavens, who ever thought of such a thing?" cried Doctor Fabian, aghast at the very idea of so great exaltation. "Not I, indeed; and I am all the more deeply wounded at being reproached with ambition and unwarranted intrusion into learned circles, because I have simply written an historical work, which adheres closely to the subject, insults no one, encroaches upon no one's rights, and--"

"And is, moreover, one of the best ever written," interposed Waldemar. "You ought to believe in its excellence, since Professor Weber has so emphatically indorsed it. You know that he is absolutely impartial, and that you have always looked upon him as an undisputed authority."

"Professor Schwarz is also an authority."

"Yes, but an atrabilious one, who concedes no merit outside himself. Why should *you* come out with a book upon Ancient Germany, when that is his especial province? Has he not written upon the subject? Woe to the man who dares venture upon that sacred ground; his anathema is pronounced beforehand! But don't look so downhearted; such a mien ill becomes a new-fledged celebrity. What would Uncle Witold, with his contempt for that 'heathen rubbish,' have said to all this? If we had known, in those old days at Altenhof, the brilliant future that lay before you, we should all have treated you with more respect. It was a sacrifice for a man of your talents to stay with me."

"No, no; a thousand times no!" cried Doctor Fabian, excitedly. "The sacrifice was all on your side. Who obstinately insisted upon keeping me with him when he no longer needed my instruction? Who always declined receiving the slightest service which would take me from my books? Who gave me the means to devote myself for years to historical research, to collect and arrange my desultory acquirements? Who almost compelled me to accompany him upon journeys, because close application had injured my health? The hour when your Norman wounded me was a beneficent hour to me. I owe to it all I hoped or longed for in this world."

"Then your longings were few indeed," returned Waldemar, "so few that it would have been a great pity had they not been gratified. But, to change the subject, I have just met in the hall that exemplary representative of the police department of L----. He came from you, and I see him now prowling about the yard. His visits cannot be on our account, since we have proved that we are not conspirators. Why, then, is he here so much?"

Fabian cast down his eyes and seemed greatly embarrassed. "I do not know," he said, "but I fancy there is a personal reason for his frequent visits at the superintendent's. He has made me a visit before."

"And did you receive him kindly? Doctor, you are strictly obedient to that Christian precept, 'If a man smite you on the right cheek, turn to him the other also.' I really believe you would not hesitate to do the greatest favor in your power even to Professor Schwarz. But be upon your guard with this formidable assessor; he is again upon the chase for conspirators, and, insignificant as he is, chance may yet favor him. There really are conspirators in Villica."

"Have you made any unpleasant discoveries?" asked Doctor Fabian. "I have thought it might be so, although you tell me nothing."

Waldemar seated himself and leaned his head wearily upon his hand. "I do not like to speak of matters concerning which I am not fully informed," he said; "and it will require time to gain perfect knowledge of affairs in Villica. How was I to know that the superintendent had not a personal interest in misrepresenting things, or that he had not exaggerated? In such matters one can only trust his own judgment, and I have used mine during the last few weeks. Unfortunately, every word Frank wrote me has been confirmed; order prevails as far as his absolute authority extends, but upon the other estates, and especially throughout the forests, I find a perfect chaos."

Fabian pushed aside his books and papers, and listened with anxious sympathy as Waldemar went on:

"Uncle Witold always thought that my Polish estates could be managed from a distance, and, unfortunately, he reared me in that belief. I did not love Villica, I do not love it now; too many unpleasant reminiscences of the fatal misunderstandings between my parents, and of my friendless childhood, are connected with it. I was accustomed to regard Altenhof as my home, and when I attained my majority and should have come here as master, reasons which I cannot name prevented me. I must now atone for past neglect. The twenty years of deputized rule allowed by my guardian have resulted in many evils; but they are nothing when compared with the perhaps irreparable injuries resulting from my mother's management. I am alone to blame; I have never troubled myself about my estates: I now stand cheated and betrayed upon my own soil."

"You were very young when you came into possession of your estates," said the doctor, apologetically. "The three years at the university were indispensable to you, and then, as we travelled a year, we could have no suspicion how things were going on at Villica. We came here immediately upon receiving the superintendent's letter, and I really think that with your good sense and energy, you will overcome the most formidable obstacles."

"They are greater than you dream," returned Waldemar. "The princess is my mother, and she and Leo are wholly dependent upon my generosity. This ties my hands. If there should be a serious breach between us, they would have to leave Villica, and Count Morynski's house would be their only refuge. I do not wish to subject them to such humiliation, but there must be an end to this underhanded game, especially to proceedings here in the castle. Doctor, you have no idea of the state of affairs. I know a great deal already, and I am resolved to make a thorough investigation. I shall now speak with my mother."

A long pause followed. Fabian ventured no reply; he knew by the expression of the young man's face that this was no trifling matter. He at length approached his pupil, laid a hand upon his shoulder, and asked, gently,--

"Waldemar, what occurred yesterday at the chase?"

"At the chase?" repeated Waldemar. "Nothing. Why do you ask?"

"Because you returned in such ill humor; and besides, at the dinner-table, I heard some hint of a dispute between you and your brother."

"Ah, indeed!" replied Waldemar, indifferently. "Leo was irritated because I treated his favorite horse rather harshly; but the matter is not of the least consequence--it is already settled."

"Then it was something else."

"Yes--something else."

Another silence followed: then the doctor began again:

"Waldemar, the princess recently called me your only confidant; I might have replied that you have no confidant. Perhaps I am somewhat nearer to you than others, but you never open your heart to me. Must you endure and fight through everything alone?"

Waldemar smiled, but it was a cold, joyless smile. "You must take me as I am," he said; "but why this solicitude? I may well be out of sorts, so many anxieties and difficulties beset me here."

The doctor shook his head. "These things no doubt irritate and embitter you beyond measure, but the sorrow that oppresses you has another cause. I have seen you in this mood only once before, Waldemar; it was at Altenhof, when--"

"Spare me these recollections, I implore you!" interrupted Waldemar, so abruptly and impetuously that Fabian started back in terror. Waldemar immediately mastered his emotion, and continued, in a calmer tone, "I am sorry that you, too, must suffer from my vexation; it was selfish in me to bring you to Villica. You should have returned to J----, to remain until I had restored order here and could offer you a quiet asylum."

"I would not have left you alone under any consideration," said Fabian, gently but decidedly.

Waldemar grasped his hand. "I knew you would not; but do not torture yourself any longer about my troubles; if you do, I shall repent having been so frank with you. Your own affairs should engross you now. Remember me to Professor Weber when you write to J----, and tell him that I am about to reduce your work to practice, and impress something of the 'History of Germany' upon my Slavonic estates. Villica needs it. Good-bye."

Doctor Fabian looked after him as he left the room, and sighed, "He is impenetrable and silent as a rock whenever I attempt to approach this one subject, but I know that to this day he has not mastered that sentiment, and he never will. I fear that the baleful influence which kept us so long from Villica is beginning to re-assert its power. Let Waldemar deny it as he will; I saw him yesterday when he returned from the chase; he is even now under the old spell."

CHAPTER XVI.

CASSANDRIAN WARNINGS.

Night had fallen, and profound silence reigned throughout Villica Castle; a silence in striking contrast to the tumult of the preceding day, when the house had been full of guests. A great supper had followed the return of the hunting-party, and as it was prolonged far into the night, most of the guests had remained until dawn. Count Morynski and Leo had left with them to pass a few days at a neighboring estate, and Wanda staid to keep her aunt company.

The two ladies sat alone in the drawing-room, which, with its brilliant lights and closely-drawn curtains, bore no trace of the rough November storm that was raging without. The princess sat upon a sofa; the young countess had risen, and was pacing up and down the room, evidently in great perturbation.

"Wanda, spare me these Cassandrian warnings, I implore you!" said the elder lady; "I tell you once more that your judgment is warped by your antipathy for Waldemar. Must he necessarily be an enemy to us all because you and he are at war?"

Wanda stopped short in her rapid walk, and gazed angrily at her aunt. "You may one day regret the scorn with which you treat my warnings," she said. "I still believe that you are deceived in your son; he is neither so blind nor so indifferent as you think."

"Will you not cease these obscure prophecies, and tell me plainly what you fear? You know that I do not trust to appearances or opinions; I require proofs. Whence arises this suspicion of yours to which you cling with such tenacity? What did Waldemar say to you when you met him yesterday at the rendezvous?"

Wanda was silent. She had mentioned only their meeting at the ranger's place, not wishing to inform her aunt of that solitary interview by the forest-lake. Not for the world would she have repeated the details of that meeting, and yet Waldemar had said nothing to give her the slightest ground for the assertions she had just made. She had no proof save that strange instinct which from the first had guided her in her estimate of a character which had escaped her aunt's keen penetration. She could not offer these mere impressions as evidence, her aunt would deride them.

"Waldemar had but little to say to me," she answered at length; "but that little convinced me that he knows more than he ought."

"Very likely," replied the princess, with perfect composure. "I doubt if Waldemar has made any investigations himself. He knows what the superintendent knows, and, what is no longer a secret in L----, that we take sides with our own people. Deeper insight into our affairs is as impossible to him as to others; we have taken all necessary precautions. His whole conduct shows his indifference to matters which do not concern him personally in the least, and he has too nice a sense of honor to compromise his nearest relatives. He has proved this in the case of Superintendent Frank; although he would prefer to have the man remain, he sides with me."

"You will not listen!" said Wanda, resignedly. "Let the future decide which of us is right. Now grant me one favor, dear aunt; allow me to return home to-morrow morning."

"So soon? It was arranged that your father should come for you."

"I remained only to have an undisturbed conversation with you upon this subject. It has been in vain,--so let me go."

"You know, my child, that I like your company," said the princess, "but I cheerfully consent to your immediate departure. You and Waldemar did not exchange two syllables at dinner; if you cannot be a little more courteous at these unavoidable interviews, you had better go."

"Then I will inform papa that he need not come here for me: will you allow me a few moments at your writing-desk?" Wanda went into her aunt's study, which was separated from the drawing-room by a half-drawn *portière*, and seated herself at the writing-desk. She had scarcely written a line when the drawing-room door opened hastily, and she heard a well-known step, so firm and heavy that it was not drowned like other footfalls in the soft, thick carpet. Then Waldemar's voice resounded close beside her, on the other side of the *portière*. She laid down her pen, and as she could not make her escape without passing through the drawing-room, she remained motionless in her place. Not a word spoken in the next room escaped her.

After a hurried good evening, Waldemar sat down at his mother's side, and began to converse upon indifferent matters. He had taken an album of water-color paintings from the table, and was turning over the leaves, while the princess reclined against the sofa-cushions, and mentally asked herself what could be the cause of this unusual and unexpected visit.

"Have you heard that your superintendent Frank is about to purchase an estate?" she asked at length. "His situation here must have been very lucrative, for, so far as I know, he was without property when he came."

"He has had a large income for the past twenty years," said Waldemar, without raising his eyes from the album, "and he must have saved fully half of it."

"And he has, no doubt, made good use of his opportunities. Have you chosen his successor?"

"No."

"One of your tenants, the man who rents the Janowo estate, has become financially embarrassed, not through any fault of his own, and is obliged to return to a salaried position. I believe him especially fitted for Villica."

"I do not think so," replied Waldemar, very deliberately. "His management has been inexcusably bad, and he has brought on his own ruin."

The princess bit her lip. "Who told you this?" she asked, at length. "The superintendent, most likely."

Waldemar made no reply, and his mother went on in an irritated tone:

"I have no desire to influence you in the selection of your subordinates, but for your own interest I warn you not to give full credence to Frank's calumnies. He does not want this man for a successor, and he is intriguing against him."

"That can hardly be," returned Waldemar, coldly; "he knows that I have decided to dispense with a superintendent, and take the management of my estates into my own hands."

"You yourself? I am astonished."

"You need not be; I have been trained for the position. Frank will remain until spring, and initiate me into all the details."

He said this very calmly, not taking his eyes from the album, whose paintings seemed to absorb his whole attention. He did not notice the look of anxious scrutiny with which his mother scanned his face as she said,--

"But you led us to infer that your visit would be very short."

"I intended to make it so, but I find that my estates need a master's care; and besides--I have something to say to you, mother."

He closed the album, and laid it on the table. Now, for the first time, the princess felt that Wanda's instinct had been more correct than her own penetration. She saw the storm coming, and prepared to meet it.

"Speak," she said, coolly, "I will listen."

Waldemar rose and gazed reproachfully at his mother. "When I offered you Villica as a home," he said, "I gave you entire control of the castle, but the estates were my own."

"Has any one disputed your right to them?"

"No one; but I now see what it meant to leave them for years in Polish hands."

The princess also rose, and confronted her son proudly and defiantly. "Do you hold me responsible for this mismanagement?" she asked. "Lay these grievances rather to the charge of your guardian, who for twenty years pretended to control your estates. You must deal with your subordinates, and not with me."

"Frank is the only one of them who still recognizes me as master," exclaimed Waldemar, bitterly; "all the others are at your beck and call. They do not openly refuse to obey me, but they evade my orders whenever they conflict with yours."

"You are dreaming," said the princess, with an air of affected superiority; "Frank has prejudiced you even against your mother."

"I have not trusted to his reports, I have made close scrutiny with my own eyes; and now I ask you, who has transferred the leased estates from German to Polish hands, and that, too, upon ruinous terms and without guaranties or security? Who has confided the management of the forests to a body of men who care nothing for my interests, but who will render good service to your cause? Who, finally, has made the superintendent's position so intolerable that his only alternative was resignation? Fortunately he had the energy to summon me to the rescue, and I have come at this late hour to find all in revolt against me. You have recklessly sacrificed everything to the interests of your family and your cause,--my servants, my property, and even my reputation, for I am supposed to be in league with you. Your four years' control of my estates has brought them to the verge of ruin. You know this as well as I; you have known it all along, but your only aim has been to prepare Villica for the Revolution."

The princess had listened in silent and ever increasing astonishment; this was not the first time that she had heard just such words in these very rooms. The elder Nordeck had often enough reproached his wife with sacrificing everything to family traditions, but bursts of fury had been his only method of opposition. He had sought to attain his end by torrents of threats and rude invective which had only elicited contemptuous smiles from his proud, fearless wife. She had well known that this *parvenu* possessed neither mind nor character, that both his likes and dislikes sprang from the basest impulses, and her disdain for the man was only equalled by her indignation that she had been compelled to accept him as a husband. She would not have been at all surprised if Waldemar had enacted a similar scene before her eyes; the fact that he did not, confounded her. He faced her with perfect composure, and with annihilating certainty hurled at her accusation after accusation, proof after proof. That mental excitement which he so powerfully repressed was only too evident; the vein on his right temple swelled portentously, and he clutched convulsively at the back of the chair near which he stood. His look and voice, however, betrayed nothing; they were entirely under control.

Some moments elapsed before the princess answered; her pride would stoop to no denial or concealment, and both, in fact, would have been useless. She could rely no longer upon Waldemar's blindness; she must resort to new tactics.

"Your fears are exaggerated," she said; "do you really apprehend that all Villica will break out in revolt, merely because I have now and then used my influence in favor of my protégés? I am sorry if any of them have abused my confidence and failed in their duty to you; but unreliable people abound everywhere, you have only to discharge all such as are in your service here. Why do you reproach me? When I came here, the estates were virtually without a master; as you did not concern yourself about them, I felt justified in assuming control, and my management has been better than that of your agents. I have certainly managed in my own way. I have always openly sided with my family and my country. My whole life bears witness to this, and I require no justification at your hands. You are my son, as well as the son of your father; the blood of the Morynskis also courses through your veins."

Waldemar started as if impelled to protest vehemently against this assertion, but controlled the momentary impulse.

"For the first time in your life you concede to me a share in your own blood," he rejoined, bitterly; "hitherto you have only regarded me as a Nordeck, and despised me accordingly. What if this sentiment has never been expressed in words, are not looks fully as eloquent? I have often observed the glance with which your eyes have turned from Leo or from your brother to rest upon me. You have sought to banish every remembrance of your first marriage as a humiliation and a disgrace; as the wife of Prince Zulieski, and the mother of Leo, you did not trouble yourself about me; you would never have come to me if circumstances had not compelled you. I do not censure you in the least; my father may have wronged you deeply, so deeply that you cannot possibly love his son; let us not therefore appeal to emotions and sympathies which have never existed between us. I shall very soon be compelled to prove to you that not a drop of the Morynski blood courses through my veins. You may have bequeathed it to your Leo--I am made of other material."

"I see it," said the princess, half despairingly,--"of other material than I thought. I have never known you."

Waldemar did not seem to notice the remark. "You understand perfectly that I shall henceforth assume control of my estates," he said. "I have one question to ask you: What was the object of the conference you held last evening, and which was protracted until nearly dawn?"

"That is my own affair," replied the princess, in an icy, repellent tone. "I am at least mistress in my own apartments."

"Certainly, in so far as you yourself are concerned; but I shall not allow Villica to be used any longer as an insurrectionary focus. Here you have held your conclaves, from here orders have been sent to and fro over the frontier. The castle-cellars are full of arms; you have collected a whole arsenal."

The princess turned deathly pale, but this blow did not shake her confidence. Not a muscle of her face moved as she asked, "Why do you say all this to me? Why do you not go to L---- and reveal your discoveries? You have displayed such remarkable talent as a spy that it would be very easy for you to turn informer."

"*Mother!*"

This one word, a furious, indignant outcry, escaped the young man's lips, and his clenched hand descended upon the back of the chair in a blow that crushed the frail, delicately carved wood to atoms. The old passion again blazed forth, threatening to bear along with it all that self-command so painfully acquired through these four past years. The princess saw that this her eldest son, who stood before her, was his father's true heir in violence and fury; his whole frame trembled, and his face was so distorted by rage that his mother involuntarily placed her hand upon the bell-knob to summon help. This movement brought Waldemar to his senses; he turned hastily away and walked to the window.

A few silent, painful moments followed. The princess felt that she had gone too far; she saw how mightily her son wrestled with his anger and what the struggle cost him; she also saw that the man who could thus control an unfortunate natural disposition, the fatal inheritance he had received from his father, was an opponent not easily silenced or overthrown.

When Waldemar again stood face to face with his mother, the struggle was over, the victory won. His arms were crossed over his breast, his lips still quivered, but his voice was calm and steady.

"When you confided my brother's future to my 'magnanimity,' I did not dream of this result. '*Spy!*' You call me so because I seek to unveil the secrets of my castle. I could apply to you a word of more evil import. Who enjoys hospitality in Villica, you or I, and who has betrayed it?"

The princess frowned. "We will not contest this matter," she said. "I have merely done what right and duty demanded, and now, what do you intend to do?"

Waldemar, after a moment's silence, replied in a subdued voice, and with an emphasis upon every word: "To-morrow I shall go to P---- on business, and remain a week. Before my return, Villica must be freed from every semblance of disloyalty. Transfer your arms and your secret assemblies to Radowicz or wherever you will, my domains must be rid of them. Shortly after my return I shall give a large hunting-party, in which the governor of the province and the officers of the garrison at L---- will participate; as mistress of the house, you will of course have the courtesy to join your name with mine in the invitations."

"No!" replied the princess, emphatically.

"Then I will sign them alone, as the invitations must be issued in any event. The time has come for me to take my stand upon the question now agitating our whole province. You are at liberty to keep your room from feigned illness on that day, or to go to your brother's; but you must consider whether it is best to have the breach between us become public, and therefore irreparable. It is in our power to forget this interview. If you comply with my demands, I shall never again remind you of the matters we have discussed to-day. You must decide upon your own course of action. You can tell Leo and your brother what I have said to you,--they had better hear it from your lips than mine; I certainly desire no rupture."

"And what if I will not obey the orders you so tyrannically impose upon me?" asked the princess defiantly. "Supposing I should contest your claim to the entire inheritance, and assert my right to Villica, which should have been my widow's dower? The courts would never do me justice, but there is a public opinion higher than all law; do you dare defy it by breaking your word to your mother and brother, and exposing them to the bitterest poverty and dependence, while you revel in luxury?"

"Do as you please," returned Waldemar; "but do not hold me responsible for what may happen."

They stood face to face, eye to eye, and that similarity between the two which had hitherto escaped the notice of all but Wanda, was now fully evident. Both faces wore the same expression: an iron will that was ready to stake everything in the furtherance of its plans. Now, as they stood there confronting each other, ready to engage in a life-and-death conflict, for the first time they showed that they were really mother and son, perhaps for the first time they felt this truth.

Waldemar stepped close to the princess, and laid his hand upon her arm.

"I have left the way open for my *mother* to retrace her steps," he said, emphatically; "but I forbid the Princess Zulieski's concocting party schemes upon my estates. If she goes on doing this, if she forces me to extreme measures, I shall carry them out, even if I must see you all--"

He stopped suddenly. His mother saw how he trembled, how the hand which held hers with an iron grasp instantly relaxed and fell powerless at his side. In mute surprise she followed the direction of his glance which was fixed upon the study-door. Wanda stood upon the threshold. Unable longer to keep back, she had come forward with a sudden impulse, and thus revealed her presence.

A flash of triumph shot from the eyes of the princess; she had found at last the vulnerable spot in her son's heart. Although the next moment he had mastered his emotion, and stood there self-poised and imperturbable as before, it was too late--that one unguarded moment had betrayed him.

"Well, Waldemar," she asked, and a tone of irony vibrated through her voice, "are you offended because Wanda has been a witness of our interview? A large portion of it concerned her. For her sake as well as mine, you must complete your threat: 'Even if you must see us all--'"

"As the Countess Morynski has witnessed our interview, no explanation is needed; I have none to make." Then turning to his mother, he added, "You have a week for your decision. I leave early to-morrow morning." He then bowed formally to Wanda as was his wont, and left the room.

Wanda had stood motionless on the threshold. She now entered the room, and approaching her aunt, she asked in a low and strangely tremulous voice,-
-

"Do you believe me *now*?"

The princess had sunk back upon the sofa. Her eyes were still fixed upon the door through which her son had passed; she seemed neither able nor willing to comprehend what had just taken place.

"I have always judged him by his father," she said as if speaking to herself; "the error is a fatal one to us all. He has shown that he is--"

"That he is more like you, Aunt Maryna," interrupted Wanda. "Leo inherits your features, but Waldemar is the true heir of your character. You have just been confronted by an energy and a will that are your very own. Waldemar resembles you more closely than Leo ever did."

There was a tone in Wanda's voice that arrested her aunt's attention.

"And who taught you to read this character so accurately?" she asked. "Was it your enmity toward Waldemar which made you see so clearly when all the rest of us were deceived?"

"I do not know," returned Wanda, casting down her eyes. "I think it was intuition rather than observation that guided me, but from the first I knew that he was our enemy."

"That does not matter," replied the princess, confidently; "he is my son and must remain so. You are right; he has shown me to-day for the first time that he really is my son, but for this very reason his mother can cope with him."

"What will you do?" interposed Wanda.

"I will take up the gauntlet he has thrown down. Do you imagine that I shall yield to his threats? We will wait and see if he really means to resort to extreme measures."

"He means what he says, depend upon it. Do not count upon any relenting or submission in this man. He will sacrifice you, Leo and us all, to what he considers right."

The princess gazed searchingly into the excited face of her niece. "He may perhaps sacrifice his mother and brother," she said, "but I now know where his strength falters; I know what he will not sacrifice, and it shall be my care to present this test at the decisive moment."

Wanda gazed at her aunt without comprehending her; she had observed nothing further than Waldemar's sudden silence, which her unexpected appearance fully accounted for, and his cold, repellent manner toward her and his mother.

"Prompt action is necessary," said the princess. "My brother first of all must be informed of the state of affairs. Waldemar's unexpected departure removes the necessity of your leaving us at once; you will therefore remain, and immediately summon your father and Leo back to Villica. No matter what other business demands their attention, they must come, for vital questions are at stake. I will send your letter this very day by a courier, and they can be here by to-morrow evening."

Wanda assented. She re-entered the study, took a seat at the escritoire, and again wrote to her father, little suspecting the part she was to act in the execution of her aunt's schemes. That "childish folly" long since overcome and forgotten, assumed a new importance when it became evident that Waldemar still remembered it, and was influenced by it. It had once aided the princess in obtaining control of Villica, why should it not again aid her?

The mother could not forgive her son for having so decidedly and offensively disclaimed all ties of kindred with the Morynskis. For this very reason he should be thwarted by a Morynski, even if he could not be thwarted by his mother.

CHAPTER XVII.

THE FRENCH LESSONS.

Doctor Fabian and Margaret Frank sat in the superintendent's library with an open book before them. The French lessons had really begun. The teacher was grave, earnest, and enthusiastic, but the pupil seemed listless and indifferent. She had agreeably relieved the monotony of the first lesson which had been given a few days before, by asking the doctor all sorts of questions about his past history, his position as Waldemar Nordeck's tutor, the manner of life at Altenhof, etc. To-day she was bent upon finding out what study so absorbed this incorrigible book-worm, and the retiring scholar, who wished to keep his "History of Ancient Germany" a profound secret, was driven almost to distraction by her pointed questions.

"Would it not be well for us to begin our lesson now, Fräulein Frank?" he asked, imploringly. "We shall accomplish nothing if we go on in this way; we are not speaking French at all."

"Pshaw! who wants to pore over stupid French lessons, when so many interesting and amusing things are going on here?" exclaimed Gretchen, impatiently turning over the leaves of her French reading-book. "My head is full of entirely different things; life at Villica is wonderfully exciting just at present."

"*I* do not think so," returned Doctor Fabian, patiently turning back to the page, where they had left off reading.

The young lady gave him an inquisitorial glance.

"Then you must be blind and deaf, Doctor Fabian," she said. "You, above all others, ought to know what is going on in the castle, for you are Herr Nordeck's friend and confidant. Something has occurred, you cannot deny it; now that the young landlord has left, everything over there is in a great commotion. Messengers are flying to and fro, Count Morynski and Prince Leo are passing back and forth from Villica to Radowicz, and our haughty, domineering princess looks as if the end of the world were just at hand. And such goings-on as there are all night in the park! There is a constant fetching and carrying, a continual tramping up and down. You must know all about it, for your windows open on the park."

Herr Frank had stipulated that French only should be spoken at his daughter's lessons, and here Gretchen was rattling on glibly in her native tongue, as if no French phrases were in existence.

Doctor Fabian turned uneasily on his chair, and said, despairingly, in his best French, that he knew absolutely nothing of these matters, and that they were no concern of his.

"Papa says the very same thing," persisted Gretchen, "whenever I ask him; he cannot possibly be involved in any conspiracy, and yet his silence would lead one to believe that he was, Don't you think so?"

"My dear mademoiselle, my best efforts to teach you will be useless if you are constantly absorbed in these outside things. I have been here half an hour, and we have not read a single page. Attend to your lesson, I entreat you."

He offered her the book certainly for the sixth time. She finally took it with a resigned air, and said in an injured tone,--

"Ah, I understand! I am not to be let into the secret; but I shall discover it, and then you will all be sorry you placed so little confidence in me. I certainly know how to keep a secret."

She began to read a French poem, but in an exasperated tone and with a purposely wretched pronunciation which almost drove her teacher to despair.

She was in the midst of the second stanza, when a carriage entered the yard. No one was in it, but the coachman seemed perfectly well acquainted, for he unharnessed immediately. A maid-servant entered with the announcement that Assessor Hubert, being detained by business in the village, had sent on his coachman to inquire if he might again presume on the superintendent's hospitality.

There was nothing unusual in this request. The assessor always passed the night at the superintendent's house when official duties' brought him to Villica, and he managed that this should occur pretty often. Herr Frank had driven out into the country, but would return at evening. Margaret gave orders that the coachman and his horses should be cared for, and that the guest-chamber should be put in order.

"When the assessor comes, our French lesson will be over," said Margaret to the doctor; "but, never mind, he shall not disturb us long. Before he has been here five minutes, I will drop a remark concerning the secret doings in the park, and he will hurry over there and hide behind a tree; then we shall be rid of him."

"For heaven's sake, don't do that! Don't send him over there!" cried Fabian, in the greatest terror. "Keep him here by all means."

Margaret was startled. "What does this mean, Doctor Fabian? I thought you knew nothing, absolutely nothing; why, then, are you so alarmed?"

The doctor lowered his eyes and looked like a detected criminal with no hope of escape. But he was incapable of falsehood, and finally said, looking the young girl full in the face,--

"I am a peace-loving man, Mademoiselle Frank, and I never intrude into the secrets of others. I actually know nothing of what is going on in the castle, but during the last few days I have been forced to see that something is going on. Herr Nordeck has only given me a hint now and then, but I have no doubt that the proceedings here involve great danger."

"Not for *us*?" replied Gretchen, with a feeling of the utmost security. "Herr Nordeck is away, the assessor cannot seize him; you are beyond suspicion; and as for the princess and Prince Leo--"

"They are Waldemar's mother and brother; do you not see that every blow directed against them will strike him too? He is master of the castle, and responsible for all that occurs there."

"And so he should be," exclaimed Gretchen, excitedly. "Why does he go away, leaving every gate and door open to conspiracy? Why does he side with his relatives?"

"He does not side with them," returned Fabian; "on the contrary, he opposes them. His journey has the sole purpose--but, my dear young lady, do not force me to speak of things which I dare not mention even to you. This much I do know: it is Waldemar's earnest wish to protect his mother and brother. At his departure he made me promise to see and hear nothing of what took place in and around the castle; your father received similar instructions. I heard Waldemar charge him to see that the princess remained unmolested during his absence; and now, when the superintendent is away, some ill chance brings the assessor here; he is bent upon making discoveries, and will do so, unless we can manage to prevent it. I am perfectly helpless."

"That comes from concealing things from me," pouted Gretchen. "If confidence had been placed in me, I should have had a timely quarrel with the assessor, and he would not have come here for many a day. But I shall think of some plan."

"Do so by all means!" entreated the doctor. "You have great influence over the assessor; keep him here; he must not go near the castle."

The young girl shook her head dubiously. "You do not know Hubert," she said; "nothing will detain him here if he once scents conspiracy or mischief, as he surely will if he stays at Villica. He must not remain in this house. Ah, I have it now! I'll let him make a proposal to me, (he always begins one, but I never allow him to finish it,) and then I will refuse him. He will be so furious that he will rush headlong back to L----."

"I will upon no consideration consent to such a thing," protested the doctor. "Whatever happens, your life's happiness must not be sacrificed."

"Do you suppose that my life's happiness is at all dependent upon Assessor Hubert?" asked Gretchen, with a scornful curl of the lips.

Fabian certainly believed this to be the case; he had received the assurance from Hubert's own lips.

"Such things are too sacred for trifling," he said, reproachfully. "The assessor would sooner or later learn the truth, and would be deeply wounded, perhaps estranged from you forever."

Although nothing would so much have delighted Gretchen as an eternal estrangement from the assessor, her conscience reproved her for the trifling part she had contemplated acting. After a moment's reflection, she said: "Then the only alternative left us is to set him upon the wrong track. All Villica is involved in intrigues, why should we not follow suit? But, seriously, do we not conspire against our own government when we prevent its representatives from doing their duty?"

"The assessor has no special orders," replied the doctor, growing courageous all at once. "In coming here he pursues only his own ambitious schemes. We do no wrong in averting an unnecessary calamity which might result from the inordinate zeal of an official."

"Well, then we will have recourse to a little piece of strategy. The assessor must not remain here over fifteen minutes; if he does, he will be out on the chase for conspirators. There he is now coming across the yard. Leave all to me;--now let us resume our French lesson."

When the assessor entered a few moments after, Fräulein Frank was reading the third stanza of her French poem. He was delighted to find that Doctor Fabian had kept his word, and that the future counsellor's wife was diligently acquiring that higher culture so indispensable to the exalted position she would one day occupy. He greeted both tutor and pupil very graciously, and after some polite inquiries after the superintendent, took the proffered seat.

"Your former pupil has surprised us all," he said, complaisantly, to Doctor Fabian. "Do you know that on his way through our town he called upon the governor on official business?"

"I knew that he proposed doing so," replied Fabian.

"His Excellency was much gratified by the visit," continued Hubert, "for he had abandoned all hope of aid from this side. Herr Nordeck was also so amiable as to invite the governor to take part in a hunt at Villica, and he hinted of other invitations no less surprising."

"Did his Excellency accept?" asked Gretchen.

"Certainly! He considered the invitation a great concession on the part of a man who has so long been under hostile influences, and felt in duty bound to accept it. Really, Doctor Fabian, you would do me a great favor if you would give me some definite information concerning the actual position of Herr Nordeck--"

"You will learn nothing from Doctor Fabian; he is more reserved even than our young landlord himself," interrupted Gretchen, feeling bound to come to the rescue of her accomplice, who was no actor and could not play his part properly. A sense of guilt almost choked him; he could not banish the thought that the assessor was to be deceived, and that he was to aid in deceiving him. Gretchen, however, took the matter less seriously, and marched straight on to her purpose.

"Will you take tea with us, Herr Assessor?" she asked. "You undoubtedly have business over at Janowo?"

"Not that I know of. Why just there?"

"Well, I only meant--We have heard so much of the proceedings over there for some days past, that I thought perhaps you had been commissioned to make a search in that place."

The assessor was fully aroused. "Conceal nothing from me, I beseech you!" he said, eagerly. "Tell me all you know about Janowo."

The doctor pushed back his chair unobserved. In his own eyes he was the blackest of conspirators, while his pupil showed a surprising talent for intrigue. She allowed herself to be questioned, and little by little she revealed all she had learned in the last few days, but with one important variation--she changed the field of operations from Villica to Janowo, the adjoining estate. Her plan succeeded far beyond her expectations. The assessor bit eagerly at the bate, and when Margaret had told all she knew, he sprang to his feet in feverish excitement.

"Excuse me, Fräulein Frank," he said, "for not awaiting your father's coming. I must return to E---- at once."

"But not on foot; it is half an hour's walk."

"I must go *incognito*," whispered Hubert, mysteriously. "I will leave my carriage here, so that it may appear as if I were still at your house. Do not expect me to supper. Good-bye, Fräulein Margaret." So saying, he hurried away.

"He is going to E----," said Gretchen, exultingly, "in search of the two gendarmes stationed there; he will hasten with them to Janowo, and all three will pry about there until late at night. Villica is well rid of them."

Her anticipations were realized; the assessor returned from his expedition at a very late hour. As it had naturally been unsuccessful, he was out of humor, and, besides, he was chilled through and through. Unaccustomed to the night-air, he had taken such a severe cold that even Gretchen felt some sympathy for him. She made him herb teas, and nursed him the whole day with a solicitude that more than consoled him for his affliction. Unfortunately, Gretchen's thoughtful care and evident anxiety strengthened his conviction of her devoted love for him. Doctor Fabian also called upon the invalid, and showed so much sympathy for him, that the assessor was much affected and greatly comforted. He did not know that all these attentions sprang from the remorseful feelings of the two conspirators, and he finally returned to L----, not cured of his cold, but in the best of spirits.

The inmates of the castle little dreamed to whom they owed their security upon that night, when all their secret doings were in danger of being unveiled. At the very moment when Doctor Fabian and Margaret Frank were arranging their plan, a grave family consultation took place in the apartments of the princess. Count Morynski and Leo were in full travelling costume; the carriage which brought the count and his daughter half an hour previously, stood waiting at the door. Leo and Wanda had withdrawn to the deep recess of the central window, and were engaged in earnest conversation, while the princess and her brother also conversed apart, in a half audible tone.

"As matters stand," said the princess, "it is fortunate that circumstances require your immediate departure. I am glad to have Leo go with you, for he could not remain at Villica if Waldemar should assume an attitude of open hostility."

"And will you remain, Maryna?" asked the count.

"I must; it is the only thing I can do for you at present. I believe with you that an open conflict with Waldemar would be useless and dangerous. We have, for the time being, abandoned Villica as the centre of operations; but you and Leo can still send messengers here, and receive tidings from us in return. The castle will also be your refuge in case the worst should happen, and you be obliged to recross the frontier. Peace will not be violated on this side. When do you think of crossing?"

"Probably to-night, and the last transport of weapons will follow us. We must take them all away before Waldemar's return day after to-morrow, for he will be likely to have the castle searched."

"He will find nothing," said the princess; "we have obeyed his orders. But he shall atone for his tyranny. I have in my hands the means of retribution, and also those of arresting his course if he should attempt to go further."

The conversation was here interrupted by the approach of Leo and Wanda. "Mamma, it is impossible for me to change Wanda's determination," said Leo, in an exasperated tone. "She persists in remaining at home, and positively refuses to come to Villica."

"What foolishness is this, Wanda?" asked the princess, gazing at her niece in astonishment. "Months ago it was arranged that you would come to me when the long contemplated absence of your father should occur. You can not and ought not to remain alone at home. I am your natural protector, and you ought to stay with me."

"I beg your pardon, Aunt Maryna, but I can not and will not be a guest in a house whose master stands in open hostility to us."

"Do you suppose it is agreeable to your aunt to remain here?" asked the count, reprovingly. "She makes the sacrifice for our sakes; can you not be as magnanimous as she?"

"But my presence here is not needed," replied Wanda, excitedly. "The reasons that influence my aunt do not affect me at all. Let me go home, papa."

"Yield, Wanda," entreated Leo; "stay with my mother. For my sake, overcome your hatred for Waldemar, and remain at Villica."

He seized her hand, but she forcibly withdrew it. "Let me go, Leo," she said. "If you knew why your mother desires to have me near her, you would be the first to oppose it."

"Bronislaw, assert your paternal authority, and command your daughter to stay at Villica," said the princess, sternly.

"If you force me to remain," returned Wanda, highly incensed at these harsh words, "my father and Leo shall know the reason. You wish to place me as a shield between you and your son. You think me the only one Waldemar will not sacrifice, the only one who can restrain him. I do not believe it, for I know him better than you do; but it is immaterial which of us is right. I will not make the trial."

"No, you shall not make it," broke out Leo; "you shall remain at home. If Waldemar's old passion is not buried and forgotten, you shall not pass a day in his presence."

"Control your anger, Leo; it is quite uncalled for," said Wanda; but her own voice indicated anything but composure. "I shall not again permit myself to be a tool in my aunt's hands. I once trifled with this man and with his love--I shall not do so a second time. He has made me feel his contempt; I know how the remembrance stings him; but that was the mere whim of a thoughtless child. I would rather die than become the instrument through which any of my aunt's schemes could be carried out. I could not live to read in his eyes the contempt I should merit."

"Do you then care so much for Waldemar that you would rather die than incur his contempt?" asked Leo. "Can you read the language of his eyes so well?"

Wanda drew herself up to her full height; her cheeks glowed, her eyes flashed, she gave the young prince a look of withering scorn, and was about to reply to him, when her father interposed,--

"Don't be jealous, Leo! Why embitter our parting, and wound Wanda's feelings at the last moment? Since you insist upon it, my daughter shall remain at home. Your mother will yield to you on this point, but you must cease harassing Wanda by your suspicions. Time is passing, and we must say good-bye."

He embraced his daughter tenderly, and seemed loth to release her from his sheltering arms. The princess waited in vain for the approach of her son, who stood before her with sullen brow and downcast eyes, biting his lips until they bled.

"Will you not bid me adieu, Leo?" she asked.

He started from his gloomy revery. "Not now, mamma. I am not needed just yet; I will remain a few days."

"*Leo!*" exclaimed the count, angrily, while Wanda, with the same indignant outcry, released herself from her father's embrace. But these protests only strengthened the young man in his determination.

"I shall remain!" he persisted; "two or three days can make no difference. I shall accompany Wanda home, and assure myself that she is to remain there; and, above all, I shall await Waldemar's return, and obtain an explanation from him. I shall question him in regard to his sentiments for my betrothed. I shall--"

"Prince Leo Zulieski will do his duty," interposed the princess, in a clear, cold voice, contrasting strangely with the excited tones of her son. "He will accompany his uncle as he has promised to do, and not for one moment leave his side."

"I cannot," said Leo, vehemently,--"I cannot leave here with this anguished suspense gnawing at my heart. Wanda's hand has been promised to me, but

I am never allowed to assert my rights; she has always coldly sided with my mother, saying that she would be the prize of the contest in which I am about to engage. I now demand that she shall be publicly and solemnly declared my betrothed bride, in Waldemar's presence--before his very eyes. He has lately undergone a surprising transformation from an obedient vassal to lord and master; ere my return, I might find him transformed into Wanda's ardent lover."

"No, Leo, that will never happen," replied Wanda, contemptuously; "but your brother certainly would not hesitate to do his duty, even at the cost of love and happiness."

She could not have uttered words more exasperating; Leo completely lost his self-control.

"O, not he! but it might cost me both if I should now leave you, with your boundless admiration for his character and his patriotism. Uncle Bronislaw, I ask only a three days' postponement of my departure; I shall claim it, even without your consent. I know that nothing of importance will occur immediately, and I shall be with you in season."

The princess was about to interfere, but the count forestalled her, saying peremptorily and authoritatively, "It is for me to decide this matter, Leo, and not you; I demand the obedience you have promised me as your commander. You must either go with me now or be dismissed from my service. Take your choice."

"He will obey you, Bronislaw," said the princess, solemnly, "or he is no longer my son. Decide, Leo! Your uncle will keep his word."

Leo had a violent conflict with himself. His uncle's threat and his mother's command would have alike proved powerless, now that his jealousy was so thoroughly aroused, if he had not known that by remaining he would incur Wanda's scorn; that decided him. He sprang to her side, and again seized her hand.

"I will go," he said; "but promise me that during my absence you will avoid Villica, and see my mother only at your own home. Promise me, above all, that you will keep aloof from Waldemar."

"No such promise is needed," she said, mildly; "I have already refused to remain at Villica."

Leo breathed more freely. Yes, it was true, she had positively refused to endure his brother's presence.

"Some day I may apologize to you for wounding your feelings," he said; "but I cannot do so now, Wanda." He pressed her hand convulsively, and added,

"I do not believe you could betray yourself and us by loving this Waldemar Nordeck, who is our enemy and our oppressor. You must cherish no sentiment of respect or admiration for him. It is bad enough for me to know that he loves you, and that you are near him."

"Leo's impulsive nature will give you great trouble," said the princess in an undertone to her brother. "He cannot comprehend the meaning of the word 'discipline.'"

"He will learn it," replied the count, firmly. "And now good-bye, Maryna; we must go."

The parting was brief, and less tender than it would have been but for the discord which had preceded it. Wanda received Leo's embrace in silence and did not return it, but she threw herself with passionate devotion upon her father's breast. As the mother bade her son good-bye, she whispered some words of warning in his ear of so grave a character that he immediately released himself from her arms. The count once more silently pressed his sister's hand, and then both men passed into the hall, wrapped their cloaks around them, and entered the carriage which awaited them. There was one more greeting to the two ladies who stood at the window, and then they were whirled rapidly away.

The princess and her niece were alone. Wanda threw herself upon a sofa and buried her face among the cushions; the princess stood at a window and gazed long and wistfully after the carriage that was bearing her darling into conflict and danger. When she turned toward Wanda, her white face and agitated manner plainly told what parting with her son had cost her.

"It was unpardonable in you, Wanda," she said, "in an hour like this, to arouse Leo's jealousy in order to make him obey you; you know how susceptible he is upon this point."

Wanda raised her head; there were traces of tears upon her cheeks.

"You forced me to it, aunt," she said; "I had no other alternative. And, besides, I had no idea that Leo could be jealous of Waldemar."

"My child," replied the princess, in an icy tone, "I have never taken Leo's part when he has tormented you with his jealous suspicions, but to-day I see that they are well founded. I fully concur in your determination not to remain here, where you will be thrown into daily association with Waldemar. For Leo's sake and your own, you had better go."

Wanda started from her reclining posture. She gazed at her aunt with dilated eyes, and white lips that were incapable of speech; she felt like one on the brink of a precipice; almost fainting, she grasped the arm of the sofa for support.

"You deceive yourself," she at length found strength to say; "or you wish to deceive me. I have not deserved this insult."

The princess gazed long and searchingly into the face of her niece. "I know that you have no premonition of your danger," she said, "and therefore I warn you. Somnambulists must be wakened before they reach those giddy heights where awakening will cause their destruction. Energy and an iron will have always been the traits of manly character you most admired; Waldemar undeniably possesses these, while Leo, who is endowed with so many brilliant qualities, unfortunately is wanting in them both. Do not place too much reliance upon your hatred for Waldemar; some day you may find it quite another sentiment. I seek to open your eyes before it is too late, and I believe that the day is not distant when you will thank me for so doing."

"I already thank you," replied Wanda, in a low voice.

"Let us dismiss the subject, then; I hope there is no danger as yet. To-morrow I will accompany you home. I must now see that the necessary precautions are taken to-night, so that no harm may befall us in these last moments of our stay at Villica. I will myself give the orders, and superintend everything in person."

So saying, the princess left the room, firmly convinced that she had done her duty and averted an imminent danger by thus boldly rending asunder the veil which had covered Wanda's heart. If she could have seen the young girl sink back upon her seat as if crushed by remorse and sorrow, she would have discovered that the giddy height where an outcry might prove fatal had been reached already. No cry of alarm could now avail, either to warn or to rescue. The awakening came too late.

CHAPTER XVIII.

THE ASSESSOR'S WOOING.

It was mid-winter. Thick snows enveloped field and forest, icy fetters stayed the rejoicing flow of brook and river, and chill blasts swept over the frozen, desolate earth.

Another storm had broken loose and was raging more fiercely than the warring elements of nature. Over the border the long dreaded insurrection had at length begun. All Poland was in commotion, and many provinces were in open revolt. All was quiet as yet on the Prussian frontier, and bade fair to remain so, although many Polish families lived on this side the border, and many Germans of Polish lineage had gone to swell the ranks of the insurrectionists.

Villica suffered most. Its position rendered it one of the most important advance-posts of the whole province, and for four years it had been the seat of Polish plots and intrigues. Its great extent rendered it impossible to guard the whole estate fully; and although Waldemar had taken a decided stand in favor of his father's country, it was difficult for him to circumvent and thwart the secret plans of his mother, who was resolved to give all the aid and comfort in her power to her own people. The princess kept her word. Believing herself rightfully entitled to Villica, she did not leave it, and from her present influence Waldemar saw what it had meant to give her that sole control of the estates which she had enjoyed so long. He was now bitterly atoning for his former neglect and indifference.

His castle was no longer the theatre of party machinations, but the estate was mostly in the hands of Poles who had been systematically organized by the princess and were working in her interest. The young landlord found himself betrayed and sold on his own soil. He was nominal master, while his mother was the real mistress. Although she did not openly assume control, her subordinates were well trained, and executed her orders rather than Waldemar's. All Villica stood in secret but determined opposition to its master. He was the victim of intrigues and subterfuges; everything was done to evade his commands and thwart his plans, but he could never discover the culprits, or bring them to punishment. None refused obedience to his face, but he knew that disobedience was the watchword all over his estates. If he enforced submission in one place, resistance raised its head in ten other places; if he triumphed one day, new obstacles confronted him on the next. If he should begin to dismiss his subordinates, all must go, for all were alike at fault. Besides, unless open proofs could be brought against his employés, his contracts with them were binding, and even could he have been rid of them, he would find none to supply their places. Any act of violence at the present crisis might prove fatal.

The young landlord was thus forced into a position exceedingly difficult for a nature like his, because it required patient and quiet endurance. His mother had taken this into account in forming her plans; she thought that Waldemar must soon grow weary of the contest in which they were about to engage. He must surely learn that he could do nothing when all Villica sided with her and opposed him, and he would in his impatience and vexation resign the reins he had so violently wrested from her.

Patience had never been a prominent virtue in Waldemar Nordeck's character, but his mother was again deceived in him. He showed that he had inherited her own indomitable will and energy; no obstacles, no opposition could move him, he was forever on the alert, he was resolved to take the control of everything into his own hands. This course of action made him many enemies. He had been hated merely as a German, he was now hated for his own sake. His servants ere long began to fear him, and fear compelled their obedience.

The relations between Waldemar and his mother grew more and more intolerable, but they maintained a show of outward politeness. Neither questioned nor upbraided the other, and so it was possible for them to remain together in the castle without revealing the mutual rancor and bitterness that filled their hearts. Waldemar became more reserved than ever; he met his mother only at meals, and then not every day, for she passed a great deal of time at Radowicz with her niece. Wanda kept her word, she never came to Villica, and Waldemar in like manner avoided Radowicz.

More than three months had passed since the departure of Count Morynski and his nephew. It was generally known that they were both involved in the insurrection, the count being one of its leaders, while Leo held an important command under his uncle. In spite of distance and all other obstacles, each held unbroken intercourse with the princess and Wanda. Both ladies had reliable and accurate information of all that occurred, and messages constantly passed to and fro.

At the hour of noon, on a cold, blustering day, Assessor Hubert and Doctor Fabian were coming from the village where they had chanced to meet. The assessor wore several wrappings, his recent painful experience having taught him to beware of taking cold. The doctor also was well protected from the severe climate which did not seem to agree with him; he was pale, and evidently ill at ease. Hubert, on the contrary, wore a most satisfied expression; the state of affairs along the border brought him often to Villica, and he now designed remaining for several days in the neighborhood. He had quartered himself, as usual, at the superintendent's, and this fact was no doubt one reason for his exuberant spirits.

"There is a grandeur, an absolute grandeur in Herr Nordeck's character," he said, in his pompous, official tone. "We of the government well know how to appreciate it. This accursed Villica would long since have given the signal for revolt if its master had not stood firm as a rock against insurrection. All L---- admires him and respects him."

Doctor Fabian sighed. "I wish he deserved that admiration less; it is counterbalanced by the hatred he has to confront here. Every time he rides out alone I tremble, for he can never be persuaded to use the slightest precaution."

"Your fears are well grounded," replied the assessor, gravely; "Nordeck's employés here in Villica are capable of any crime, even of firing a shot from some ambush. I think that his only protection thus far has lain in the fact that he is the son of the Princess Zulieski, but who knows how much longer this may be a safeguard against that national fanaticism which is now at its height? What a life they must be leading in the castle just now! It is strange that the princess remains there. Terrible scenes occur between the mother and son, I suppose. Tell me all about them."

"I would not like to gossip about family affairs."

"O, I can use discretion," said Hubert, curious to find out something he could relate in L----, where the young landlord and his mother were a frequent topic of conversation. "You have no idea what prodigious stories are being told in the city. It is said that young Nordeck broke up a band of conspirators who had been wont to assemble in the cellars of the castle, with Count Morynski and Prince Leo at their head; that as the princess was about to interfere, her son placed a pistol at her breast, and then she cursed him, and both of them--"

"How absurd!" interrupted the doctor. "I give you my word that not a syllable of all this gossip is true. None of these violent scenes ever took place between Waldemar and his mother. They are not that kind of people; they are very *polite* to each other."

"Are they really?" asked the assessor, doubtfully. He was very reluctant to give up that story of the pistol, and the maternal curse; it was far more telling and dramatic than Doctor Fabian's unadorned statement. "But conspirators were in the castle," he said, "two hundred of them, and the young landlord put them to flight. O, if I had only been there! Unfortunately I was over at Janowo where I made no discoveries. How could Fräulein Frank, who is usually so shrewd, be deceived in such a matter?"

The doctor was silent. The mention of Janowo embarrassed and confused him. Fortunately for him, they at this moment reached the spot where their ways parted; Fabian bade his companion good day, and the assessor proceeded to the superintendent's house.

Meantime a serious interview had taken place between the superintendent and his daughter. Gretchen had at last assumed a decidedly warlike attitude; she stood before her father with her arms folded, her blonde head thrown back; she even stamped violently to give due emphasis to her words.

"I tell you, papa, I don't like the assessor, and even if he should sigh around me for another six months, and you should encourage him ever so much, I could never be compelled to say yes."

"My child, no one wishes to compel you. You very well know that you can do just as you like, but the matter must be finally settled. If you are determined to persist in your refusal, you must not give Hubert any more encouragement."

"I don't give him the least encouragement," replied Gretchen, almost crying with vexation. "I treat him just as hatefully as I know how, but it is of no use. Ever since I nursed him so faithfully through that cold, he persists in thinking I am in love with him. If I should refuse him to-day, he would smile, and say, 'You don't mean it, Fräulein Frank; you love me, you know you do!' and he would be here again to-morrow."

Herr Frank took his daughter's hand, and drew her close to his side. "Gretchen, now be serious," he said, "and tell me what you really have against the assessor. He is young, rather good-looking, and possessed of some property; he can give you a very good social position. I admit that he has his peculiarities, but a woman of the right sort can make something of him. His highest recommendation is his unbounded love for you. What has changed you so toward him? You did not at first look upon him with such unfavorable eyes."

This question embarrassed Gretchen somewhat. She did not answer it immediately. At length she said,--

"I do not love him; I do not want him; I will not marry him!"

This positive declaration disarmed the father; he answered, with a shrug,--

"Well, do just as you like. I shall tell the assessor the plain truth before he leaves us. I shall, however, wait until the moment of his departure; perhaps your reason may return to you by that time."

"I shall never be of any different opinion," the young girl said, indifferently; then seating herself at her sewing-table, she took up a book and began to read.

The superintendent paced impatiently up and down the room; at length he paused before his daughter.

"What thick volume is that I see constantly in your hands? Is it a grammar, and are you studying French so very diligently?"

"No, papa; grammar is a very tiresome study to me. At present I am studying the 'History of Ancient Germany.'"

"Studying what?" asked the superintendent, scarcely believing his ears.

"The History of Ancient Germany," repeated Gretchen, emphatically. "It is an excellent work, full of the profoundest learning. Would you like to read it? Here is the first volume."

"Don't bother me with your Ancient Germany!" exclaimed the superintendent. "I have all I can do with ancient Slavonia. How do you come by such learned rubbish? Doctor Fabian must have lent you the book; but that is not according to agreement: he promised to teach you French, and instead of doing so, he brings you musty old books out of his library, not a word of which you understand."

"I understand every word," retorted the young girl, angrily. "And this is not a musty old book; it is an entirely new work, and Doctor Fabian himself wrote it. It is creating a great sensation in the literary world, and two of our greatest scholars, Professors Weber and Schwarz, are having a controversy about the book and its author. You will very soon see that he has become a greater man than either of them."

"Schwarz?" said the superintendent, thoughtfully. "That must be our assessor's celebrated uncle at the university of J----. Doctor Fabian may consider himself fortunate if his books attract even the hostile attention of so renowned a man."

"Professor Schwarz knows nothing at all," declared Gretchen, with the infallibility of an academic judge. "He will disgrace himself as much by his criticism of Fabian's book, as the assessor did by his attempted arrest of our young landlord. You might know they were uncle and nephew--for they are both fools!"

A new light appeared to dawn upon the superintendent; he gazed searchingly at his daughter. "You seem perfectly well informed in these university matters," he said; "you must enjoy the unlimited confidence of Doctor Fabian."

"And so I do," replied Gretchen, proudly; "but it has cost me great effort to win his confidence. In spite of his great talents, Doctor Fabian is the most modest and reticent of men. I had to question him a great deal before I found all this out, and it was a long time before he would lend me his book; but I became angry at last, and sulked and pouted, so that he did not dare refuse me any longer."

"My daughter," said the superintendent, gravely, "I fear the assessor made a stupid blunder in advising you to take French lessons of this learned doctor. That quiet, pale-faced tutor, with his soft voice and timid manners, has really bewitched you, and is the sole cause of the shameful treatment poor Hubert receives at your hands. Are you sure you are not acting foolishly? Doctor Fabian is nothing but an ex-tutor, who lives with his old pupil and draws a pension from him. He may write learned works for recreation, but they will bring him little money; they will certainly insure him no certain income. It is fortunate that he is too timid and too sensible to base any hopes upon your predilection for him; I think it best, however, for the French lessons to end, and I shall arrange this in a way that will wound no one's feelings. When you, who scarce have patience to read a novel, study the 'History of Ancient Germany,' and grow enthusiastic over such dry stuff merely because the doctor wrote it, I can but have my suspicions."

Gretchen was highly displeased at her father's words, and was about to utter a vehement protest, when the superintendent was called from the room. Assessor Hubert could not have come at a more inopportune moment, but the evil star which had always controlled this young man's wooing, now guided him into the presence of his beloved. He was, as usual, all politeness and attention, but Gretchen's ill-humor was so marked that he could not refrain from alluding to it.

"You appear out of sorts, Fräulein Margaret," he began, after several ineffectual attempts to enter into conversation. "May I inquire the cause?"

"I am vexed that the most talented people should be the most timid, and show so little self-confidence."

The assessor's face lighted up at these words. '*Talented people--timidity--no self-confidence!*' Ah, yes! One day he had drawn back when in the very act of kneeling, and to this day he had not ventured upon a formal proposal. In truth, the young lady herself was to blame for it all, but still she was vexed because he had so little self-confidence. He must redeem himself without delay; no hint could be plainer or more direct.

Gretchen saw at once the effect of her thoughtless words which Hubert had naturally applied to himself. She made haste to conceal her "History of Ancient Germany," as Doctor Fabian had charged her not to mention it to the nephew of his literary rival. As the assessor's glance rested upon her, she said, sharply, "You need not follow me around with a detective's eye, sir; I am engaged in no conspiracy, and I don't want to be watched so narrowly."

"My dear young lady," replied the assessor, in a dignified and yet an injured tone,--for he was conscious of having given only tender glances to the mistress of his heart,--"you reproach me unjustly; I gave you no such glance, and you are inclined to deride my zeal in the performance of official duty, when you should consider it my greatest merit. The security and welfare of the nation rest upon us public servants; thousands have to thank us that they can lie down in peace at night; without us--"

"If you had been our only safeguard, we here in Villica might have been murdered long ago," interrupted Gretchen; "Herr Nordeck is a more powerful protection than the whole police force of L----."

"Herr Nordeck seems just now to be the object of universal admiration," remarked the assessor in an irritated tone; "I see that you, too, are infatuated with him."

"Yes, very much so; with him and no other!" exclaimed Gretchen, throwing a mischievous glance at the assessor; but he only smiled.

"No momentary infatuation would content me," he said. "I hope for quite another feeling in the one soul which is akin to mine."

Gretchen saw that she had gained nothing by this harsh treatment of her admirer. Hubert was evidently on the point of making a direct proposal, but the young girl was determined not to hear it. She did not want to refuse him; she preferred delegating that unpleasant duty to her father. She therefore asked the first question that occurred to her.

"You have not for a long time told me anything about your renowned uncle, Professor Schwarz. What is he doing now?"

The assessor saw from this question that his future wife felt a deep interest in his relatives, and it gave him intense satisfaction.

"My poor uncle has suffered great vexation of late," he replied. "A rival party has sprung up against him at the university (what great man does not suffer from the envy and jealousy of others?) Professor Weber stands at its head. This gentleman literally hankers after popularity; the students are blindly infatuated with him, everybody speaks of his amiability, and my uncle, who disdains such artifices and never caters to public opinion, encounters ill-will on every side. The rival party have brought forward an obscure individual solely to annoy him, and are trying to compare his book on Ancient Germany with my uncle's works."

"Is it possible?" observed Gretchen.

"Yes, with my uncle's works!" repeated the assessor, indignantly. "I know neither the name nor the antecedents of this insignificant rival; my uncle does not enter into details in his letters, but the affair has so enraged him, and his controversy with Professor Weber has reached such a height, that he thinks of tendering his resignation. Of course, this is a mere threat, the resignation would not be accepted; the university would meet with an irreparable loss if he should leave it, but he thinks it necessary to intimidate his opponents."

"I hope they are duly intimidated," said Gretchen in such an indignant tone that the assessor started back; but the next moment he approached nearer, and said,--

"It affords me great pleasure to see you take so deep an interest in the welfare of my uncle. He is already interested in you; I have often written to him of the house and the family where I have found such a friendly welcome, and it would delight him to hear that I had formed a--"

Again he was on the way to a proposal. Gretchen sprang up despairingly, rushed to the open piano, and began to play. She under-estimated the perseverance of her suitor, for the next moment he stood at her side, listening attentively.

"Ah, the Longing Waltz! My favorite piece! Yes, yes; music, far better than words, expresses the longings of the heart--is that not so, dear Margaret?"

Gretchen saw that everything conspired against her to-day. This happened to be the only piece she could play without notes, and she could not venture to rise and fetch her music, for the assessor's manner plainly indicated that he was only awaiting a pause in the playing to give utterance to the emotions of his heart. She therefore rattled off the Longing Waltz with all her might, and to the time of a military march. The discord was horrible, a string snapped, but the tumult was loud enough to thwart any attempt at a declaration of love.

"Is *fortissimo* proper in a sentimental piece like this?" interposed the assessor at the top of his voice. "I think it should be played in *pianissimo.*"

"I prefer to play it in *fortissimo,*" retorted Gretchen, thumping still more forcibly at the keys. A second string broke.

The assessor grew nervous. "You will ruin this splendid instrument," he said, in his loudest key.

"There are plenty of piano-tuners in the world," cried Gretchen; "I want to help one of them;" and seeing the assessor's discomfiture, she banged at the keys with all her might, and coolly sacrificed a third string. This proved effectual. Hubert saw that speech would be impossible to him to-day, and he beat a retreat, vexed at the girl's coquetry, but still with unshaken confidence in himself and in the final success of his suit. This wilful young lady had nursed him so tenderly when threatened with that lung-fever, and only an hour ago she had called him talented, and reproached him for his lack of self-confidence! Her obstinacy was indeed incomprehensible, but she loved him in spite of all.

When he was gone, Margaret rose and closed the piano. "Three strings are broken," she said, regretfully, and yet with an air of great satisfaction; "but I have kept him from proposing, and papa can arrange matters so that he never will." She then seated herself at her work-table, took from one of its drawers the "History of Ancient Germany," and was soon absorbed in its contents.

CHAPTER XIX.

THE FOREST DRIVE.

Some hours later, Waldemar Nordeck was returning from L----, whither He had ridden in the morning. Intercourse between Villica Castle and the city was becoming quite frequent, and Waldemar often went to L----, where he always received the most polite attentions from the government officials, who well knew what a powerful ally they had in him, the master of a frontier estate, whose disloyalty might prove very dangerous.

Waldemar knew that his disagreement with his mother was the topic of daily conversation in L----, and that exaggerated reports were in circulation. Firmly resolved to furnish no material for gossip, he presented a firm front and a quiet brow to strangers; but now, when alone and unobserved, his forehead, which had just seemed perfectly calm and unruffled, grew corrugated and anxious. He rode along heedless of all around him, and upon arriving at a cross-road, he reined up mechanically to allow passage to a sleigh which was advancing at full speed.

Norman reared suddenly; his rider had jerked the reins so violently that the animal was frightened, and sprang wildly to one side of the road. In so doing, his hind-feet caught in a rut hidden beneath the snow; he stumbled, and nearly fell with his master.

Waldemar quickly guided his horse into the road, where a sleigh, in which a lady sat, had stopped short at her command.

"Pardon me, Countess Morynski," he said, "if I have frightened you; my horse shied upon suddenly meeting yours."

"I hope you are not injured," said Wanda, turning pale.

"O, not at all; but my Norman--"

He did not finish the sentence; he sprang quickly from the saddle. Norman was evidently injured in one of the hind-feet. Waldemar made an examination, and said, coldly but politely, "I beg you not to delay your journey on account of this slight mishap, Countess Morynski." He bowed, and stepped aside to allow the sleigh to pass.

"Shall you not mount again?" asked Wanda, as she saw Waldemar throw the reins over his arm.

"No; Norman has injured his foot, and limps badly; he cannot possibly carry me."

"But Villica is nearly a dozen miles distant from here," said Wanda; "you cannot possibly walk there."

"No other alternative is left me; I must at least take my horse to the nearest village, and leave him there until I can send for him."

"But it will be dark before you reach the castle."

"No matter--I know the way."

Wanda knew that the road to Villica led most of the way through a dense forest full of dangers to the young landlord, who was the object of so much secret hostility.

"Would it not be better for you to take a seat in my sleigh?" she asked, in a low, timid voice, not daring to lift her eyes. "My coachman can take your horse to the village."

Waldemar gazed intently into the young girl's face; her proposition seemed to surprise him greatly.

"No, I thank you; you are doubtless on your way home?"

"Radowicz does not lie far out of your way--you can leave me there, and then take the sleigh and drive home." These words were uttered in a subdued, almost anguished tone. Waldemar let the reins fall slowly, and some moments passed before he replied,--

"I think it will be better for me to go directly to Villica."

"But I implore you, do not walk there alone; ride along with me."

There was such a tone of anxiety in Wanda's voice, that the refusal was not renewed. Waldemar resigned his horse to the coachman's care, and took his seat. The place at Wanda's side remained vacant.

They drove on in profound silence. Waldemar gave his whole attention to the reins. Wanda wrapped her furs more closely about her, and, apparently absorbed in herself, did not pay the least heed to her companion, who sat on the driver's box, which was at the back of the sleigh.

Although it was the beginning of March, winter still held undisputed sway over the earth. Far and near, the whole landscape was enveloped in snow and ice; tempestuous blasts swept over it, whirling the snow and sleet in all directions.

The wind went down at last, but the air was raw and cold as upon the bleakest December day. The horses flew over the smooth road, the keen, frosty air lending them new life and vigor, but a chill, oppressive atmosphere seemed to envelop the two inmates of the sleigh, who sat there silent and wrapped in their own contemplations. They had not met for three months, and this was the first time they had been alone since that interview by the forest-lake. Melancholy and depressing as that autumnal evening had been, with its fallen leaves and its flitting shadows, yet nature, even in dying, had then shown some signs of life; now, the pangs of dissolution were over; a deathly silence pervaded the broad fields stretching out so white and boundless. Nothing but snow met the eye, while overhead floated leaden clouds, and all nature lay stark and dead in this wintry solitude and desolation.

The road ere long turned into the forest, where the snow was so deep that the horses were compelled to slacken their pace. The driver relaxed the reins which he had thus far held so tightly. On both sides of the way, dark, giant pines bent beneath their burden of snow; one of the boughs grazed Waldemar's head, and a cloud of snowflakes fell over him and his companion, who for the first time turned half around, and remarked,--

"The road to Villica lies all the way through an unbroken forest just like this."

Waldemar smiled. "I am fully aware of that," he said; "I make the journey very often."

"But not on foot and at dusk. Do you not know, or will you not believe, that it is dangerous for you to do so?"

Waldemar's face grew grave. "If I had entertained any doubts of that," he said, "they would have been dispelled by the ball that grazed my hair as I was passing along here a few days ago."

"After that experience, your constant venturing forth alone is an actual challenge," exclaimed Wanda, unable to conceal her alarm.

"I am always armed; no escort can protect me against a secret shot. As matters now stand, if I should manifest fear and surround myself with safeguards, my authority would be at an end. My best course is to continue to face attacks alone."

"And what if that ball had hit?" asked Wanda, in a tremulous voice. "You see how near the danger came."

The young man bent forward toward her seat. "In insisting upon my accompanying you, did you wish to shield me from a similar danger?" he asked.

"Yes," was the scarce audible answer.

Waldemar seemed about to reply, but as though a recollection had suddenly flashed upon his mind, he seized the reins, and said, in a bitter tone,--

"You will have to pay dear for this to your party, Countess Morynski."

She turned quite around, and her eyes met his. "No," she said; "for you have proclaimed open enmity to us. It lay in your power to offer us peace; you declared war."

"I did what I was forced to do. You forget that my father was a German."

"And your mother is a Pole."

"You need not remind me of it in that reproachful tone. That unhappy difference of nationality has cost me so much that I cannot forget it for a moment. It caused the separation of my parents; it poisoned my childhood, it embittered my youth and robbed me of my mother. Perhaps she would have loved me as she loves Leo if I had been a Zulieski. She, more than all others, made me cruelly atone for being--the son of my father. Our present political antagonism is simply the result of the past."

"You carry out this antagonism with an iron will," said Wanda, excitedly. "Any one else would have sought a reconciliation, an adjustment, which would certainly have been possible between a mother and son."

"Between any other mother and son, perhaps, but not between the Princess Zulieski and me. She forced me to the alternative of submitting unconditionally to her interests, or of declaring war against her. Were it not for this struggle for the mastery, she would have left me long ago. I certainly did not request her to remain."

Wanda did not reply; she knew that Waldemar was right, and the certainty forced itself upon her that this man, who was universally considered cold and forbidding, was grieved and pained at his mother's want of affection for him. In those exceptional moments when he disclosed his inner nature, he always reverted to this subject. The indifference of his mother toward him and her love for her younger son, had been the dart which had pierced the heart of the boy, and in the man's heart the wound had never healed.

They had passed through the forest; the horses quickened their pace, and soon Radowicz appeared in sight. Waldemar was about to turn into the main avenue leading to the castle, but Wanda pointed in another direction.

"Let me alight at the outskirts of the village," she said; "I prefer to walk the short distance to my home. You can keep on in the road to Villica."

"Then you dare not appear at Radowicz in my company," said Waldemar, after a moment's silence. "You could never be forgiven if you did so--we are enemies."

"It is your fault alone that we are so; our struggle is not against your fatherland, it is to be fought out on a foreign soil."

"It is better not to discuss this matter," said Nordeck, resignedly. "Necessity may have driven your father and Leo into the conflict, but the same necessity drives me to opposition. Birth and family traditions point out but one way to Leo, and he has taken it, but I was forced to choose between the two sides. I must belong to one party or the other; I could not oscillate between both. No one cares to ask what the step I have taken costs me; but no matter. I have chosen, and shall maintain my position. Leo throws himself enthusiastically into the contest for his highest ideal, spurred on by the love and admiration of his kindred; he knows that his safety is their daily concern, and even danger has a charm for him; but I stand alone at my post, in daily peril of assassination. All Villica hates me, and my mother, my brother, and you, Wanda, hate me more bitterly than all others. Fate has not dealt equally with Leo and me, but I have never been spoiled by love and indulgence, and I can endure anything. So continue your hatred, Wanda; doubtless it is best for us both."

Upon reaching the entrance to the village, Waldemar reined in the horses, sprang from the seat, and offered to assist Wanda in alighting. She declined the proffered aid. No parting word came from her compressed lips; she merely bowed.

"I shall send back the sleigh to-morrow, with my thanks," Waldemar said, coldly, "if you will not reject *them*."

Wanda seemed to be passing through an inward conflict; she should already have been on the way, but she still lingered.

"Herr Nordeck!"

"What is your pleasure, Countess Morynski?"

"I--you must promise me not to be so rash as to again expose yourself to danger as you were on the point of doing to-day. You are right: all Villica hates you; do not make it so easy for your enemies to attack you, I entreat."

Waldemar's face flushed deeply--he cast only a single glance at her's, and all his enmity vanished. "I will be more cautious," he said, in a low voice.

"Then farewell!"

Wanda turned and took the way leading to the village; Waldemar gazed after her until she disappeared in the distance; he then resumed his seat and drove swiftly to Villica. The road soon entered the forest; he drew his pistol from his pocket, and laid it beside him. While he held the reins with his usual firmness, his eyes glanced in all directions. The daring, fearless man had all at once become cautious and vigilant; he had promised to be so, and he now knew that there was one person who trembled even for his life.

CHAPTER XX.

THE CONFLICT BETWEEN LOVE AND DUTY.

Radowicz, embracing a tract of land only one tenth as large as Villica, could in no respect compare with that magnificent estate. It had no splendid castle, no extensive forests, no grand and noble park. It was situated only a few miles from L----, in the midst of an open country, and possessed little to distinguish it from the small estates of the neighboring gentry.

Wanda had lived alone upon the estate since her father's departure. Under other circumstances, she would have remained at Villica with her aunt, but now it seemed proper and natural that the daughter of Count Morynski should avoid the castle whose master maintained so hostile an attitude toward her people. The stay of the princess there excited much comment. The aunt made her niece frequent visits and was now her guest. She had arrived upon the evening of Wanda's return, and as yet knew nothing of her meeting with Waldemar. Upon the morning of the second day of her visit, the two ladies sat in Wanda's apartments. They had just received letters which evidently brought them gloomy tidings, for both looked grave and anxious.

"Again repulsed!" said the princess, with suppressed emotion; "they had advanced to the very heart of the country, and now they have been driven back to the border. There has been nothing decisive, no noteworthy result. We may almost despair of ultimate success."

"My father also writes in a very despondent tone," said Wanda. "He is vexed and discouraged at this eternal conflict with so many opposing elements. All seek to command, none are willing to obey; dissension among the leaders is constantly on the increase. Where will all this end?"

"Your father looks upon the dark side, as he is wont to do," said the princess, reassuringly. "The order and discipline of a well-drilled army cannot be expected from a body of volunteers who at the first call rush to arms. All this will come in time."

Wanda shook her head doubtingly. "The fighting has gone on for three months," she said, "and we have atoned with three defeats for every slight success. I now for the first time understand my father's depression when he left us; it was not merely the grief of separation,--he went away cheered by no hope of victory."

"Bronislaw has always taken life too seriously," replied the princess. "I hope much from Leo's constant presence and influence over his uncle. He has all the elasticity and enthusiasm of youth; he regards every doubt of our ultimate success as treason. It would be well if he could infuse into others his unshaken confidence in victory. We all have need of it."

She re-read her son's letter. "In any event, Leo is happy," she said; "his uncle has at last yielded to his entreaties, and intrusted him with an independent command. He is stationed with his troops only a few miles from the boundary,--and yet his mother and his betrothed bride may not see him for a single moment."

"For heaven's sake, do not put such thoughts into Leo's head!" interposed Wanda. "In his present frame of mind he might commit the maddest folly in order to obtain an interview."

"Never fear for him!" replied the mother, confidently. "He has positive orders not to leave his post, and he will obey. But what does he write to you? His letter to me is brief and hasty, yours seems longer."

"It contains very little," replied Wanda, with apparent displeasure; "very little of importance to us who must remain here inactive and in suspense. Leo prefers to write me about his love; he finds time in the midst of a bloody conflict to torment himself and me with his jealousy."

"That is a strange reproach from the lips of an affianced bride!" returned the princess, sharply. "Any other girl would be proud and happy to be the centre of her lover's thoughts at a time like this."

"Leo is engaged in a life-and-death struggle. I demand deeds from him, not vows of constancy."

The mother's brow grew dark. "Now that my son has at last the opportunity, deeds will not be wanting. Do you think coldness and taciturnity are essential to the performance of great deeds?"

Wanda rose and walked to the window. She knew the purport of her aunt's words, but she could not and would not expose herself to the gaze of those penetrating eyes which rested pitilessly upon her face as if they would discover the most secret emotions of her heart. In her dealings with her niece, the princess acted upon the discovery she had made in Waldemar. She had alluded to it but once; she considered repetitions useless and dangerous, and yet the conviction that she was subjected to constant surveillance, that her every word and look was carefully noted and inwardly commented upon, robbed Wanda of all freedom in intercourse with her aunt.

"We are likely to have fighting near the boundary in a few days," resumed the princess. "Villica might be of great advantage to us,--but what is it now?"

Wanda turned and fixed her dark eyes upon her aunt. "I know the necessity that detains you in Villica," she said; "but *I* could not submit to it. I would make any sacrifice rather than live day after day in determined opposition, as you and Waldemar live."

"We two are the only ones who could endure such a life," returned the princess, with bitter irony. "I confess, Wanda, that your judgment of Waldemar was correct; the conflict with him is more obstinate than I had anticipated. Instead of wearying him, I am myself on the point of yielding; he is more than a match for me."

"He is your own son," replied Wanda; "you always forget that."

The princess, with an air of deep dejection, rested her head on her hand. "He takes pains that I shall not forget it," she said; "he daily proves to me what these four years of absence have made him. I should never have thought it possible that this incredible strength of character could result from a youth so wild and uncontrollable. He has learned to subdue himself, and he subdues all around him. The employés on the estate are all devoted to me, and yet when he opposes my orders I can no longer enforce them, he overawes all at Villica; there is authority in his glance, his will is more imperious than even mine. I only wish that Nordeck had given me this boy! I would have trained him for our cause, and perhaps he would have become something more than master of Villica. He now belongs body and soul to his father's people, and he will not renounce them for the highest prizes our side can offer. I deeply feel the misfortune of never having been allowed to be a mother to my eldest child. Both of us are atoning for this injustice."

There was a tone of remorseful self-accusation in these words; the princess had never before spoken in this manner of her eldest son. The tenderer emotions of her nature had hitherto been called forth only by her younger child, her Leo. She made a violent effort to overcome this unusual emotion, and rising abruptly, she said in a cold, hard voice,--

"It is immaterial; we are enemies and shall remain so. We must endure strife and enmity, as we endure other unavoidable evils."

A servant entered with tidings that the head steward of Villica had arrived, and urgently requested an interview with his mistress. The princess was startled. "Something must have happened," she said; "show him in immediately."

The next moment Paul entered. He had been the valet of the late Prince Zulieski, and had followed his master's family into banishment; he was now head servant at the castle. The old man appeared hurried and excited, but he did not neglect the usual tokens of respect as he approached his mistress, who said impatiently,--

"Waive all formalities, Paul. What news do you bring? What has happened in Villica?"

"Nothing in Villica, my lady, but at the border-forester's place--"

"Well?"

"There has been another skirmish, and the forester has placed all manner of obstacles in the way of the military authorities. He finally insulted the patrols, thereby provoking an open attack."

"Will the indiscretion of these subordinates eternally thwart our plans?" cried the princess, angrily. "Just now, when everything depends upon attention being diverted from that forester's place, our men literally court observation. I have ordered this Osiecki to conduct peaceably, and to restrain his servants. I will dispatch a messenger to renew that command."

"Unfortunately, Herr Nordeck has anticipated us," said Paul, hesitatingly. "He has ordered the forester to leave the house with all his servants, and to report at Villica. A German overseer is to be stationed at the boundary until a substitute can be found."

"And what has the forester done?" asked the princess.

"He has refused to obey; he sent back word to the young landlord that you had placed him there, and that whoever wished to drive him away might attempt it."

"And what has my son resolved upon?" asked the princess, her face white with terror.

"He has declared that he will himself ride over there this afternoon."

"*Alone*?" asked Wanda, who had been an attentive listener to the whole conversation.

"He always rides alone," said Paul.

The princess had seemed lost in revery. "Paul," she said, rousing herself, "have the horses harnessed immediately; you will accompany me to Villica. If anything happens, I must be there."

Paul left to execute the order. The door had scarcely closed behind him, when Wanda was at her aunt's side.

"Did you hear, aunt, that Waldemar intends to go to the border-forester's place?" she asked.

"Yes, child, I heard; what of it?"

"Do you believe the forester will submit?"

"No, he dares not. His district is the most important of all for us; it is doubly important now in view of impending events. We must have a reliable man in charge there. The fools, to jeopardize the post just at this crisis!"

"We have lost it!" exclaimed Wanda, excitedly. "Waldemar will enforce obedience."

"He will not do so in this case," replied the princess. "The forester will yield only to superior force, and Waldemar will not resort to violence. Have we not just heard that he is going over alone?"

"You certainly will not permit it. Are you not going to Villica to warn him--to keep him back?"

The princess gazed at her niece in surprise. "What are you thinking of, Wanda?" she said. "A warning from me would betray everything to Waldemar, and he would at once perceive that the men obey me and not him. He would then absolutely insist upon the overseer's removal, which may yet be prevented,--and it shall be, cost what it may."

"Do you believe that your son will tolerate open disobedience? He has not done so as yet, I do not believe that he ever will. This overseer is a desperate man capable of anything, and I do not believe that his subordinates are any better."

"Waldemar knows his character," returned the princess, "and will be careful how he irritates him. He has perfect self-control, and will always maintain that attitude toward his subordinates."

"They hate him," said Wanda, with quivering lips. "One ball has already missed him, the second may fulfil its mission better."

The princess was startled. "Who told you this?" she asked.

"I learned it from some one at Villica."

"It is a myth," said the princess, disdainfully, "and was probably invented by that cowardly Doctor Fabian, who no doubt has taken a random shot in the forest for a murderous attack upon his beloved pupil. He is constantly anxious for Waldemar's safety; but the master of Villica is my son, and that shields him from all danger."

"When the murderous passions of these men are once aroused, this circumstance will not protect him," exclaimed Wanda, in evident alarm and excitement. "You ordered the overseer to keep quiet, and you see in what manner he has obeyed you."

"Would it not be better for you to save your extreme solicitude for your own friends?" asked the princess cuttingly. "You seem to forget that Leo is hourly exposed to mortal danger."

"Knowing this, if it lay in our power to protect him, we should hasten to his rescue," broke out the young girl passionately. "And, besides, wherever Leo is, he is at the head of his own followers, while Waldemar confronts alone those savage, unrestrained bands of men whose hatred toward him you yourself have provoked, and who will not scruple to turn their hostility against their own master, if he exasperates them."

"And they will do perfectly right in that case. But he knows the danger, and he will not exasperate them. If he resorts to violent measures--let the consequences fall upon his own head."

Wanda trembled at the glance which accompanied these words. "Does a *mother* say this?" she asked.

"They are the words of a deeply offended mother whose son has driven her to the last extremity; in the present posture of affairs, there can be no peace between Waldemar and me. Wherever I set my foot, I find him in my way; whatever I attempt, he confronts and opposes me. How many of our plans he has already thwarted! How much we have been forced to sacrifice just for his sake! He has carried his opposition so far that we stand in the relation of mortal enemies. Yes, he stands alone--let him endure alone what the enmity he has provoked brings upon him."

Her voice had an icy tone; it bore no longer a trace of the maternal feeling, of that tenderness which had thrilled it a moment before; it expressed the real feeling of the Princess Zulieski, who never forgave nor forgot an injury, and against whom no greater offence was ever committed than to deprive her of authority. This was Waldemar's offence, and his mother could not forgive it.

She was about leaving the room to make preparations for departure, when her glance fell upon Wanda, who stood gazing at her, motionless and speechless, but with such a look of determination in her face that the princess paused, and said,--

"I would like to impress one thing upon you before I go: If I do not warn Waldemar, no one else should dare warn him; it would be *treason* to our cause. Why do you shudder at that word? What would you call it if any one of our party revealed our secrets by a spoken or a written word to the master of Villica? It would thwart our plans and cost us the loss of the forester's place. Wanda, the Morynskis have never had cause to regret taking the women of their house into their confidence--a traitoress has never been found among them."

"*Aunt Maryna!*" cried Wanda in such a tone of horror that the princess withdrew the hand she had laid heavily on her niece's arm.

"I only wished you to know what is at stake here," she said. "You do not want to be ashamed to look your father in the face when he returns; as to the manner in which you will settle with Leo for the mortal terror concerning his brother which now tortures you, that is your affair, not mine. If I had known that this blow threatened Leo, I should have opposed his fatal love for you instead of fostering it. Now it is too late for him and for you. This present hour has proved to me--"

The sentence was cut short by Paul's announcement that the carriage was at the door. At parting, Wanda silently placed her ice-cold hand in her aunt's, and the latter seemed content with the unspoken promise.

Wanda fled to her own room: she was finally alone with herself, alone with her apprehension of danger to Waldemar, of which his mother had no fear. Love alone could foreshadow such peril, and the princess did not love her eldest son. If she had known that Waldemar's life was in danger, she would not have uttered a word to save him, for this word might have jeopardized the interests of her party.

Wanda seated herself at her writing-desk. A brief warning, a few written lines, sent to Villica, might save Waldemar; he need not know whence they came. If he went to the forester's place, he would go accompanied by others, and no one would venture to attack him. He would, thus sustained, easily enforce obedience; he could have the forester arrested, and the forest-house guarded by soldiers. Then Waldemar would have peace.

But what would be the result to her own party? This forester's place was now used for the same purpose which Villica Castle had so long served; a portion of the weapons which had been removed from Villica were concealed there, it was the focus of the insurrection, the point whence all messengers went and to which they came. It was of the utmost importance that the present forester should remain, as firm reliance could be placed upon his loyalty and his silence. His removal would be the loss of this central point of operations; he knew that fact as well as his mistress, and he resolved to remain at all hazards.

Nordeck himself came but seldom to this remote house in the forest; his idea in going there now was to enforce obedience by his personal authority. He had often been called to such duties of late, and he probably did not regard the present affair as one of any great importance. If his authority should meet with opposition at the forester's place, if he should discover that a systematic resistance had been organized against him, he would act with his wonted energy, and deprive his mother of her last foothold. Discovery could no longer be prevented if he were told that danger threatened him from that quarter.

All this was terribly clear to Wanda's mind, and Waldemar's danger was just as clearly revealed to her. She was firmly convinced that the ball which had recently imperilled his life had come from the forester's rifle; that the man whose bitter hatred had culminated in an attempt at assassination, would not hesitate to slay his master should opportunity offer. Knowing this, must she allow Waldemar to rush unwarned perhaps into the very jaws of death? But before that terrible word *Treason* her resolution faltered; hitherto she had been her father's confidant, he relied implicitly upon his daughter, and would have scorned the thought that she could divulge a word of the secrets he had committed to her, in order to rescue an enemy. She herself had treated Leo with contempt when in a fit of jealousy he had hesitated to do his duty. The same duty that had forced him from her side to deadly conflict, now bade her do the most difficult of all things: remain silent and inactive, a witness of an impending danger she could avert with a single stroke of the pen--a single word from her lips.

All these thoughts surged in wild commotion through Wanda's breast, and almost overwhelmed her. In vain she sought to silence the voice of her heart, and let reason alone decide this conflict between love and duty; in vain she looked about her for some means of rescue compatible with her own loyalty and honor,--that inevitable and terrible "*either--or*" still confronted her. If she had not already understood her own heart, this hour would have revealed it to her. For months she had known that Leo was exposed to danger, and she had been anxious for him as for a dear relative, with a brave composure and a silent heroism. Now Waldemar was in peril, and her composure and heroism were at an end; they vanished before the mortal agony that convulsed her whole being at thought of the danger of the man she loved.

There is a point where even the most violent and anguished suffering yields to stupefaction, at least for a time, because the capacity to suffer is completely exhausted. For more than an hour Wanda had been alone in her chamber, torn by conflicting emotions; her face bore traces of the agony she had endured; she had reached that place where she could no longer dispute or question, where she could not even think. She sank helplessly upon a chair, leaned back her head, and closed her eyes.

The old dream-picture reappeared--that vision once conjured up by the sun's golden beams and the ocean vapors, and which had thrown its magic spell around two youthful hearts as yet ignorant of its deep significance. Since that autumnal evening at the forest-lake it had often appeared before their eyes, and all their strength of will had not availed to exorcise its haunting presence. It had accompanied them on that lonely drive through the wintry forest, it had hovered around them as they sped over those broad fields of snow, it had taken shape and hue from the mists rising in the zenith, it had floated on the lowering clouds away at the horizon's verge; no desolate waste, no icy atmosphere hindered its appearance. And now it suddenly rose again in its olden beauty and splendor, as if evoked by supernatural powers.

Wanda had not invoked this vision. She had placed distance and estrangement between herself and the man she wished to hate because he was not the friend of her people; she had sought a way of escape from an infatuation which she was resolved to conquer, in the fierce strife that had broken out between two hostile nations. This desperate conflict with herself had been unavailing, it had ended only in defeat. She was under the influence of no dream, no self-delusion; she knew the nature of the spell that had first been thrown around her at the beech-holm, that had been renewed at the forest-lake, that had deepened and strengthened day by day.

In one thing surely the old tradition had spoken truth: the remembrance would not vanish, the longing would not be stilled. In the midst of strife and hatred a fairy vision rose before her, beautiful as Vineta emerging from its ocean-depths,--the vision of a love truer and deeper than any other earth could offer, of a happiness that might have been hers if kindlier fates had smiled upon her life, and in fancy she heard a chiming as of bridal bells from the old city towers sunken beneath the wave.

Wanda rose slowly. The conflict between love and duty which had raged so long in her breast was over; the last ten minutes had decided it. The pen upon her writing-desk remained untouched, the words of warning were not written. She leaned for support against the desk; her hand trembled, but her face bore the serenity of an unalterable purpose.

"I will go to the forester's," she said, "and if the worst happens, I will interpose. His mother coldly and indifferently allows him to rush into the midst of danger. I will rescue him!"

CHAPTER XXI.

THE RESCUE.

The border-forester's place was situated in the midst of dense forests, and close to the boundary. The once large and stately house, which had been erected here by the elder Nordeck, showed signs of dilapidation and decay, as it had not been repaired for twenty years. The present occupant owed his position to the Princess Zulieski. He had been here three years, his bad management being entirely overlooked by his mistress, because she knew that he was devoted body and soul to her interests, and could be relied upon in any emergency. Waldemar seldom visited this distant portion of his estate, and had only a very slight acquaintance with the forester. He had, however, of late felt obliged to interfere, on account of the conflicts between this man and the soldiers who guarded the German frontier.

Winter still held undisputed sway. Forest and forest-house lay wrapped in snow, and the dim light of a gray, cloudy sky fell around the chill, desolate landscape. The forester and his men, numbering three or four assistants and as many servants, were gathered in a large room upon the ground-floor. They were all armed, and were awaiting the landlord's arrival. Waldemar had ordered the forester, Osiecki, and his men to depart quietly from the place, but appearances did not indicate an intention to obey. The lowering faces of the subordinates boded nothing good, and the forester's aspect was that of a man capable of any act of desperation. These men, who had passed their lives in the solitude of the forest, were little disposed to law and order, and their leader was known as one who placed but slight restraint upon his lawless, passionate nature.

They all maintained a respectful attitude at this moment, for the young Countess Morynski stood before them. She had thrown back her cloak, and her pale, beautiful face bore no traces of the agonized conflict through which she had just passed. Its ruling expression was a stern, cold gravity.

"You have led us into an unfortunate position, Osiecki," she said. "Instead of seeking to avert suspicion from this quarter, you provoke collision with the patrols, and you imperil us all by your indiscretion. My aunt is displeased with you, and I come to forbid your again committing any act of violence against any person whomsoever."

The reproof did not fail of its effect. The forester cast down his eyes, and his voice had an apologetic tone, as, with mingled defiance and penitence, he answered,--

"What is done cannot be helped; I could restrain neither my men nor myself. You do not know what it is to remain inactive here upon the frontier, while every day there is fighting over yonder,--to be obliged to endure the presence of these domineering soldiers, and not dare to act, even when we have loaded muskets in our hands. I do not think our patience will hold out much longer; we lost it entirely day before yesterday. If I did not know that we were needed here, I should long ago have been with the army. Prince Zulieski is stationed only a few miles from here--we can easily find our way to him."

"You must remain," said Wanda, resolutely. "You know my father's orders. This forester's place must be retained at all hazards, and you can do more for us here than you could in battle. Prince Leo has men enough under his command. But now to the main point: Herr Nordeck is coming here to-day."

"Yes," replied the forester, jeeringly; "he says that he will enforce obedience. He orders us to Villica Castle, where he can watch us constantly, and lay his finger upon us at any moment. Nordeck can command, but the question is, Shall we obey? If he intends driving us away from here, he will have to call a whole regiment of soldiers to his aid; otherwise, things may end worse than he imagines."

"What do you mean?" asked the young countess; "do you forget that Waldemar Nordeck is the son of your mistress?"

"Prince Leo Zulieski is her son and our master," broke out the forester. "It is a shame for the princess and all of us to be ruled by this German, just because his father twenty odd years ago intruded here, and compelled the young Countess Morynski to marry him. The marriage brought her misery enough, but the son is even worse than his father. We know the life they lead together; she really would not mourn his loss any more than she did the loss of his father, and his death would be the best thing that could happen. Then there would be no need of issuing secret commands from the castle; the princess would rule, and our young prince would be the heir and the future master of Villica, as he ought to be."

Wanda turned pale. The unhappy strife between this mother and son had gone so far that the tenants on the estate were deliberately estimating the advantages Waldemar's death would bring to his nearest relatives--that they even counted upon the forgiveness of the princess for his assassination! Wanda's worst fears were confirmed, but she knew that she dared not betray her anxiety by word or manner. She was respected here as the daughter of Count Morynski, as the niece of the princess, and she was supposed to speak in the name of the latter. If her purpose in coming should be discovered, her authority and her ability to protect Waldemar would end.

"Do not venture to attack your master," she said, with a commanding air, and as calmly as if she were delivering a message intrusted to her. "Whatever happens, the princess will spare her son at any cost. The man who attacks him need hope no mercy. Your disobedience, Osiecki, has already exasperated your mistress; do not attempt rebellion a second time."

The forester set down his gun reluctantly, and the other men followed his example. Wanda, acting as the representative of their mistress, could have gained her object if more time had been granted her; but Waldemar's sleigh now drew up before the door, and all eyes were turned to the window.

Wanda started. "Is the landlord already here?" she said. "Osiecki, open the side-door for me, and do not betray my presence by a word. I shall go as soon as he leaves."

Wanda entered a small, dimly lighted room, and closed the door behind her. Two minutes after, Waldemar appeared in the house. He paused upon the threshold, and with one sweeping glance scanned the circle of foresters, who, still grasping their weapons, gathered around their leader. This was not a very encouraging spectacle for the young landlord, who had come entirely alone to enforce obedience from his rebellious subordinates, but his voice and manner betrayed no alarm as he turned to the forester, and said,--

"I did not notify you of my coming, and yet you seem prepared for it."

"Yes, we are awaiting you," was the laconic answer.

"Armed? And in this attitude? Why are weapons in your hands? Set them down!"

Osiecki set down his musket, but not beyond his reach; the others did the same. Waldemar advanced to the middle of the room.

"I come to seek explanation of an *error* that occurred yesterday," he said. "My order could not have been misunderstood, for it was sent to you in writing. The messenger, however, might have misapprehended your answer."

The forester hesitated; he had not the audacity to repeat to his master's face what he had said to the messenger the day before.

"I am frontier forester," he answered, "and I intend to remain so as long as I am in your service, Herr Nordeck. I am responsible for my district, and must have the management of it."

"You have shown yourself incapable of management; you cannot or will not hold your men in check. I have warned you repeatedly; yesterday was the third time, and it is also the last."

"At a time like the present, I cannot prevent my men from coming in conflict with the patrols," said the forester, defiantly. "My authority does not extend so far."

"For this very reason you should go to Villica, and leave the control here to me."

"And my district?"

"Will remain under charge of Overseer Fellner until the arrival of the new forester. You will leave this place to-morrow, and if you do not report at Villica with all your men, you will be dismissed."

A threatening murmur was heard. The men pressed close together, and the overseer confronted his landlord. "That is not so easily done," he said; "I am no common laborer, to be hired to-day and discharged to-morrow. You can give me notice to leave if you wish, but I and the men I have engaged have a right to remain until autumn. I do not wish to take any other district, and I will not; whoever attempts to drive me away will repent it."

"The forest is my property," returned Waldemar, "and the foresters must submit to my authority. Appeal to no right you yourself have forfeited! If justice were done you, you would receive a severer punishment than mere transferral. You will either comply with my orders, or I shall to-day tender this place to the government as a post of observation, and to-morrow troops will occupy the house."

The overseer made a hasty movement as if to grasp his musket, but he checked himself.

"You will not do that, Herr Nordeck," he said.

"I shall do it in case of disobedience or opposition. Now tell me plainly, will you appear at Villica to-morrow, or will you not?"

"No, and a thousand times no!" replied the forester in a towering passion. "I have orders not to leave here, and I shall go only when forced to do so."

Waldemar was startled. "Orders? From whom?"

The forester saw his blunder, but it was too late to recall the hasty words.

"From whom have you received orders?" repeated the young landlord. "Is it from the princess, my mother?"

"Well, what if it were so? The princess has ruled us for years, why should she not rule us now?"

"Because the master is himself at hand, and two persons cannot hold the reins. My mother is my guest; I am ruler of Villica. You say you have orders not to leave unless forced to do so? Here is something more than mere insubordination."

The forester maintained an obstinate silence. Through his own indiscretion he had been guilty of what the princess would have called treason, and what Wanda's hasty mission was intended to prevent. That one unguarded word betrayed to Waldemar that the opposition to which he had thus far attached little importance, was the result of a deep-laid scheme on the part of his mother.

"We will not discuss the matter further," said Waldemar. "To-morrow this district will be in other hands. The rest of our business can be arranged at Villica Castle."

He was on the point of leaving, but the overseer seized his musket and intercepted him.

"I think we had better come to a final settlement now," he said. "Once for all, I tell you I shall not leave my place; I shall not go to Villica; and you shall not go from here until you have revoked your command!"

The foresters, like well-drilled soldiers, each seized his weapon, and in an instant the young landlord was surrounded by sullen, threatening faces--faces which indicated plainly that the men would shrink from no deed of violence. The man[oe]uvre had been so quick and so well executed, that it must have been planned. Waldemar, perhaps, regretted that he had come alone, but he retained his usual composure.

"What does this mean?" he asked. "Am I to take it as a threat?"

"Take it for what you please," said the border-forester, beside himself with rage; "but you shall not stir from here until you comply with our terms! It is now our turn to say '*either--or.*' Take care, you are not bullet-proof!"

"You have already made the test, perhaps," the young landlord said, riveting his gaze upon the forester. "From whose gun did the ball come that was fired at me when I left here on my last visit?"

The only answer was a gleam of deadly hatred from Osiecki's eyes.

"I have another ball, and so has each of my men. We are ready to put them to the proof. To come to the point: you must either give us your word--your word of honor, (for this is more binding with people of your rank than any written agreement,)--that all of us shall remain here unmolested, that no soldier shall set foot here, or--"

"Or?"

"You shall not leave this place alive!"

This menace was followed by ominous mutterings from the men. They pressed more closely around the young landlord, six rifle-barrels raised threateningly backed the overseer's words, but not a muscle of Waldemar's face moved as he deliberately eyed the group.

"You are fools," he said, contemptuously; "do you not know that if you kill me you must suffer the consequences? Such deeds never escape discovery."

"We are not afraid," replied Osiecki, derisively; "in half an hour we should be beyond the boundary, in the thick of the fight. None would call us to account; our own party would thank us for having rid it of a bitter and powerful enemy. Besides, we are tired of staying here; we want to join our comrades in the army. Now, I ask you for the last time, will you give us your word of honor?"

"No!" said Nordeck, without moving from his place, or taking his eye from the speaker.

"Bethink yourself, Herr Nordeck," cried the overseer, in a voice half stifled with rage; "consider ere it is too late!"

With a few rapid strides, Waldemar reached the wall, and braced himself firmly against it.

"No! I repeat; and since we have gone so far, you had better think what you are about before attacking me. A couple of you at least will pay with your lives for an attempt to murder me. I can hit as well as you!"

These words let loose the storm which had been so long impending. A wild tumult arose; angry mutterings, curses, and threats came thick and fast. More than one man placed his finger upon the trigger of his gun. The overseer was about to give the signal for a simultaneous attack, when the side-door opened, and the next instant Wanda stood close to the imperilled landlord.

Her appearance for the moment restrained the would-be assassins; she stood so near their master that to fire upon him would endanger her life. Waldemar was at first confounded by the young girl's mysterious presence, but the truth soon flashed upon him. Her death-like pallor, the expression of desperate energy with which she took her position at his side, told him that she had learned of his danger and was here for his sake alone.

The danger was too imminent to allow time for explanation. Wanda confronted the assailants and by turns threatened and commanded them. Her efforts were fruitless; she resorted to entreaty, but that was alike unavailing. The men gave her angry and menacing answers, the forester emphasizing his words with furious stamps and gesticulations. This vehement conversation, which had been carried on in Polish, a language little understood by Waldemar, lasted only a few moments; no one retreated a step, no one lowered his weapon. The men, exasperated to fury, no longer heeded any authority or control.

"Go away, Wanda," said Waldemar, in an undertone, as he tried gently to push her aside. "They are about to fire on me, they can no longer be restrained; give me room to defend myself."

Wanda did not stir, she only kept her place more resolutely; she knew that Waldemar, if left alone, must succumb, that his only chance of escape lay in her remaining close at his side. They would not like to harm her, but the moment was near when even this forbearance would end.

"Stand aside, Countess Morynski!" cried the forester's voice, rising above the tumult; "stand aside, or I shall hit you too."

He levelled his rifle. Wanda saw his finger on the lock, she saw his face distorted by fury and hatred, and her self-control vanished. Her mind harbored only one lucid thought--Waldemar's peril,--and as a last resort she threw herself upon his breast, and shielded him with her trembling form.

It was too late; the forester fired, and the next instant Waldemar's revolver answered. With a hollow cry, Osiecki threw up his arms and fell lifeless on the floor. Waldemar's ball had hit its mark with terrible accuracy, but he himself stood upright, and Wanda with him. The movement she had made in trying to shield him had drawn him out of the range of the overseer's deadly shot, and had saved both him and her.

All this had occurred so quickly that none of the men had taken part in the murderous affray. It seemed that in one and the same moment they had seen Wanda throw herself on Waldemar's breast, their leader lying on the ground, and the landlord confronting them ready for a second shot. A deathlike silence of some moments followed; no one moved.

Immediately after the firing, Waldemar stationed himself before Wanda. He comprehended the situation at a glance. The door was blockaded, six loaded muskets opposed his single weapon. If the firing should be renewed and Wanda attempt to shield him, both would be lost. An effectual defence was out of the question. Courage even to rashness alone could avail.

Summoning his whole resolution, he threw himself into the midst of his assailants; his tall figure towered above them all, and his infuriated glance flamed down upon the cowards who sought to assassinate him.

"Put down your guns!" he cried, in a loud, imperious voice. "I tolerate no rebellion upon my estates. The first man who has attempted it lies there; the next will share his fate. Down with your arms, I say!"

The men stood as if paralyzed, and stared speechless at their master. They hated him, they were in revolt against him, and he had just shot their leader. To avenge Osiecki's fall would be their next and most natural step. They had intended to attack Waldemar, but as he strode among them and with his bare hand thrust aside their weapons, they recoiled before him. That old habit of blind obedience, which, without asking any reason, submits to all commands, asserted itself; it was the instinctive submission of inferior natures to a superior. They trembled, and shrunk back from these flaming eyes which they had long since learned to fear,--from this threatening, commanding brow. The forester's never-failing ball had passed by this man harmlessly, and he lay dead upon the floor, shot through the heart. The men cowered back with a sort of superstitious dread. The levelled guns were gradually lowered, the circle around the landlord grew wider; he had passed unharmed through this great peril--he had parried six weapons with one.

Waldemar approached Wanda, and taking her arm, drew her gently to his side. "Out of our way!" he said to the men, in a commanding tone; "make room for us!"

The men moved sullenly aside, opening a passage to the door. Not a word was uttered; in silence they allowed their master and the young countess to pass through. Waldemar did not hasten in the least; he knew that the danger was over only for the moment, that it would return with redoubled force as soon as the men recovered their self-possession and were conscious of their advantage; but he also knew that the slightest indication of fear must prove fatal. The power of his eye and voice still ruled these savage men. He must break away from them before the spell was over, and this might happen at any instant.

He left the house with Wanda. The sleigh was standing outside, and the driver, with a terror-stricken face, ran to meet them. Waldemar assisted Wanda in and sat down by her side.

"Drive slowly as far as those trees," he said to the coachman, in an undertone, "then give your horses the whip, and make all possible haste."

The man obeyed; the trees were soon passed, and they flew on like the wind. Waldemar held the revolver in his right hand, and firmly grasped Wanda's hand with his left. He retained his defensive attitude until they were a long distance from the forest-house and all danger of attack was over. He then turned to his companion, and saw that the hand he held in his was covered with blood. Heavy drops trickled down the young girl's sleeve; and the man who had just faced death with such iron composure, trembled and grew pale.

"It is nothing," said Wanda, in reply to his inquiry; "the overseer's ball must have grazed my shoulder. I feel the wound now for the first time."

Waldemar hastily drew out his handkerchief and bound up the wounded arm. His look and manner betrayed all that was in his heart, and he was on the point of speaking, when the young girl lifted her pallid face to his. She said nothing, yet there was such an expression of anxious entreaty in her eyes, that Waldemar kept silent; he saw that he must forbear, at least for the present. He uttered only her name, but this one word conveyed more than a passionate declaration of love.

"WANDA!"

He sought her gaze in vain, her hand lay heavy and cold in his.

"*Wanda!*" he repeated. "Greater love hath no one than this, that he should lay down his life for his friend. You have imperilled your life for mine."

"Yes, and I would have died for you," she said, in a faint, hollow voice that fell upon his ear like an expiring gasp. "But you are the enemy of my people--and I am the betrothed of Leo Zulieski!"

CHAPTER XXII.

THE NEW UNIVERSITY PROFESSOR.

The forester's death prevented any concealment of the tragedy at the border-house, and all Villica was in commotion. Nothing could have been more unwelcome to the princess than this open and bloody conflict. Doctor Fabian and the superintendent were horror-stricken, while the tenants were divided into two parties, and discussed the affair with angry vehemence. One person only was elated at this melancholy event, and that person was Assessor Hubert. As he chanced to be stopping at the superintendent's, he seized his opportunity, and went at once to the castle in his official capacity, forcing Herr Nordeck into a personal interview, a consummation he had long devoutly wished.

Waldemar told him, very briefly, that he had shot the forester in self-defence, and declared himself ready to proceed at once to L----, to undergo an examination by the civil authorities; meanwhile Hubert could obtain all the information in his power.

The representative of the police department of L---- was right in his element, and set about his duties with a very consequential air; but he was doomed to disappointment; the witnesses he had hoped to seize and bear in triumph to L---- had eluded his grasp; the men concerned in the affray had seen fit to escape all judicial investigation by flight beyond the border where they had long desired to be. They had escaped by night, and had already joined the insurgent army. Hubert was inconsolable.

"They have gone!" he said, despairingly, to the superintendent. "Not a single one of them remains behind."

"I could have told you that before," rejoined Herr Frank; "it was the wisest thing they could do. Over there they are secure from indictment as accomplices."

"But I wanted to arrest them--I wanted to bring them all to justice."

"And I am glad they are out of the way; they are a wild, dangerous set, and we are well rid of them. Herr Nordeck does not want a great ado made about it."

"It is none of Herr Nordeck's business," said Hubert, in his most pompous, official tone; "he must submit to the majesty of the law, which demands the most thorough and searching investigation. Of course he will not be compromised; he fired in self-defence, after the forester had aimed at him. He will only have to submit to an examination which will end in an honorable acquittal; but there is something else involved: we are dealing with a conspiracy, with an insurrection--"

"For heaven's sake, are you on that track again?"

"Yes, an insurrection!" repeated Hubert, with unshaken equanimity; "all the facts go to prove it."

"Nonsense!" ejaculated the superintendent; "it was a revolt against the landlord personally--nothing more. The forester and his men were accustomed to acts of violence, and the princess allowed them great liberty because they implicitly obeyed her commands. They would learn obedience to no other, and when their master sought to teach it to them, they rebelled. Any other man would have been killed, but his energy and presence of mind saved him. He shot down the would-be assassin without ceremony, and this paralyzed the others. The affair is as clear and simple as possible, and I do not comprehend how you can see a conspiracy in it."

"And how do you explain the presence of the Countess Morynski?" asked Hubert, triumphantly, as if he had just proved an accused person guilty of some heinous crime. "What business had she at the forester's place? We all know the part she and the princess take in the Polish movement. The women of that nation are very dangerous; they know everything, they are capable of everything, most of the political intrigues are in their hands, and the Countess Morynski is her father's own daughter, the apt pupil of her aunt. Her presence at the forest-house proves the existence of a conspiracy as clear as noonday. She hates her cousin with all the fanaticism of her nation, and she must have planned that murderous attack. That is why she suddenly appeared in the midst of the tumult, why she endeavored to disarm Herr Nordeck when he levelled his revolver at Osiecki, why she urged on the forester and his men to assassination. Waldemar Nordeck is a remarkable man; he not only put down the revolt, but he secured its instigator and carried her forcibly to Villica; in spite of all resistance, he tore his treacherous cousin from the midst of her followers, placed her in his sleigh, and dashed away with her as if life or death were at stake. Just think of it! during the whole journey he did not vouchsafe her one solitary word; he held her firmly by the hand so as to frustrate any attempt at flight. I have all this from a reliable source. I have questioned the coachman very minutely--"

"You had him on the rack for three hours, until the poor man became confused and said 'yes' to everything," interposed the superintendent, dryly. "He really knows very little about the matter; he only told what you put into his mouth. Herr Nordeck's story alone is reliable."

The assessor was deeply offended, but ere he gave vent to his indignation, he bethought himself that the person who indulged in such censure was his prospective father-in-law and must be treated accordingly, even though he were wanting in proper respect to his own official wisdom and dignity. So he swallowed his indignation, and replied in his usual self-possessed tone,--

"Herr Nordeck conducts himself like a sovereign as usual. He made his report as laconic as possible, would enter into no details, and refused to allow me to question the Countess Morynski on the plea that she was ill. Then he went on giving orders and making arrangements as if I were not present, and as if no other person had a right to say a word upon a matter he would prefer to keep secret. 'Herr Nordeck,' said I to him, 'you greatly deceive yourself if you look upon this affair as a mere outbreak of personal hatred. I perceive that it has a deeper significance: it was a deliberately planned insurrection which broke out prematurely; it was not designed merely as an attack upon you, it was a plot against order, law, and government. We must sift the matter to the bottom.' What do you suppose he said in reply? These were his words:

"'Herr Assessor, you deceive *yourself* in regarding the violence of a brutal man against me personally as a conspiracy against the state. As the main actors have escaped, in the absence of other conspirators you will be obliged to fall back upon Doctor Fabian and me. For your own sake, I advise you to restrain your ardor. I have given you the necessary materials for your report to the police department of L----, and you need not feel concerned about law and order here in Villica, for I consider myself competent to maintain both.' He then made a cold, polite, and incredibly haughty bow, and left me standing there alone."

The superintendent laughed. "He is just like his mother. I know this manner in the Princess Zulieski, and I have often enough been enraged by it. It is a sort of superiority which awes you in spite of yourself, and which Prince Leo does not at all possess. Herr Nordeck was right, however, in advising you to restrain your ardor; it has often enough brought you into difficulty."

"That is my fate," said the assessor, in a resigned tone. "With the noblest motives, with self-sacrificing devotion to the state and untiring zeal for its welfare, I reap nothing but ingratitude, misrepresentation and neglect. I had finally grasped the clew to a conspiracy, but it slipped through my hands. Osiecki is killed, his men have fled, no evidence can be obtained from the Countess Morynski; I can make an ordinary report and nothing more. If I had only been at the forest-house yesterday! When I arrived there this morning, it was empty. Yes, it is my destiny always to arrive too late!"

The superintendent, thinking that this would be a favorable opportunity to introduce the subject of the assessor's suit, and to inform him distinctly that he must cherish no hopes of obtaining his daughter's hand, cleared his throat portentously; but at this moment the landlord's coachman appeared with a message from his master. This was the man who had driven Waldemar to the forest-house on the preceding day, and who had already been subjected to an exhaustive examination from the assessor. Hubert now lost sight of everything else, he forgot misrepresentation and neglect, and suddenly recollected that he had some very important questions to ask. Heedless of Frank's protestations, he took the coachman to his own room, with a view to prosecuting the examination with renewed ardor.

The superintendent shook his head; he began to incline to the opinion that there was something morbid in the assessor's nature, and to feel that his daughter was not so greatly at fault for rejecting a suitor whose frantic official zeal could no more be moderated than his fixed belief in a general insurrection.

Gretchen meantime was following the assessor's example by putting very pointed questions to Doctor Fabian, who sat near her in the parlor of the superintendent's house. The doctor could tell her nothing of recent events that she did not know already, and he was not at all informed upon the point which most excited her curiosity,--the part the Countess Wanda had played at the house of the border-forester. She placed small reliance upon Hubert's assertion that the young countess hated her cousin, and that she had planned the attack. With true womanly intuition, she imagined that the relations between these two were of an entirely different nature, and she was vexed and indignant because she could learn nothing further.

"You do not know how to use your influence, Doctor Fabian," she said, in a reproachful tone. "If I were the intimate friend of Waldemar Nordeck, I should be better informed in regard to his affairs."

The doctor smiled. "I hardly think you would," he said; "Waldemar has a reticent nature, he does not feel the need of confiding in any one."

"That is because he has no heart," said Gretchen, who was very hasty in her judgments. "One can see at a glance that he is heartless; a freezing atmosphere surrounds him, he chills me whenever he speaks to me. He has taught all Villica to fear him, and he is loved by none. In spite of his friendly regard for my father, he is as cold and distant to us now as he was upon the day of his arrival here. I am convinced that he has never loved a human being--and least of all a woman. He is perfectly heartless."

"My dear young lady, you do my friend great injustice. He has a heart, a warmer one than you think,--warmer perhaps than that fiery Prince Leo. He does not wear his heart upon his sleeve, however. I thought as you do about Waldemar Nordeck, until an accident which happened to me and nearly caused my death taught me to know him as he really is."

"Well, one thing is certain," said Gretchen, decidedly, "he possesses very little amiability, and I do not understand your great affection for him. Yesterday, you were almost beside yourself on his account, and something must have occurred to-day, for you are again excited and depressed. Does any danger still threaten Herr Nordeck?"

"No, no," replied the doctor; "my excitement concerns only myself. I received letters from J---- this morning."

"Has that scientific and historic monster, that Professor Schwarz, again caused you vexation?" inquired the young lady, with a belligerent air, as if she were all ready to begin a contest with the aforesaid gentleman.

Fabian shook his head. "I fear," said he, "that it is I who now cause him the greatest vexation, although I do so sorely against my will. You are aware that it was my 'History of Ancient Germany' that first gave rise to that unfortunate strife between him and Professor Weber,--a strife that has grown more and more bitter, until it has resulted in estrangement. Professor Schwarz, who has a very impetuous nature, was exasperated at the popularity of my book, and resorted to personalities against his colleagues. Seeing that the whole university sided with his rival, he threatened to resign, but the threat was merely for effect, as he supposed that his services could not be dispensed with. His irascible nature, however, had made him so many enemies among the regents of the university, that no attempt was made to retain him, and his resignation was accepted. He is soon to leave."

"That is a lucky thing for the university," coolly remarked Gretchen; "but I really believe you censure yourself for it; it would be just like you."

"And this is not all," said Doctor Fabian, hesitatingly and half audibly; "there is a desire that I--that I should take his position. Professor Weber writes that I am to be offered the professorship--I, a mere private tutor, without academic experience, and whose sole merit lies in his book, the first he has ever published. This is an occurrence so unusual, so unprecedented, that at first I was taken completely by surprise."

Gretchen looked neither surprised nor confounded; she seemed to think this proceeding the most natural thing in the world. "They are very wise in offering you a professorship," she said; "you are a greater man than Professor Schwarz; your work stands far above his writings, and when you once occupy his chair, your renown will overshadow his."

"But, Fräulein Frank, you are acquainted neither with the professor nor with his works," protested the doctor, timidly.

"That does not matter; I am acquainted with *you*," said the young girl, in a manner that forbade all protest. "You will of course accept?"

"I hardly think I shall. Honorable as the position is, I scarcely dare accept it, for I fear I am not fitted for it. Years of seclusion and a solitary life with my books, have almost disqualified me for public life, and have totally unfitted me for the social requirements of such a station. But my main objection is that I do not wish to leave Waldemar now, when so many dangers and difficulties environ him. I am the only one whose absence he would regret; it would be the height of ingratitude if, for the sake of mere personal advantage, I should--"

"And it would be the height of selfishness in Herr Nordeck to accept the sacrifice of your whole future," interrupted Gretchen. "Fortunately, he will not do it; he will never oppose your entering upon a path which would insure your happiness and prosperity."

"My happiness," repeated Doctor Fabian, in a tone of deep dejection; "there you are in error. I have sought and I have found perfect satisfaction in my studies, and I considered it an especial favor of fortune when my pupil, who had once been so cold and distant toward me, became my warm, true friend. I have never known what is called real happiness,--a home, a family; I probably never shall. It would be presumption in me to dream of that higher bliss now that so great and unexpected a success has been granted me. I am content with my lot."

For all their resignation, these words had a very melancholy tone, and yet they did not seem to awaken much sympathy in the youthful listener. Her lips curled in scorn.

"You have a peculiar nature, Doctor Fabian," she said; "the prospect of a life of renunciation would fill me with despair."

The doctor smiled sadly. "It is very different with you," he said. "One who, like you, is young and charming and has grown up under easy and fortunate circumstances, has a right to expect happiness from life. That it may be yours in fullest measure is my most ardent wish. You will be happy, for Assessor Hubert loves you, and--"

"What has Assessor Hubert to do with my happiness?" broke out Gretchen. "You have hinted at such a thing once before; what do you mean?"

Fabian was greatly embarrassed. "I beg your pardon if I have been indiscreet," he stammered; "the words escaped me ere I was aware. I know that there has been no public betrothal, but my heartfelt interest in you must be my excuse, if I--"

"If you *what*?" cried the young lady, passionately, seeing that the doctor hesitated. "I really believe that you seriously consider me the betrothed of this silly, tiresome Hubert, who talks to me all day long of nothing but conspiracies and his future title of government counsellor."

"But, my dear young lady," said the doctor, in profound astonishment, "the assessor himself informed me, last autumn, that he had positive encouragement from you, and could with certainty reckon upon your consent."

Gretchen sprang from her seat so violently that the chair fell over. "Ah, he said that to you, did he! But you alone are to blame for it, Doctor Fabian. Do not look so terror-stricken. It was you who induced me to send him to Janowo, where he caught a severe cold. Fearing a serious illness, I nursed the assessor, and ever since that time he has had a fixed idea that I love him. He is one who never gets rid of his fixed ideas--we know that from his everlasting talk about conspiracies."

She almost cried from vexation, but the doctor's face lighted up at sight of her unfeigned indignation.

"Do you not love the assessor?" he asked, breathlessly. "Do you not intend to give him your hand?"

"I never dreamed of such a thing," replied Gretchen, very decidedly; and she was about to add some remarks not at all complimentary to poor Hubert, when her eyes met the doctor's ardent gaze. She blushed deeply, and was silent.

A long pause followed. Fabian had a hard struggle with his timid nature; several times he sought in vain to speak; but meanwhile his eyes spoke, and so plainly that Gretchen could not remain in doubt as to what was coming. She now felt no impulse to run away, or to break piano-strings, as at that moment when Hubert had been on the point of making a declaration. She resumed her seat, and awaited the inevitable.

After a while, the doctor approached her timidly and anxiously.

"My dear young lady," he began, "I really believed--that is--I supposed--the ardent affection of the assessor for you--"

He stopped, and bethought himself that it was very unwise to be speaking of the assessor's ardent affection when he ought to speak of his own. Gretchen saw that he was becoming hopelessly involved in his phrases, and that she must come to his rescue. It was only a glance she gave her bashful wooer, but it spoke as plainly as his own had spoken a few moments before. The doctor all at once took courage, and went on with incredible boldness:--

"That error has made me very unhappy," he began. "Still I would not have ventured to confess it to you, even so short a time ago as yesterday. Dependent as I was upon Waldemar's magnanimity, how could I give utterance to the dearest wish of my heart? A moment ago, Fräulein Margaret, you reproached me for possessing a too self-sacrificing nature; if you knew the life of renunciation I have led, you would take back the reproach. I have passed through life neglected and solitary from my childhood; I have pursued my studies only through the greatest self-denial, and they have yielded me nothing but dependence upon the whims and generosity of strangers. It is galling to a man, spurred on by high and noble purposes and possessed of a heart glowing with enthusiasm for science, to descend, day after day, to the intellect of a boy, and instruct him in the rudiments of learning. This was my lot until Waldemar made it possible for me to devote myself to study, and paved my way to the career which is now open before me. I had, in truth, resolved to sacrifice this career for his sake, and also to keep the fact of my call to it a secret. Then I looked upon you as the affianced bride of another, but now,"--he took her hand, all his embarrassment vanished, while words came thronging to his lips,--"but now that my future is so full of promise, it depends upon you whether it shall bring me happiness. Decide for me, Margaret; shall I accept or decline the position?"

He had reached the very place where the assessor had made his great dramatic pause preparatory to falling upon his knees, and where he had been checked by the precipitate departure of his adored. The doctor, however, made no attempt at kneeling; he spoke on without hesitation, while Margaret sat near him with downcast eyes, and listened with intense satisfaction. Formal proposal, acceptance, and betrothal kiss followed in quick succession, and Doctor Fabian's future was decided.

Assessor Hubert came down the stairs. He had subjected the coachman to a detailed and lengthy examination, until both were weary; he now proposed to rest from fatiguing official duties, and give free course to the emotions of his heart. Poor Hubert! As he had said, it was always his misfortune to arrive too late. He had as yet no suspicion of the way in which the words would be verified to-day. He was to leave this afternoon, and he had resolved to come to a positive understanding with Margaret before his departure. He was resolved to leave Villica as her accepted lover, and in the ardor of this resolution he opened the hall-door so boisterously, that the newly-betrothed couple found time to assume an unembarrassed attitude. As he entered the room, Margaret sat at a window, and the doctor stood near her in front of the piano, which to Hubert's relief was closed. Hubert greeted the doctor graciously, but condescendingly; he had always treated him in a patronizing manner, as a mere salaried tutor of no consequence whatever excepting as the chosen friend of the master of Villica. Now, as he had resolved to propose at once, he thought Fabian's presence a great intrusion, and took no pains to conceal that fact.

"I regret disturbing you," he said; "you are doubtless giving your pupil her French lesson."

He said this in a tone so supercilious, that even Doctor Fabian, so accustomed to being addressed by him as a hired teacher, was offended. Hitherto he had not resented Hubert's treatment, but to-day, his new dignity as Margaret's accepted lover would brook no slight or insult. Drawing himself up, he said with an emphasis that delighted Margaret,--

"You mistake; we are taking lessons in an entirely different science."

The assessor paid no heed to the words; he was wholly absorbed in devising some way to get rid of this tiresome, intrusive man.

"Are you giving lessons in history?" he asked, maliciously. "I believe that is your hobby; but unfortunately, it is not a science pleasing to young ladies. I fear you will weary Fräulein Frank with it, Doctor Fabian."

A reply was on the doctor's lips, but Gretchen anticipated him. Thinking it high time to silence the assessor, she undertook that duty with no small delight.

"You will soon have to address Doctor Fabian by another title," she said. "He is about to accept a professorship in the university of J----, which has been offered him on account of his great literary and scientific acquirements."

"Wh--a--t are you saying?" cried the assessor, with a start, and an expression of utter incredulity. He could not reconcile himself to this sudden transformation of the neglected Fabian into a university professor.

The doctor's amiable disposition had again won the mastery. His sympathetic nature was troubled at thought of the double wound he must necessarily inflict upon the nephew of his rival and the unsuccessful wooer of his betrothed.

"Herr Assessor," he began, believing that Hubert was acquainted with recent events at the university, which was by no means the case,--"I regret that your uncle has so misunderstood me. No one can be more sincere than myself in recognition of his great ability. Let me assure you that I have not taken the least part in the strife which my 'History of Ancient Germany' has provoked. Professor Schwarz seems to believe that I instigated the dispute and carried it to its present pitch from selfish motives."

A terrible light now began to dawn upon the assessor. He had not known the name of the obscure man whom the opposition had chosen for its champion, and whose first book had begun to be compared with, and even placed above his uncle's works; but he was aware that a "History of Ancient Germany" was the prime cause of the dispute, and Fabian's words left him in no doubt that the author of this book, this intriguer, this assailer of his family renown, stood before him. He was on the point of giving vent to his astonishment and indignation, when Gretchen, who felt called upon to assert her dignity as the future wife of the professor, interposed,--

"Yes," she said, "the professor may well believe this, since Doctor Fabian has an urgent call to replace him, and accept the chair of History at L----. You already know, I suppose, that your uncle has tendered his resignation?"

The assessor struggled so desperately for breath, that Fabian cast a look of entreaty upon his betrothed: but she remained inexorable. She could not forget that Hubert had boasted for months of her readiness to accept his suit, and she wanted to teach him a lesson. She therefore played her last card by formally grasping Doctor Fabian's hand and leading him up to the assessor with these words:--

"And furthermore, Herr Assessor, I have the pleasure of introducing to you in the person of Professor Fabian, the successor of your renowned uncle,--my future husband!"

"I believe the assessor is deranged," remarked Superintendent Frank to his overseer, as the two were standing in the yard. "He has just dashed out of the house like a lunatic, and rushed to his carriage without greeting me. He was in high spirits this morning. I fear this new chase after a conspiracy has turned his brain. Go and look after him, and see that no harm befalls him."

The overseer shrugged his shoulders, and pointed to Hubert's carriage, which was already in rapid motion. "It is too late," he said; "there the madman goes!"

Frank entered the house, and there learned the cause of the assessor's headlong flight, while the coachman, who stood gazing after the fugitive, said with a sigh of relief,--

"Thank Heaven, he has gone, and will quiz me no more!"

CHAPTER XXIII.

BROTHER AGAINST BROTHER.

An ominous atmosphere brooded over Villica, filling all its inmates with gloomy foreboding. Since the return of Waldemar and Wanda from the border-forester's the night before, a storm had raged in the upper apartments of the castle, and it had not yet subsided. The young countess after an interview with her aunt, had shut herself up in her chamber, where she still remained. The princess also sought seclusion, and when she appeared, which was but seldom, her look and manner frightened the servants, who well knew that this knitted brow and these compressed lips boded no good. Waldemar also had lost that icy composure which he retained outwardly whatever storms might rage within his breast; he seemed dejected and irritated. Perhaps this was due to the fact that Wanda had twice to-day denied him an interview. He had not seen her since that moment when he had laid her swooning and unconscious in the arms of his mother. She refused to see him, and yet he knew that she was not seriously ill; the physician had repeatedly assured him that her wound was not dangerous.

Waldemar, however, had but little time for personal matters, so many outside things demanded his attention. The forester's corpse was brought to Villica, and with it came tidings that all his men had fled beyond the border. The forester's range was confided to other hands. In the midst of all these preoccupations, Assessor Hubert kept coming with inquiries and advice, until Waldemar lost all patience, and summarily dismissed the troublesome official. Scarce was he rid of the assessor, when other concerns demanded his immediate attention.

The authorities of L---- had been informed of the position and the plans of the insurgent forces over the border; a fight was daily expected, and orders had been given to reinforce the frontier garrison. A large detachment of soldiers passed through Villica, and during a brief halt in the village its officers called upon Herr Nordeck, who was obliged to entertain them alone. Now that he had taken an open stand against her party, his mother refused to receive his guests. Late in the afternoon the detachment moved on in season to reach the designated post before dark; and now came Doctor Fabian, the accepted lover and future professor, with his double tidings, which he hoped would call forth the interest and sympathy of his former pupil, compelling him to rejoice in another's happiness while he saw his own sinking into irretrievable ruin. It required an iron nature like Waldemar's to preserve a semblance of equanimity under so many trying circumstances.

Two days had fled since the tragedy at the forester's house. The princess, having passed a restless night, had risen early, and was alone in her private parlor. The gray, misty dawn only partially lighted the lofty room, half of which still lay in shadow. The fire on the hearth threw an uncertain, flickering light upon the carpet and around the form of the lady who sat before it.

Lost in gloomy reflection, she rested her head upon her hand; her heart and mind were full of that event in which her niece had played so prominent a part. The woman who had hitherto shown herself equal to any emergency, was not equal to the present situation. The ruthlessness with which she had unveiled her niece's heart so as to arm her against the passion that had begun to enthrall her, the months of entire separation, that last warning at Radowicz,--all had been in vain; all had vanished before a danger that menaced Waldemar. Wanda had informed her aunt of everything that had occurred at the forester's house; she was too proud, too thoroughly identified with the cause of her people, to allow the least suspicion of treason to rest upon her. She assured her aunt that she had sent no warning, had awakened no suspicion, that she had intervened only at the last moment when nothing else would have saved Waldemar. The wound on her arm attested the manner in which she had intervened.

Waldemar's entrance aroused the princess from these torturing reflections. She knew the reason of his coming. Paul had informed her that after three futile attempts to gain an interview with Wanda that morning, Herr Nordeck had at last succeeded. He approached slowly, and paused before his mother.

"Do you come from Wanda?" she asked.

"I do."

The mother gazed intently into her son's face, which was flushed with excitement, and yet wore an expression of intense but suppressed sorrow.

"Then, in spite of her remonstrances, you forced your way to her! You have at least learned that it was not my command which closed Wanda's door against you. She expressly declared that she did not wish to see you."

"I had a right to see and to speak with Wanda, who has risked her life for me," he said; "I was compelled to speak with her. O, remain calm," he added, bitterly, as the princess was about to make an angry reply; "your niece has fully justified your expectations, and done her best to deprive me of all hope. She insists that she is following her own wishes, while she is blindly submissive to yours; she only echoes your words and opinions. She would have yielded to my influence, if she had not been so completely under yours. You have persuaded her that the promise, which as a mere child you almost forced her to give my brother, is an irrevocable vow, and that to break it would be a deadly sin. You have so inoculated her with your national prejudices--"

"Waldemar!" interposed the princess.

"With your national prejudices," he repeated, emphatically, "that she thinks it would be treason to her family and to her people to consent to be my wife, because I chance to be a German, and circumstances compel me to oppose your party schemes. Yes, you have attained your wish; she would sooner die than lift her hand to free herself from her engagement, or give me permission to free her. For this I have to thank you alone."

"I have certainly reminded Wanda of her duty," replied the princess, coldly. "I hardly needed to do so, for she had already come to her senses; I hope that you may soon do the same. Since that day when you in this very room declared yourself my enemy, I have known that your former boyish fancy had grown into an ardent passion, and the events of the last two days have taught me to what an extent that passion is returned. It would be useless to censure you for what has happened, the past cannot be recalled, but you and Wanda must now be conscious that you owe Leo nothing less than absolute separation. Wanda already understands this, and you must submit to it."

"Must I?" asked Waldemar. "Mother, you know that submission is not one of my virtues, and can I submit here, where my life's happiness is at stake?"

The princess gazed at him with an expression of surprise and terror. "What does this mean?" she asked. "Will you attempt to rob your brother of his bride, after having robbed him of her love?"

"Leo has never possessed Wanda's love; she knew neither herself nor her heart when she yielded to his affection, yielded to her father's wishes and to yours, and to family plans. Her love belongs to me; and now that I have this certainty, I shall know how to assert my claim to what is rightfully my own."

"Do not be so positive, Waldemar!" said the princess, almost derisively. "Have you considered what response your brother will give to such presumption?"

"I would release my betrothed if she declared to me that her love belonged to another; I would do it, no matter what such renunciation cost me. I know Leo, and I am sure he will adopt no such course; he will be beside himself, he will goad Wanda to desperation, and inflict a series of terrible scenes upon us all."

"Will you give him precepts upon moderation, you who are inflicting such a mortal wound upon him?" returned the mother. "Leo is absent, he is battling for the holiest rights of his people, and while he is hourly staking his life for his country, he does not suspect that his brother, at home, behind his back--"

She paused, for Waldemar's hand was laid heavily upon hers. "*Mother*," he said, in a voice that was full of warning, for in him this hollow, suppressed tone always preceded an eruption; "stop these accusations which you do not yourself believe! You know better than all others how Wanda and I have fought against this passion, you know what finally unsealed our lips. Behind Leo's back! The letter I wrote to him before my interview with Wanda is in my room; read it if you will. That interview changes nothing. He must know that we have confessed our love to each other, we have no wish to conceal it from him. I would like to confide my letter to you; you know where Leo is to be found, and can forward it to him."

"By no means!" cried the princess, excitedly. "I know too well the fiery temper of my son to inflict this torture upon him. To remain away perhaps for months, while all his jealousy is aroused and his dearest hopes are jeopardized, might be beyond his powers of endurance; and he must remain steadfast, he dares not leave his post until the contest there is decided. No, no; Leo must not be informed! Wanda has promised silence, you also must promise it. She will go home to-day, and when she has fully recovered, she will visit our relatives in M----, and remain with them until Leo returns to assert his rights in person."

"I know all this," returned Waldemar, sadly; "she herself has told me; she cannot place miles enough between us. I have tried every argument at the command of love and despair, but in vain, she always meets me with that inevitable *no*. Let the matter rest, then, until Leo's return. Perhaps you are right--we had best settle it face to face. I am ready to confront him at any moment. What may then happen between us is quite another question."

The princess rose and approached her son. "Waldemar, abandon this insane hope," she said. "I tell you that Wanda would never be your bride even if she were free; too many insurmountable obstacles stand between you. You deceive yourself when you expect any change of mind in her. What you call national prejudice is the very life-blood which has nourished her from infancy, and which she can renounce only with life itself. Even though she loves you, this daughter of our race knows what duty and honor demand from her; if she did not remember this, we are here to remind her of it,--her father, myself, and Leo above all!"

A disdainful smile played around the young man's lips as he replied: "And do you really think that either one of you could hinder me if I had Wanda's consent? The fact that she herself refuses me, that she forbids me to contend for her hand, robs me of my self-control; but even that shall not deter me! One who has never known love, and to whom that sentiment so suddenly, so entirely, and so enrapturingly reveals itself as it has to me, does not subdue and renounce it so easily. The prize is worthy of my highest and most persistent efforts. Where I have everything to win I venture everything, and although tenfold greater obstacles interpose, Wanda will be mine."

His words expressed a determination that would never yield nor falter. The red glare from the hearth lighted up Waldemar's features, which at this moment seemed cast from bronze. The princess was forced to acknowledge once more that this was her own son who stood before her, with an inflexible determination, with a glance and bearing so like her very own. She had hitherto vainly sought to comprehend why the cold, melancholy, unattractive Waldemar should be preferred to Leo, why in the contest for a woman's love he should come out conqueror over his handsome, chivalrous brother. She comprehended now.

"Have you forgotten who your rival is?" she asked, gravely. "Brother against brother! Must I witness a hostile, perhaps deadly encounter between my sons? Have you no thought for a mother's anguish?"

"Your sons!" repeated Waldemar. "In speaking of a mother's anguish and affection, you refer to but one son. You do not forgive me for intruding upon the happiness of your darling, and I know a means of deliverance that would cost you few tears. But cease your apprehensions; I shall do all in my power to avert the result you dread, and you must seek to render it possible for me to see a brother in Leo. You have unbounded influence over him, he will listen to you. I have learned to restrain my impetuous nature, but my self-control has its limits, and Leo must not force me beyond them. He has little regard for another's honor when he believes himself affronted."

They were interrupted; an officer of the detachment which had passed through Villica the day previous, was without, and desired an immediate interview with Herr Nordeck. Waldemar met him in the ante-room. After presenting the compliments of his commanding officer, he reported that the detachment had been forced into action immediately after reaching its new post. A severe conflict had taken place during the night, and ended in the defeat of the insurgents, who had fled in great disorder, closely pursued by the victors. A portion of the fugitives had taken refuge upon German soil, where they had been disarmed. They were to be taken to L----, but among them were a few men so severely wounded that it was feared they could not endure the journey, and a temporary asylum was asked for them at Villica. Waldemar cheerfully consented, and ordered all needful preparations for their reception.

The princess remained alone. She had scarcely noticed her son's departure, and knew nothing of the tidings. Entirely different thoughts occupied her mind.

What now? This question arose continually like a haunting spectre which would not depart; the decisive moment might be postponed, but it must come at last. The princess only too well knew what to expect if her sons should meet as enemies, and they must become mortal enemies from the moment when Leo discovered the truth. If Leo, whose jealousy at the first suspicion had nearly caused a breach of duty, should now learn that his brother had actually robbed him of the love of his betrothed, if Waldemar's violent temper which now lay slumbering under restraint should break out anew--the mother shuddered at the abyss that opened before her at the thought. She knew that her usual control over her younger son would be at an end, that Waldemar as well as Leo had the blood of her ancestors in his veins, and whatever contrasts there might be between a Nordeck and a Zulieski, they were alike in one respect: neither could restrain his passion when it was once aroused.

The door of the adjoining room opened. Waldemar, who had been called away in the midst of the conversation, was perhaps returning. But the step was quicker and more impetuous than his; the portière was raised, and with an exclamation of mingled delight and terror, the princess sprang from her chair.

"*Leo! You here?*"

The young prince was clasped in his mother's arms. He returned her embrace, but he had no word of greeting. Silently and passionately he pressed her to his heart, but the movement betrayed nothing of the joy of reunion.

"Whence do you come?" asked the mother, recovering her self-possession, and with it an intense anxiety and alarm. "Your presence is so sudden, so unexpected! How could you be so rash as to come to the castle in broad daylight? You are liable to arrest at any moment; why did you not wait until dark?"

Leo released himself from her arms. "I waited long enough," he said. "I left yesterday afternoon, and I have been upon the rack ever since. It was impossible for me to cross the lines, and I had to lie concealed. Toward day break I arrived at Villica forest, and it was with great difficulty that I reached the castle."

His words were excited and incoherent. The mother now saw for the first time how pale and troubled he looked. She drew him almost forcibly to a chair.

"Sit down and rest," she said; "you are wearied to death with your rash venture. What a foolhardy boy you are to stake life and liberty merely for a brief interview! You must have known that our anxiety for you would overshadow all the joy of meeting. I do not understand how your uncle could allow you to leave just now, when you are in the midst of conflicts."

"No, no!" interposed Leo; "nothing will occur within the next twenty-four hours. We have exact information in regard to the plans and position of the enemy. Day after to-morrow--perhaps tomorrow--there will be a battle, but not before. If a fight had been close at hand, I should not be here; but I was forced to come to Villica even at the sacrifice of life and liberty."

The princess gazed at him anxiously, and then, as if seized with a sudden, indefinable suspicion, she asked,--

"Leo, have you your uncle's permission?"

"Yes--certainly," stammered the young man, but he avoided his mother's gaze. "I tell you that all is safe, that every precaution has been taken. I am stationed with my soldiers in the forest of A----, and our position is well guarded. My adjutant has command during my absence."

"And your uncle Bronislaw?"

"My uncle has concentrated his main force at A----, close to the border; I protect his rear. But no more questions, mother--where is Waldemar?"

"Your brother?" asked the princess, both surprised and alarmed, for she began to suspect Leo's motive in leaving his command. "Do you come on his account?"

"I am in search of Waldemar," he broke out furiously,--"him and no other! Paul says he is not in the castle, but Wanda is here. Has he really brought her here as a victor's booty, as his very own, and has she permitted it? I will teach him to whom Wanda belongs; both him and--her."

"For heaven's sake, do you know--"

"What took place at the forester's house? Yes, I know it. Osiecki's men joined my detachment yesterday, and informed me of what they had witnessed. Do you now comprehend that I was obliged to come to Villica, let the price of my absence be what it might?"

"I feared it," said the princess, under her breath.

Leo sprang to his feet and stood with flaming eyes before her.

"And have you allowed this, mother?" he cried. "Have you witnessed in silence the way in which my love and my rights have been trodden under foot,--you who usually rule every one, and enforce obedience? Does this Waldemar domineer over all? Is there no one who dares oppose him? I was a fool not to have had an understanding with him before my departure, not to have taken Wanda away, so that any further meetings between them might have been impossible. But," added he, with bitter irony, "my suspicion offended her and you, and my uncle regarded my 'blind jealousy' as a crime. You now see that it was well founded. While I am perilling my life for my country, my betrothed, risks her life for a man who openly takes sides with our oppressors, who has set his foot upon our necks here in Villica as the tyrants in our own land have done; she proves faithless to me, she forgets fatherland, people, family, everything, to guard him from an impending danger. Perhaps she is now seeking to place him on his guard against me; but let her beware! I no longer care which of us perishes, he or I,--or she with both of us!"

The mother seized his hand imploringly. "Control yourself, Leo!" she cried; "I entreat, I demand it of you. Do not rush into your brother's presence with this deadly hatred in your heart. Listen to me!"

Leo broke away from her. "I have already heard too much, enough to drive me mad," he exclaimed. "When Osiecki's ball sought Waldemar's life, Wanda threw herself into his arms; she made her breast his shield. Can I longer doubt her treachery to me? Where is Waldemar? I must and will have an interview with him."

The mother sought to pacify her son; he would not listen. While she was considering how she might prevent the fatal meeting, the event she had most dreaded took place. Waldemar returned.

CHAPTER XXIV.

THE FATAL VENTURE.

Waldemar entered hastily, and was approaching his mother, when his glance fell upon Leo. His face expressed something more than astonishment; it blanched suddenly and a deathly terror crept over it. For some moments he seemed incapable of speech; he measured Leo from head to foot, and his eyes flashed scorn and contempt as he at length asked slowly and emphatically,--

"*Are you here, Leo, at a time like this?*"

Leo's face betrayed a sort of malignant satisfaction as he saw the object of his hatred right before him.

"You certainly were not expecting me," he said, with a sneer.

Waldemar did not answer; he paid no heed to the sneering tone, he was thinking only of the danger to which Leo had exposed himself in coming to Villica in the open day. He turned away to close the door leading to the next room, and then approaching his brother, he said,--

"No, I did not expect you; neither did our mother."

"I wished to congratulate you upon your heroic exploit at the border-forester's house, for you doubtless think it heroic," said the young prince, mockingly. "You shot the forester and overawed all the others; the cowards did not venture to touch you."

"They crossed the boundary that very night," replied Waldemar; "did they reach you?"

"Yes."

"I thought so. When did you leave your command?"

"Why do you catechise me in this way?" cried Leo, furiously. "I am here to call *you* to an account. Come! We two have a settlement to make."

"You will remain here," said the princess, imperiously. "If a meeting between you must take place, let it be in my presence. Perhaps you will not then entirely forget that you are brothers."

"Brother or not," cried Leo, beside himself. "Waldemar has dealt treacherously with me. He knew that Wanda was my betrothed, but he has not hesitated to rob me of her and of her love. None but traitors and ren--"

The mother tried to check him, but in vain. The word renegade fell from his lips, and Waldemar started as if struck by a ball. The princess turned pale. It was not the insane fury of her younger son that frightened her, it was the expression in the face of the elder, and his menacing attitude. She feared him, and tried to restrain him, although he was unarmed, while Leo wore a sword at his side. With all the authority of a mother she stepped between them, and cried, in a commanding voice,--

"Waldemar--Leo--control yourselves! I demand obedience!"

Whenever the Princess Zulieski assumed this voice and manner, she was always sure to enforce submission. Her sons obeyed her involuntarily. Leo's hand slipped from the hilt of his sword, and Waldemar restrained his fury. He had been passing through a terrible conflict with rage and indignation, but his mother's words had brought him back to reason, and nothing more was needed to restore his self-control.

"Leo," he said, "I have borne insult enough from you; one word more, one single word, and no settlement between us can be possible except by a resort to arms. If yesterday you had the right to censure me, it is forfeited to-day. I love Wanda more than you suspect, for you have not, like me, fought against an ardent passion for years, and been driven through hatred and separation and mortal peril, to the consciousness that it is stronger than yourself; but not even for Wanda's sake would I have neglected my duty and sacrificed my honor. I would not have deserted my post and the soldiers who were intrusted to me; I would not have broken my oath of allegiance. You have done all this: our mother may decide which of us deserves the opprobrious name you hurl at me."

"What is this, Leo?" cried the princess, starting up in terror. "You are here with the knowledge and consent of your uncle? You had his express permission to come to Villica? Answer me!"

The face of the young prince had been colorless, it now became crimson; not daring to meet his mother's eye, he turned in a towering passion to his brother,--

"What do you know of my duties? Why should they concern you? You belong to our enemies. I have thus far held my place at the front, and I shall be there when needed; on this very account our business demands prompt action. I have not much time for settlement with you, I must return to my soldiers in a few hours."

"You are too late," said Waldemar, coldly; "you will not find them."

Leo apparently did not understand the import of these words; he gazed bewildered at his brother as if he were speaking in a foreign tongue.

"When did you leave your command?" repeated Waldemar, and with such terrible earnestness that his brother answered him half involuntarily,--

"Yesterday afternoon."

"The attack took place in the night; your detachment is dispersed--annihilated."

A shriek broke from the lips of the young prince. He rushed upon the speaker. "It is impossible--it cannot be! You lie! You only seek to frighten me away with such tidings," he cried.

"No, no, it cannot be!" interposed the princess, with quivering lips. "Waldemar, you can have no tidings of what occurred over the border during the night; I must have received them sooner than you. You are deceiving us; do not resort to such ignoble subterfuges!"

For some moments Waldemar gazed silently at his mother, who would sooner accuse him of falsehood than believe his brother guilty of a breach of faith. It must have been this consciousness that made his voice so icy and his words so pitiless, as he said,--

"Prince Zulieski was intrusted with an important position, and had the strictest orders not to leave it. He was in command of a detachment which protected his uncle's rear. When the attack was made, the prince was missing from his post. The subordinate officers proved unequal to the emergency; they had no definite plan of defence, and a massacre ensued. Some twenty men saved their lives by flight across the border, where they fell into the hands of our patrols. Three of the refugees lie out in the yard severely wounded; I have learned these facts from them. The rest of Prince Leo's soldiers are dispersed or slain."

"And my brother?" asked the princess, with forced composure. "What has become of the Morynskian corps?"

"I do not know," answered Waldemar. "It is said that the victors went on to W----. I have no intelligence of what has occurred there."

He was silent. A momentous, breathless pause followed. Leo had buried his face in his hands, hollow moans issued from his breast, and his whole frame was convulsed with anguish. The princess stood erect, her eyes were fixed upon him, she struggled for breath.

"Leave us alone, Waldemar," she said at last, in a hollow voice, but with her usual firmness.

Waldemar hesitated. His mother had always appeared cold, and often enough hostile to him; here in this very spot she had stood opposed to him as an embittered rival, when the strife for supremacy in Villica had broken out; but he had never seen her hard and pitiless as she appeared at this moment, and he, the stern, relentless Nordeck, was seized with apprehension and sympathy, as he read his brother's sentence in her face.

"Mother," he said gently.

"Go!" she repeated; "I have to deal with your brother; no third person must come between us. Leave us alone!"

Waldemar obeyed and left the room, but bitter and painful emotions swelled his heart to bursting as he went. He was banished when the mother wished to speak with Leo; it mattered not that she was now to let her younger son feel her anger, as she had so often allowed him to feel her affection; the elder son had no participation in either her joy or sorrow; he had always been a stranger to her, and such he must remain. He was told to go, he must not intrude between this mother and son, whether they met in love or hatred. But an emotion of pity touched this heart so cruelly defrauded of a mother's love: Waldemar knew that he was more than avenged, that his mother's love and pride were suffering the most cruel punishment in her favorite child, her idol.

He closed the door behind him, but remained in the ante-room to guard the entrance, for he knew the danger to which Leo was exposed. Prince Leo Zulieski had taken too prominent a part in the insurrection to escape even here, and he was liable to arrest and trial. He had acted very rashly in visiting the castle in broad daylight, and his presence was likely to become known. The guard that had brought the wounded prisoners was still in the village, and an escort with the other refugees might pass at any moment. Precautionary measures must be taken.

Waldemar stood at a window as far as possible from the door; he did not wish to hear anything of a conversation from which he was excluded, and it was impossible to catch a word, for the heavy folds of the velvet portiére shut out every sound. The interview was a lengthy one; more than half an hour had passed, and it still went on. Neither the mother nor Leo seemed to realize that the young soldier's danger was every moment increasing. At length Waldemar felt obliged to interrupt them. He entered the parlor, but was surprised at its silence.

The princess had left, and the door leading to her study was closed. Leo was alone in the room, and lay upon a sofa with his face buried in the cushions. He seemed completely crushed, and did not notice his brother's entrance. Waldemar approached and called him by name.

"Arouse yourself!" he said, in a low, earnest voice. "Care for your own safety! We are in close communication with L----, and I cannot guard the castle from visitors who might be dangerous to you. For the present, withdraw to your own chamber, which may be kept closed, as it has been during your absence. Paul is reliable. Come!"

Leo slowly raised his head; his face was white as death, every drop of blood seemed to have left it. He stared wildly and vacantly at his brother, but did not comprehend his words. His ear caught only the last.

"Where?"

"First of all, leave these reception-rooms, which are accessible to so many. Come, I entreat you!"

Leo rose mechanically; he stared around vacantly as if he did not recognize the familiar rooms, and did not know where he was, but as his eyes fell upon the door leading to his mother's study, a shudder passed over him.

"Where is Wanda?" he at length asked.

"In her room; do you wish to see her?"

"No; she would repel me with aversion and contempt. I can endure no more."

He leaned heavily against the chair; his usually clear, joyous voice was hollow and broken. That scene with his mother had completely unmanned him.

"Leo," said Waldemar, remorsefully, "if you had not enraged me so, I should have broken the news to you more gently; but that fatal word, '*renegade*,' exasperated me beyond endurance."

"You are avenged; my mother has hurled it back at me. In her eyes I am a traitor and a renegade. I was forced to hear her and to be--silent."

There was something ominous in the rigid, unnatural composure of this fiery, passionate youth, whose whole nature seemed to have undergone a transformation within the last half-hour.

"Follow me!" urged Waldemar. "You must conceal yourself in the castle."

"No; I shall go immediately to W----. I must know what has become of my uncle and his men."

"In heaven's name, do not make the foolhardy attempt to cross the boundary in broad daylight. It would be deliberate suicide."

"I must," persisted Leo. "I know the place where passage is still possible. If I found the way this morning, I shall be able to do so again."

"I tell you that it is impossible. This morning our guards were strengthened, we have now three lines of outposts. Our men have orders to shoot every one who does not know the password. In any event, you will be too late; the conflict at W---- has already been decided."

"No matter!" cried Leo, recovering from his prostration, and breaking out into the wildest despair. "There will be a light somewhere yet,--one fight, at least, and that is all I need. Ah, you do not know what my mother's terrible words have done for me! She is fully conscious that if I am responsible for the overthrow of my soldiers, I must bear the curse and torment of my crime, and she ought to pity me; but instead of that--O my God! she is still my mother, and I have been her all!"

Waldemar trembled before this outburst of agony. "Let me call Wanda," he said; "she will--"

"She will follow my mother's example. You do not know our Polish women, and therefore"--a sort of grim triumph broke through the young soldier's despair--"therefore hope nothing from them! Wanda will never be your wife, not even after my death,--not if she dies of her love for you. You are the enemy of her people, you take sides with the oppressors of her country. This pronounces your sentence. No Polish maiden will ever become your bride. And it is well that it is so," he added, breathing more freely; "I could not die in peace, knowing that she was in your arms. Now I can die content,--she is lost to you, as well as to me."

He was hurrying away, but he paused suddenly as if rooted to the floor. For some moments he seemed to hesitate, then he went slowly and timidly to the door leading into his mother's study.

"Mother!"

All within was quiet; there was not a sign of life.

"I wish to bid you good-bye."

No answer.

"Mother!" The young man's voice faltered in agonized, heart-rending supplication. "Do not let me leave you in this way. If I cannot see you, give me one parting word--one only. It will be the last. Do you not hear me, mother?"

He fell upon his knees, and pressed his forehead against the bolted door, as if it must open to him. In vain. The door remained closed, and no sound came from within. The mother had no farewell for her son, the Princess Zulieski had no word of forgiveness for his offence.

Leo rose from his knees. His face was still rigid and colorless, but around the quivering lips and in the bloodshot eyes there was an expression of wild, intense, unutterable agony. He did not speak another word, he silently took up his cloak, threw it around his shoulders, and approached the door. His brother vainly tried to detain him.

"Let me go!" he cried, pushing Waldemar aside. "Tell Wanda--no, tell her nothing. She does not love me, she has discarded me for you. Farewell!"

He rushed away. For some moments Waldemar stood gazing after him, entirely bewildered and helpless. Then collecting his thoughts, prompted by a sudden resolution, he hastened to his mother's room. He found Paul standing at the vestibule. The old man was in great trouble at the terrible tidings he had just heard,--at the sudden departure of the young prince, who had rushed past him without a word.

"Paul," said Waldemar, "follow Prince Zulieski at once; he is rushing on to certain death. He intends to cross the boundary by daylight."

"God in Heaven!" ejaculated the old man.

"I cannot restrain him," continued Waldemar, "and I dare not aid him openly,--that would only augment his danger; but in his present desperate mood, some person must accompany him. You ride well; take a horse at once. The prince is on foot; you can overtake him before he reaches the boundary. You know the route he will take, and the place where he will attempt to cross. It is the spot where secret communication is still kept up with the insurgents, and cannot be far from the house of my border-forester."

Paul did not reply; he did not dare confirm the truth, and he had not the courage to deny it. Waldemar understood his silence.

"The strictest watch is kept at that very place,--so I hear from our officers. I do not know how my brother succeeded in passing through this morning; he cannot do it again. Hurry after him, Paul. He must not attempt to cross there. Let him try any other place, but not that. He must wait until night; he can conceal himself in the forester's house. Fellner has charge there now; he sides with me, but he will not in any event betray Leo. Hasten!"

Paul needed no urging. Intense anxiety for his young master would be sure to hurry him away.

"I shall be ready in five minutes," he said; "and I shall ride as if my life were at stake."

A few minutes after, he rode swiftly out of the yard. Waldemar, who gazed after him, breathed more freely. "This was the only resource left me," he thought. "Paul may yet overtake my brother, and save him from almost certain death."

Four, five hours passed, bringing no tidings of Leo. Communication--usually so frequent between the frontier and Villica, which was on the direct route to L----, seemed broken off to-day. Waldemar paced his room restlessly, trying to take Paul's long absence as a good omen. He must surely have overtaken Leo, and would remain at his side as far as the boundary. Perhaps both were concealed in the forester's house. At last--it was late in the afternoon--the superintendent entered hastily and unannounced.

"Herr Nordeck, will you come out into the court?" he said; "your presence is very necessary."

"What is the matter?" asked Waldemar. "Has anything happened to the wounded men?"

"O, no," returned Frank; "but I wish you to come yourself. We have tidings from the frontier; a desperate battle was fought at W---- this morning with Count Morynski's corps."

"And how has it resulted?" asked Waldemar, breathlessly.

"The insurgents are defeated, and it is said that they owe this result either to treason or to an unexpected attack. They defended themselves bravely, but were compelled to yield to superior forces. The survivors are scattered, and have fled in every direction."

"And the leader, Count Morynski?"

The superintendent cast down his eyes, and was silent.

"Is he dead?"

"No; but he is severely wounded, and in the hands of the enemy."

Waldemar had always been estranged from his uncle, but he knew how tenderly and passionately Wanda loved her father. If he had fallen in battle, she could have borne it better than to know that he was wounded, suffering, and a prisoner in the hands of his enemies. Who was responsible for the defeat of the corps which should have been protected from an attack in the rear by the detachment of Prince Zulieski?

Waldemar summoned all his self-control. "Who brought you this news?" he asked. "Is it reliable?"

"Paul brought it," replied the superintendent. "He is over yonder--"

"And why does he bring you tidings, when he knows that I have been for hours anxiously awaiting his return? Why does he not come to the castle?"

The superintendent's eyes again sought the floor. "He could not venture--the princess or the young countess might have come to the window; they must be prepared for evil tidings. Paul is not alone, Herr Nordeck--"

"What has happened? My brother--"

"Prince Zulieski has fallen. Paul brings the corpse--"

Waldemar was speechless. A great blow had fallen upon him, depriving him, for the instant, of sense and motion. All was dark around him; for some moments he covered his eyes with his hands, then he roused himself by a powerful effort, and hastened to the superintendent's house. Paul came to meet him, gazing timidly into the face of the man he had been taught to regard as an enemy, but the sorrow depicted there plainly told him that the brother of his young master, weighed down by a sorrow greater even than his own, stood before him. The old man's self-control gave way.

"Our princess!" he wailed, "she will not survive it, neither will the Countess Wanda."

"Did you not overtake the prince?" asked Waldemar.

"Yes," replied Paul, in a faltering voice; "I reached him in season, and gave him your warning. At first he would not listen; he was determined to cross the border at all hazards. He thought the denseness of the forest would protect him. I entreated, I fell upon my knees, and asked if he would allow himself to be shot down like a hunted deer. This at length moved him; he consented to wait until evening. We were just considering whether we could venture to seek admittance to the forest-house, when we were met--"

"By whom? A patrol?"

"No, by the tenant of Janowo, whom we could trust implicitly, as he has always belonged to our party. He told us that there was fighting at W----, that the battle was still in progress, and that the Morynskian corps was struggling desperately and against great odds. Our young prince now lost all reason and discretion; but one idea possessed him,--to reach W----, and plunge into the thick of the fight. We could not restrain him; he would not listen to us. Shortly after he left us, we heard shots; at first there were two in quick succession, then half a dozen all at once, and then--" The old man could not go on; his voice choked, and tears streamed down his cheeks.

"I have brought back his body," he resumed, after a pause. "The colonel who visited you at the castle yesterday gave me permission and assistance. But I dared not take him to the castle. He lies in there."

He pointed to the opposite room. Waldemar entered the chamber of death alone. The last gray beams of the departing day faintly lighted the room and revealed the lifeless form of the young prince. The landlord of Villica stood in silence by his brother's corpse. The handsome face, once glowing with animation and happiness, was rigid and cold; the dark, flashing eyes were closed, and the breast which had swelled so high with dreams, of freedom and a glorious future bore the death-wound. Whatever wrong this fiery, impulsive temperament had committed was now expiated by the blood that welled from his riddled breast, coloring his apparel with dark and fatal stains.

Only a few hours before, all the passions of youth had stormed within this lifeless frame,--hatred and love, jealousy and revenge, despair over the deed he had unwittingly committed and its frightful consequences. Now all was over, chilled in the icy repose of death. Yet upon that still, white face was stamped, as if for all eternity, that expression of bitter agony which had quivered around the lips of the son when his mother refused him a last adieu, when she let him go from her bolted door without her forgiveness, without one parting word. All else had vanished with life, but the young prince had taken this anguish with him, even into the throes of dissolution: the veil of the tomb itself would not hide it.

Waldemar left the room speechless and sad as he had entered it. As he approached those who were awaiting him without, his pallid face and trembling voice attested that he had loved his brother.

"Bring the body to the castle," he said; "I will go on before, and break the tidings to my mother."

CHAPTER XXV.

HUBERT GROWS MISANTHROPIC.

The Polish insurrection of 1863-4, whose events have already passed into history, was subdued; tranquillity reigned throughout the conquered province, but it was the tranquillity of desolation. Those wintry March days of a year ago, which had brought such calamity to the main actors in our story, had also witnessed the downfall of a nation's cause and crushed out the last hope of national freedom from the hearts of a brave, patriotic people. Russia, aided by Prussia and with the connivance of Austria, had trampled out the last embers of the revolution. The overthrow of Count Morynski's corps had been the turning-point of the revolt on the German frontier. From that moment the course of the revolution in Prussian Poland was downward.

The loss of Count Morynski, who was by far the ablest revolutionary leader in this province, and the death of Leo Zulieski, whose name and family traditions gave so much prestige to the patriot cause, were heavy blows for a faction already rent by internal discord and rivalry. Now and then the waning star, which was destined so soon to go out in utter darkness, flamed up anew; there were still battles and skirmishes animated by the courage of despair and signalized by heroic deeds; but the fact became more and more apparent that the cause for which Poland was fighting was a lost cause. The revolt, which had at first extended over the whole country, became pent up within ever-narrowing limits; one post after another fell, one division after another was dispersed or disbanded, and the insurrection, which had at first assumed such alarming dimensions, was extinguished even to the last spark. Only desolation and ruin marked the final desperate struggle of a people whose heroism and misfortunes appeal to the sympathies of the civilized world, but which was doomed to such entire defeat and ruin, that the country for which they fought exists no longer as an independent power upon the map of nations.

A long time elapsed ere the fate of Count Morynski was decided. He awoke to consciousness in a prison, and as the surgeons pronounced his wound mortal, no legal proceedings could be instituted against him. For many months he hovered between life and death, and upon his partial recovery he was condemned to execution. A revolutionary leader taken in arms upon the battle-field could expect no other fate. Severe illness alone prevented the immediate carrying out of his sentence; upon his final recovery the revolt was quelled, the rebel army annihilated, and the victors could afford to be magnanimous. His sentence was commuted to life-long banishment to one of the remotest provinces of Siberia,--a questionable act of clemency to a man whose whole existence had been one long aspiration for freedom, and whose personal liberty had never known restraint save during his brief period of exile in France.

He had not seen his family since that evening at Villica when he had bidden them adieu for the battlefield. Neither his daughter nor his sister was allowed to visit him, his rigid confinement being due to the attempts they had made to liberate him. In one of these ineffectual attempts, Paul, the old, faithful servant of the family, had been shot dead by the prison-guard. The princess and Wanda finding all attempts at rescue unavailing, had been compelled to yield to the inevitable, and leave the unhappy man to his fate.

The princess, immediately after the death of her younger son, went to live at Radowicz. It seemed only natural that the bereaved mother and the afflicted daughter should seek each others society; but Waldemar better understood the reason of his mother's departure: he knew that she could not endure the daily presence of the son who had unconsciously defrauded the other and dearer one of Wanda's love, who had goaded him on to that rash deed which led to his untimely death and to the defeat of the cause so near her heart. He knew also that his manner of ruling Villica wounded and exasperated his mother; he had seized the reins with an iron grasp, and he would not let go his hold. No sooner had the outside revolt, which had so deeply implicated his estates, been suppressed, than he set about a thorough reorganization of Villica, bringing everything under his own personal control, and holding all his subordinates to a strict account, after he had summarily dismissed those who refused to obey his commands. His aim was to create a new order of things from the ruins of the old; and although the task was a herculean one, he was equal to it. His tenants soon learned to recognize the controlling hand of the master and to yield to it; revolt upon his estates ended with the departure of the princess and the downfall of the revolution.

Superintendent Frank, at the young landlord's earnest solicitation, concluded to remain a year longer at Villica, but when affairs there were settled upon a secure basis, he carried out his long-cherished purpose and bought an estate of his own, a pleasant and well-ordered manor in another province. In two months he would take possession.

At Gretchen's marriage, her father had given her a dowry far surpassing even Assessor Hubert's selfish anticipations. The marriage had taken place in October, and the newly-wedded pair lived in J----, where Professor Fabian had entered upon the duties of his new position, and where he was meeting with very flattering success. He soon overcame his morbid fear of publicity, and fully justified the expectations he had raised as author of "The History of Ancient Germany." His modest and amiable disposition, so unlike the offensive egotism of his predecessor, won him general favor; and his handsome young wife, who was enabled by her father's generosity to make his home elegant and attractive, knew how to do the honors of her house and to maintain her husband's position so worthily, that the Fabians stood socially upon a most agreeable and enviable plane. They had not visited the old home since their marriage, but they were expected there in a few days.

Assessor Hubert had meantime suffered much from the "slings and arrows of outrageous fortune," and yet many would have considered his lot an enviable one, Professor Schwarz having died unmarried, and left him a considerable fortune. But what availed pecuniary independence, when the young lady he had chosen out of all the world, and upon whose hand he had counted with such assurance, belonged to another; when he had not reached the goal of his life-long ambition, the post of government counsellor? In spite of his untiring zeal and his laudable efforts to serve the state, he met with the most atrocious treatment. The state, far from appreciating his ability, self-sacrifice and devotion, seemed to incline to Superintendent Frank's opinion, that Assessor Hubert went on perpetrating one blunder after another, and was really unfit for the public service.

In truth, Hubert was so palpably slighted in every official promotion, that his colleagues began to jeer at him, and his aspiring soul, wounded to its depths, formed a grim resolve to leave the police department of L---- to its own destruction. His uncle's legacy placed him above pecuniary want, why should he longer endure unappreciation and neglect; why submit to non-advancement? Why longer serve a thankless government which persistently refused to recognize his brilliant qualities, while it appointed commonplace men like Doctor Fabian to the highest positions, and conferred the most honorable distinctions upon them?

The more Hubert thought upon the wrongs and slights he had endured, the deeper became his indignation; at length it carried him so far that he went to the governor and hinted at resigning. To his great chagrin the hint was received eagerly and without one word of protest. He was declared wise in laying aside the cares and fatigues of active service now that he had no need of its pecuniary rewards, and the governor added that he really was rather too nervous and excitable to perform the duties of an office which required both courage and self-control.

As Hubert went forth from this interview to draw up his formal resignation, he felt a touch of his renowned uncle's misanthropy and contempt for the world. The resignation was sent in and actually accepted. When it took effect, to Hubert's great surprise the state and police departments were not dissolved, and the world went on as usual! The ex-assessor had only imitated his uncle's stupid man[oe]uvre, like him anticipating the direst consequences; but in neither case did the expected catastrophe arrive.

CHAPTER XXVI.

A DREAM OF EXILE.

Waldemar, reined up his horse before the main entrance to Radowicz. His visits here was brief and infrequent; the breach between himself and his nearest relatives would not close, and recent events had widened it still more.

Waldemar's visit was to Wanda alone, and in a few moments the two sat side by side. The young girl was greatly changed; she had always been pale, but her face had never before been deathly white and colorless as now, when it bore the imprint of deep suffering. Leo's fate, her father's imprisonment, and the downfall of her people's cause, weighed heavily upon her heart. She knew that her father was ill and perhaps near death, but she could not see him for one brief moment, and she knew also that the hope of national freedom, for which he had perilled his life, was extinguished forever. The anguish of separation, the oscillation between hope and fear, the excitement and suspense attending these abortive attempts at liberation, had all left their traces upon her face. Wanda was one of those natures which contend against the most cruel misfortunes with unabated ardor while a gleam of hope remains, but which succumb powerlessly when the gleam is extinguished. It was evident that she had now reached that point; for the moment her manner betrayed a feverish excitement, a summoning of her last waning energies.

Waldemar had risen, and stood before the young girl stern and almost defiant. His manner was half angry, half imploring, and his voice expressed both exasperation and sorrow.

"For the last time I entreat you to abandon this idea," he said; "you will only forfeit your own life without aiding your father in the least; you will rather enhance his misery. You wish to accompany him to that frightful desert, to that climate which proves fatal even to the most robust; you, who from infancy have been indulged and petted, and surrounded by every comfort and luxury, would subject yourself to the bitterest privations. Your father's iron constitution may, perhaps, endure what would kill you in a few months. Ask your physician, question the present state of your health, and both will give answer that you cannot live there a year."

"Neither can my father live there," replied Wanda, in a tremulous voice; "but we are both indifferent to life, and we can die together."

"And *I*?" asked Waldemar, in a reproachful tone.

She turned away without answering.

"And *I*?" he reiterated, still more emphatically. "What will become of me?"

"You at least are free, and life is still before you. Endure it manfully; my burden is incomparably heavier than yours."

Waldemar was on the point of giving way to an outburst of passion, but a glance at that pale, sorrow-stricken face restrained him.

"Wanda," he said, calmly, "a year ago, when our hearts at last understood each other, we declared our mutual love. I should have won you from Leo at all hazards, but fate willed otherwise; his death removed that barrier. By Leo's new-made grave, at a time when the sword hung hourly suspended over your father's head, I did not venture to speak to you of love and marriage. I saw you only for a few moments at a time and at long intervals. You and my mother made me feel, whenever I visited Radowicz, that you still regarded me as an enemy; but I hoped for better things in the future, and now you meet me with this insane resolve, against which I will contend to my last breath: '*We will die together.*' This is easily said, and also easily done, if, like Leo, one can die instantly, pierced through the heart by a bullet. Have you a clear conception of what death in banishment really is? It is a slow decline, a lingering struggle against privations which break down the mind long before they destroy the body. To languish far from home, to be cut off from the world and its interests, to be deprived of those intellectual and social enjoyments which are vital to you as the air you breathe, to be crushed and stifled under a load of misery,--this is exile. Do you ask my consent to your voluntary acceptance of such a destiny?"

The young girl shuddered. She felt the truth of Waldemar's description, but she remained silent.

"And will your father accept this incredible sacrifice?" continued the young man, still more excitedly. "Will my mother permit it? O, yes! They want to tear you from my arms, and if they can only do that, they will not hesitate to consign you to a living grave. If I had fallen in Leo's stead, your father would have commanded you to remain, and my mother would have kept you back for him. Now they have persuaded you into this idea of martyrdom; they know it will bring you certain death, but it will make your union with me impossible, and that is just what they want."

"Cease these bitter reproaches!" interposed Wanda. "You wrong my family; no one has persuaded me, this is my own resolution. My father stands upon the threshold of age; wounds, imprisonment, and, above all, defeat, have prostrated him mentally and physically. I am the only one left him, the last tie which binds him to life. I belong to him. The frightful picture you have drawn depicts *his* lot. Do you believe that I could enjoy a moment's peace at your side, knowing that my father had gone forth alone to confront that destiny, knowing that I had caused him the last and bitterest pang of his life by marrying a man he considers an enemy? My only solace in that merciless decree of exile is the permission to accompany my father. I knew that the conflict with you would be a hard one; I have just learned how terrible it is. Spare me, Waldemar; I have not much strength left!"

"O, no, not much for me!" cried Waldemar, bitterly; "whatever strength you have belongs to your father. I was a fool to trust that outburst of emotion which, in a moment of supreme danger, threw you into my arms. My mother is right: your national prejudices are your life's blood; you imbibed them in infancy, you can resign them only with life itself. You will sacrifice yourself and me to these prejudices; to them your father will sacrifice his only child. If your lover belonged to his own nation, he would never allow you to accompany him into exile. Do you Poles know only hatred, even beyond death and the grave?"

"If my father were free," said Wanda, in a broken voice, "I might have the courage to defy him, and what you call our national prejudices, for your sake. Now I can not, and I will not, for it would be treason to my filial duty. I shall go with my father even at the cost of my life; I will not leave him alone in his adversity."

The firmness with which she uttered these words convinced Waldemar that her resolution was not to be shaken, and he ceased opposing it. "When do you leave?" he asked, after a long pause.

"Next month. My aunt will accompany me to O----, and there we shall meet my father. Some weeks are left us; our final parting need not be to-day. But promise me that you will not come again until the last moment. I need all my courage for the farewell hour, and your despair takes it from me. We shall meet once more; until then, good-bye."

"Good-bye," Waldemar replied, curtly, almost roughly, without looking at her or taking her proffered hand.

"Waldemar," said the young girl, appealingly, and with an accent of reproachful tenderness in her voice; but it was lost upon the stern man, who was excited almost to frenzy. Rage and anguish at the thought of losing his beloved outweighed every appeal to his sense of right.

"I cannot be reconciled to this sacrifice," he said, sternly; "my whole nature rebels against it; but, as you insist upon it, I must prove equal to my fate. You know that I cannot indulge in idle lamentations, and as my remonstrances and reproaches wound you deeply, I had best keep silence. Farewell, Wanda."

Wanda lingered for a few moments as if in violent conflict with herself, but she dared not give utterance to the emotions that swelled her heart almost to bursting. "Farewell, Waldemar," she said softly, and left the room.

The lover made no effort to detain her; he stood vacantly gazing out of a window. Many conflicting emotions struggled for mastery in his features, but among them all there was no trace of the renunciation his loved one had demanded of him. He remained for a long time with his face pressed against the panes, not looking up until his name was spoken.

The princess had entered unobserved. How heavily the terrible events of the past year had fallen upon this woman! Her bearing was still erect and firm, and at the first glance no striking change was noticeable in her appearance, but closer scrutiny revealed what Leo's death had cost his mother. Her features wore a quiet, rigid composure, which was the result neither of self-control nor resignation, but rather of enforced submission; it was the expression of one who has nothing more to hope for or to lose,--whose life has been bereft of every interest and charm. The once brilliant eyes were lustreless, the once smooth brow was deeply furrowed, the dark hair was flecked with gray. The blow to the maternal pride of the princess had been a mortal one, and had wrought a change in her whole nature; the defeat of her countrymen, and the fate of the brother whom she loved next to Leo, had prostrated the remaining strength of this resolute woman.

"Have you been torturing Wanda again?" she asked. Her voice, too, had changed; it had a hollow, broken sound. "You know it is useless."

"Yes, it is useless," replied Waldemar, turning around and gazing at his mother. His face was still clouded; he had not overcome his vexation.

"I told you so. Wanda is not one of those women who say no to-day and throw themselves into your arms to-morrow. When she once forms a resolution, it is irrevocable. You ought to recognize this fact, but you will not; you keep forcing her back into the useless conflict. You deal unsparingly with her. I can not and will not attempt to keep Wanda back, and you ought not. She is her father's only child, his all; in accompanying him, she only fulfils a daughter's duty."

"To die in exile," interposed Waldemar.

"Death has of late come near us so often that we no longer fear it," replied the princess. "Those to whom fate has dealt blows so merciless must learn to endure the worst that may happen. Wanda has learned this lesson. We have nothing more to lose, and therefore nothing more to fear. This fatal year has ruined more and brighter hopes than yours; you, too, must submit to the overthrow of your happiness."

"You would never forgive me if I should wrest my happiness from the ruin of your hopes," returned Waldemar, bitterly. "You need have no fear. I have learned to-day that Wanda cannot be influenced; she remains steadfast in her refusal."

"And you?"

"Well--I submit."

The mother scanned her son closely. "What do you intend to do?" she asked.

"Nothing. I have just told you so. I resign all hope, and submit to the inevitable."

The mother's eyes still rested upon his face. "You do not submit," she said. "I know my son better. Is it submission that I see written upon your brow? You harbor some scheme, some rash, dangerous venture. Take care! It is Wanda's own will that opposes you; she will yield to no compulsion, not even from you."

"We shall see!" rejoined the young man, coldly. "However, you need feel no concern. I may have some dangerous scheme in view, but it will affect me alone, and imperil only my own life."

"Do you speak of imperilling your life with an idea that this will console your mother?"

"Forgive me. I thought you would not care for my peril, now that you have lost your Leo."

The mother cast down her eyes. "From the hour of Leo's death you have made me feel myself indeed childless," she said.

"*I*?" ejaculated Waldemar. "Ought I to have insisted upon your sharing my home at Villica? I knew that you sought only to flee from my presence, that the sight of me was a torture you could not endure. Mother," he added, with deep emotion, "when you stood in such terrible agony by my brother's corpse, I did not venture to speak one word of consolation. I shall speak no such word to-day. Your heart has never found room for me; I have always been an alien and an outcast. I come to Radowicz because I could not live without seeing Wanda. I have sought you in this time of sorrow as little as you have sought me, but I shall not bear the blame of the estrangement between us; do not accuse me of deserting you in the bitterest hour of your life."

The mother had listened without interrupting her son, but now she answered, with quivering lips, "If I loved your brother more than I loved you, I have been forced to lose him, and to lose him in the most cruel manner. I sent him forth to battle for his country, and I could have borne his death if it had come at his post, or in the thick of the conflict, but to have him fall ingloriously--" Her voice faltered, she struggled for breath, and several moments passed ere she could go on:--

"I let my Leo go from me without one word of forgiveness, without that last farewell which he implored upon his knees, and that same day he was laid lifeless at my feet. His memory--all that remains to me of him--is linked eternally with that ill-fated deed which brought ruin upon my countrymen. My people's cause is lost, my brother goes forth to meet a destiny worse than death; Wanda is to accompany him, and I shall be left entirely alone. One would suppose, Waldemar, that you had been fully avenged."

The hollow voice and rigid glance of the woman were more touching than the most violent outburst of anguish. Waldemar could not resist their might; he bent over his mother, and said, significantly,--

"Mother, Count Morynski is still in his own country, and Wanda is also here. To-day she unwittingly showed me a way in which I may yet win her. I shall attempt it."

The princess was startled; she gazed anxiously at her son, and read his purpose in his face.

"Will you attempt--"

"What you have attempted. You failed--I may succeed."

A gleam of hope lighted that pale, sad face, but it instantly died out; the princess shook her head doubtingly.

"No, no," she cried; "do not undertake a rescue, it will be in vain. When I tell you this, you may rest assured that everything possible has been attempted, but without success. Paul's fidelity cost him his life."

"Paul was an old man," rejoined Waldemar; "he was too moderate and cautious. He had courage enough, but he lacked coolness and daring at the decisive moment. Youth, nerve, and above all prompt action, are needed for such a mission."

"And with all these it is full of danger. We have learned how the boundaries are watched and the prisoners guarded. Waldemar, must I lose you also?" cried the princess, in a tone of anguish and alarm.

Waldemar gazed at his mother in astonishment; his face flushed, and then grew pale, as he heard her words.

"I make the stake for your brother's freedom," he said.

"Bronislaw cannot be rescued," was the despondent answer. "Do not risk your life for our lost cause. It has already cost us sacrifice enough. Think of Leo's fall, and of Paul's fate. I will not let you go," she cried, seizing his hand and holding it fast. "I was wrong in saying a moment ago that I had nothing more to lose. I now feel that one child is still left me; I will not give up my last, my only one. Do not go, my son; it is your mother who entreats you."

This was a mother's voice and tone, this was a language of the heart such as these lips had never before addressed to Waldemar. The hour had come when this proud, resolute woman saw everything falling in ruins around her, and found herself clinging in despair to the only object fate had left her. The neglected son at last entered into his birthright, but it was not until the grave had closed over his brother.

Any other mother and son would have fallen into each other's arms, and in one outburst of affection sought to forget the long and bitter estrangement. These natures were too stern and reticent. Waldemar did not utter a word, but, for the first time in his life, he pressed his mother's hand to his lips.

"Will you remain?" asked the mother, entreatingly.

"No," he replied, firmly but gently; "I shall go, but I thank you for the words you have spoken. They make the risk far easier for me. You have always regarded me as your enemy because I have not entered into your party plans; I could not do so, I cannot now; but nothing forbids my releasing the count from an inhuman sentence. I will at least make the attempt, and I shall succeed if success is possible. You know the motive that urges me on."

The mother abandoned her opposition. This assurance awakened hope within her own breast.

"And Wanda?" she asked.

"Wanda said to me to-day, 'If my father were at liberty, I should have the courage to defy everything for your sake.' Tell her that I hope to remind her of those words some day. Do not question me further, mother. You know that I must act alone, for I only among you all am free from suspicion. You will not hear from me during my absence, for you are under close surveillance, and a message from you would endanger my undertaking. Leave all to me. I must hasten--there is no time to lose. And now, good-bye."

He kissed his mother's hand, and hastened away. She was deeply wounded at her son's hurried farewell; she went to the window, eager for one more parting recognition, but she received none. Waldemar's eyes sought another window. As he rode out of the court his glance was fixed upon Wanda's corner room, as if in that glance lay some magic power to compel from her a farewell greeting. For her sake he was about to enter upon an undertaking beset with dangers, and where Wanda was concerned, his mother and all the world were forgotten.

He saw her once more. She appeared at the window, and Waldemar's face lighted up as if illumined by a sudden burst of sunshine. For a moment their eyes met in a glance more eloquent than words. The young man bowed low, and giving Norman the rein, he dashed away like the wind.

The mother stood gazing after her son. He had not turned to give her one farewell look; she was forgotten. At this thought her soul was for the first time pierced by the same arrow Waldemar had often felt at sight of her partiality for Leo. At this moment the conviction she was still reluctant to admit forced itself upon her: that her eldest son inherited what the youngest had never possessed,--her own indomitable will and energy. She now acknowledged that, in mind and character, Waldemar was blood of her blood.

CHAPTER XXVII.

THE GOVERNMENT COUNSELLOR.

Upon the forenoon of a cool but bright and sunny day in May, Superintendent Frank was returning from L----, the nearest railway station, where he had gone to meet his son and daughter, Professor and Madame Fabian. The new academic and marital dignities well became the professor. The old, depressed look was gone, his face was no longer "sicklied o'er with the pale cast of thought;" he seemed in cheerful, almost buoyant spirits. The young wife, always intent upon maintaining her husband's position, wore a grave, important, almost solemn aspect, which was in striking contrast to her fresh, youthful appearance. Happily, she often forgot the part she had so carefully studied, and became the merry, saucy Gretchen Frank of the old girlhood days. At this moment, however, the professor's wife was in the ascendant as she sat very erect in the carriage at her father's side, and told him of the new life at the university city.

"Yes, papa, this visit home will be such a rest and recreation for us," she said, passing her pocket-handkerchief over the blooming face, which certainly indicated no need either of rest or amusement; "the university makes so many and such constant demands upon our time, and our social position involves such a round of visits and receptions and so many other cares. We German scholars, to-day, stand in the van of intellectual progress; we are the profound thinkers of the world."

"You really seem to stand very much in the van," replied the superintendent, who had listened to Gretchen's remarks in mingled surprise and amusement. "Tell me, child, who occupies the chair of Ancient History at the University of J----; you or your husband?"

"The husband and the wife are one," said Gretchen, sagely; "if it had not been for me, Emil would not have accepted the professorship, as great a scholar as he is. Only day before yesterday, Professor Weber remarked to him in my presence, 'Professor Fabian, you are a treasure for our university, but you are out of your element in practical life; you are fortunate in having a wife who so energetically represents you there.' And he was right,--wasn't he, Emil? Practically and socially, you would be lost without me,--wouldn't you?"

"Wholly and entirely so!" returned the professor, emphatically, and with a look of grateful affection at his wife.

"Do you hear, papa? he acknowledges it," said Gretchen, triumphantly. "Emil is one of the few men who fully appreciates his wife. Hubert never would have done so,--but, appropos of the assessor, how is he nowadays? Has he become government counsellor?"

"No: and I fear he never will. He has at last become indignant at the lack of appreciation paid to his great abilities, and has tendered his resignation. Next month he leaves the public service."

"What a loss for the prime ministry!" exclaimed Gretchen, laughing; "he was sure of one day attaining that position, and rehearsed his ministerial part constantly while he sat in our parlor. Is he still haunted with the idea of unearthing conspiracies and traitors everywhere?"

"I do not know," replied Herr Frank. "I have scarcely seen him since your marriage. He has not entered my house since he rushed from it so incontinently on that evening which proved fatal to his matrimonial hopes. I cannot blame him, Gretchen, but I do blame you; you ought to have told him the news more considerately. But the assessor needs no pity; he is now quite a wealthy man, being the chief heir of Professor Schwarz, who died a few months ago."

"Probably of a bilious fever," added Gretchen.

"*Gretchen!*" said the professor, imploringly and reproachfully.

"Heaven knows he had a bilious temperament!" continued Gretchen. "He was as irritable as you are patient. Only think of it, papa! Just after his call to J----, Emil wrote the professor a courteous, modest letter, in which he really apologized for being his successor, and solemnly declared his innocence of all participation in the university quarrel. The letter was never answered, and now that this unamiable celebrity has left the world, my husband feels called upon to dedicate to him a posthumous eulogy, deploring the loss to science as if this professor had been his best friend."

"I did so in good faith, and from sincere conviction," replied Fabian, in his gentle, earnest way. "The professor's morbid character often robbed him of the appreciation which was justly his due. I felt it my duty to remind the world of the loss science has suffered in his death. He was a man of great learning and ability."

Gretchen's lips curled in scorn. "I don't care what he was!" she said. "Let us change the subject. Herr Nordeck is not in Villica."

"No," said Herr Frank, curtly; "he is away."

"Yes; he wrote to my husband that he thought of going to Altenhof, and might remain there for some weeks. It is strange that he should leave Villica just now, when so many things there demand his attention."

"Altenhof is his old home," said the professor. "It has been left him by will, and nothing can persuade him to sell the estate. It is only natural that he should wish to revisit the scenes of his youth."

Gretchen looked incredulous. "Waldemar Nordeck is not a man to cling to sentimental remembrances," she said. "This visit is merely a pretext: perhaps he is seeking by change of scene to divert his mind from its passion for the Countess Wanda. Polish women are insane in their national fanaticism; this young girl will not give her hand to the man she loves because he is a German! I would have married my Emil if he had been a Hottentot. And now my dear husband is fretting continually over the supposed unhappiness of his beloved Waldemar, seriously imagining that this man has a heart like other men. Nothing can make me believe such an absurdity!"

"*Gretchen!*" said the professor a second time, and with an effort at severity which was an entire failure.

"I'm sure I don't believe it; why should I?" reiterated the young wife. "If a man has a secret sorrow he will manifest it in some manner. Herr Nordeck rules Villica in a high-handed sort of way that betrays but very little sensibility, and when he was groomsman at our wedding he did not manifest the slightest feeling."

"He is a man so reticent by nature that if he were dying of an unhappy passion he would make no sign," said Fabian.

"A man whose unhappy love is never evident has no deep feeling," persisted Gretchen. "Your woe-begone look was visible a dozen paces off. Those few weeks before our betrothal, when you really thought I was going to marry the assessor, you went about with such a rueful face! I pitied you from the bottom of my heart, but you was so timid I thought you never would muster up courage to make a declaration."

Herr Frank had taken no part in this conversation; the road which for a short distance led along by the river-bank, began to be very bad, and required careful driving. The damage done by the late high water had not yet been repaired, and passage was difficult, although the superintendent declared that it was not dangerous. Gretchen would not trust his assurance; she insisted upon leaving the carriage and going over the bridge on foot. Both gentlemen followed her example, and all three took the upper footpath while the carriage slowly passed over the bridge below.

They were not the only timid ones; another carriage had reached the opposite end of the bridge, and its inmate had also alighted. After advancing a few steps they found themselves suddenly face to face with the assessor.

The unexpected meeting was fraught with painful embarrassment to both parties, as their last interview had been upon that evening when the assessor had left Gretchen's presence in a rage at the sudden announcement of her betrothal to Doctor Fabian. All felt, however, that their friendship was of too long duration to allow them to pass each other as mere strangers. Herr Frank stepped up to the assessor as if nothing had happened, and offered his hand in the old cordial way, expressing great pleasure at seeing him again.

The assessor had assumed his most dignified attitude. He was dressed in black from head to foot. He wore a crape band around his hat and another around his left arm; he was paying due respect to the memory of his illustrious uncle, but the inheritance must have distilled some balsam into the heart of the sorrowing nephew, for he looked like anything rather than an image of despair. His face to-day wore a peculiar expression: an exalted self-satisfaction, a conscious greatness; he was evidently in the mood to forgive all the world and to make peace with all mankind. After a moment's hesitation he grasped the superintendent's proffered hand, and returned his friendly greeting.

The professor and Gretchen now advanced. Hubert threw a reproachful glance upon the young wife, who, in her travelling hat with its floating veil, certainly looked charming enough to awaken a regretful feeling in the heart of her former adorer. He bowed distantly to her and then turned to the professor.

"Professor Fabian," he said, solemnly, "you, too, sympathize with the great bereavement which our family, and with it all science, has suffered. The letter you some time ago wrote to my uncle convinced him that you had no part in the intrigues which had been set on foot against him; that you at least could recognize his great services without envy. He himself expressed this conviction to me; he did you full justice. Your beautiful eulogy of your predecessor does you great honor, and is a most gratifying source of consolation to his surviving relatives. I thank you in the name of the family."

Fabian cordially pressed the speaker's hand. The hostility of Professor Schwarz and the resentment of Assessor Hubert had pressed heavily upon his soul, although he had not done either any intentional injury. He gave his heartfelt sympathy to the afflicted nephew.

"Yes, we have deeply lamented the loss of Professor Schwarz at the university," said Gretchen, and she was unprincipled enough to add many words of sorrow and condolence for the death of the man she had thoroughly hated without knowing him, and whom she could not forgive, even in the grave, for his criticism of the "History of Ancient Germany."

"And have you really tendered your resignation?" asked Herr Frank, changing the subject. "Are you about to leave the state service, Assessor Hubert?"

"Yes, I shall leave in a week," replied Hubert, "but will you allow me to inform you that I must be addressed by a new title. I"--he again made a dramatic pause, a far longer one than that which had preceded his attempted declaration of love, and scanned the three persons before him one by one as if he would prepare them each and all for an astounding piece of news; then he drew a deep breath, and with a smile of infinite rapture illuminating his face, he added: "Since yesterday I have been Government Counsellor!"

"Thank heaven--*at last*!" said Gretchen, half aloud, while her horrified husband grasped her by the arm, to keep her from further indiscreet utterances. Hubert, fortunately, had not heard the exclamation; he received with a dignity suited to the greatness of the moment the congratulations of Herr Frank and the good wishes of the married pair. His conciliatory mood was fully accounted for: the new government counsellor stood upon a pedestal far removed from any slights and affronts that had been experienced by the former assessor. He forgave everybody, and especially the state which had so long ignored him.

"The promotion really changes none of my plans," he resumed. "The state sometimes recognizes too late the ability of its servants, but I bear no resentment. The die is now cast; but some police duties require my aid, and in the last week of my official career an important mission is confided to me. I am on my way to W----."

"Over the border?" asked Fabian, in astonishment.

"Certainly; I have to consult with the authorities there in regard to the capture and transportation of an arch-traitor."

Gretchen threw a glance at her husband, which plainly said, "There, he is beginning again!" but Frank, whose attention was all at once aroused, remarked, in a tone of assumed indifference,--

"I think the insurrection is at an end."

"But conspiracies still exist," cried Hubert, excitedly; "we have just now a striking verification of this fact. You, perhaps, do not know that Count Morynski, the leader, the very soul of the insurrection, has escaped?"

The professor and his wife were speechless with astonishment, but the superintendent said, calmly, "It really is not possible!"

The new government counsellor shrugged his shoulders. "It is, unfortunately, a secret no longer," he said; "it is a topic of common remark in L----. The Princess Zulieski is no doubt at the bottom of the affair; that woman is a menace, to the whole province. The count, you are aware, was sentenced to transportation; all such prisoners are very strictly guarded, but his friends have in some way aided him to escape. There is great excitement over the incredible boldness of the undertaking; the whole region has been searched for three days, but not one trace of the fugitive has been discovered."

Fabian had at first listened only with lively sympathy, but as Hubert dwelt upon the boldness of the undertaking, he began to grow uneasy. An undefinable suspicion seized him; he was about to question Hubert further, when he met his father-in-law's warning glance, and relapsed into an awe-stricken silence.

Gretchen had not remarked this silent understanding between her father and her husband, and she listened without embarrassment to Hubert's further remarks.

"The fugitive cannot have gone far, for his flight was almost immediately discovered. He has not yet passed the border, that is certain. He will probably first take refuge in Radowicz; Villica, thank heaven, is now closed to traitors, although Herr Nordeck is not there at present."

"No," said Herr Frank, emphatically, "he is at Altenhof."

"I know it; he informed the governor of his intended departure. It is fortunate that he is absent, and will be spared the pain of seeing his uncle captured and delivered up."

"What! will you deliver him up?" asked Gretchen, excitedly.

Hubert gazed at her in amazement. "Certainly! He is a criminal and a traitor."

The young woman glanced first at her husband and then at her father; she did not understand why neither shared her indignation, for Herr Frank looked indifferent, and Fabian did not utter a word. But our brave Gretchen was not easily intimidated. She indulged in some not very flattering remarks upon the German government and its officials, at the same time eulogizing the Poles, whose patriotism and devotion to liberty were, she declared, worthy of a better fate. Hubert listened in horror. For the first time he thanked God that he had not made this woman his wife--the wife of a government counsellor! She had just shown him that she was not fit to be the wife of a loyal officer; there was treason in her veins.

"If I were in your place I would decline such a service," she said; "you might do so, the time for your resignation being close at hand; I would not close my official career with the delivery of a poor, half-dead, hunted prisoner into the hands of his tormentors."

"I am government counsellor," returned Hubert, solemnly emphasizing the title, "and I must do my duty. My country commands--I obey. But I see that my carriage has passed the dangerous place safely. Farewell! Duty summons me." He bowed and withdrew.

"Did you hear, Emil?" asked the young wife, when they were again seated in the carriage. "Hubert has become government counsellor, and a week before resigning his police duties to enter upon the new position, he sets out on a fool's chase after another conspirator. He can never be a counsellor of the government except in name. I really believe he has bought the place with the money his uncle left him; but if he has only the title, he cannot do any more harm."

Gretchen dwelt at some length upon the details Hubert had given them concerning Count Morynski's flight, but she received only short and absent replies. Her father and husband had grown very reticent; the conversation would not flow back into its former channel. A malign influence had seemed to follow that accidental meeting with Hubert, and Gretchen was heartily glad when they at last reached Villica.

As the day passed, the "Frau Professorin" was every hour thrown into new surprise and vexation. Her father was perfectly incomprehensible. Upon meeting his children at the station he had embraced them fondly; he must be delighted with their present happiness and their future prospects; but still he seemed somewhat annoyed at their presence just now. He had a preoccupied air, and declared that he was overwhelmed with business. Immediately upon their arrival he had taken his son-in-law into his private office, and had remained alone with him for nearly an hour.

Gretchen was indignant at not being invited to this secret interview, and her indignation increased when she found that she could not learn anything of its purport from her husband. She kept her eyes and ears wide open; she recalled several incidental remarks which had been made by her father and husband during the journey, and by combining them very skilfully, she at last arrived at a conclusion which was perfectly satisfactory to her own mind.

CHAPTER XXVIII.

THE "FRAU PROFESSORIN."

Dinner was over, and the married pair found themselves alone in the family sitting-room. The professor, quite contrary to his usual habit, was pacing uneasily up and down. He tried vainly to conceal his inward perturbation, and was so deeply absorbed in thought that he did not remark the silence of his usually talkative wife. Gretchen sat upon the sofa, and for a long time gazed intently at her husband. At length having studied her mode of attack, she advanced valiantly to the charge.

"Emil," she began, with a solemnity which Hubert himself had never equalled; "Emil, I am outrageously treated here!"

Fabian stopped short, and gazed at his wife in alarm and horror. "You? Good heavens! By whom?"

"By my papa, and, what is worst of all, by my own husband."

The professor rushed to his wife's side and seized her hand, but with a very ungracious mien she snatched it from him.

"Yes, the way in which I am treated is perfectly outrageous!" she reiterated. "You show me no confidence, you have secrets from me, you treat me like an ignorant child, *me*, a married woman, the wife of a professor in the University of J----; it is atrocious!"

"Dear Gretchen," said Fabian, meekly, and then he stopped suddenly.

"What has papa been telling you? Why have you not confided it to me? Why were you two so long closeted together? What are these momentous secrets between you? O, you needn't deny it, Emil; you know that you and papa have secrets that you don't tell me."

The professor attempted no denial; he gazed at the floor, and looked very much depressed. His wife gave him a reproving glance.

"Well, then, I shall tell *you*," said Gretchen, "since you will not trust me. There is another plot in Villica, a conspiracy, as Hubert would say. Papa is involved, and is drawing you into it. The object of the plot is the liberation of Count Morynski."

"Child, for God's sake be silent!" cried Fabian, in dismay; but Gretchen paid no heed to the entreaty; she went on without a moment's pause.

"And Herr Nordeck is not in Altenhof; if he were, you would not be so anxious about him. What do you care for Count Morynski and his flight? Ah, but I know why you tremble! Your beloved Waldemar is with him. I shouldn't wonder if he himself had liberated the count; it would be just like him."

The professor was dumb with amazement at his wife's penetration, and at the clear, logical way in which she had stated the case. He thought her incredibly clever, and yet he was horrified as she counted out to him on her fingers the secrets he had believed impenetrable.

"And no one tells me a word of all these things," continued Gretchen, in ever-increasing indignation, "not a word, when you and papa both know that I can keep a secret. Who saved an outbreak at the castle by sending Assessor Hubert on a fool's errand over to Janowo; who, indeed, if not I alone? You hadn't a thing to do with it. The princess and the Countess Wanda always know what is going on; the Polish women are the confidants of their fathers and husbands; they are allowed to take part in politics, and especially in conspiracies; but we poor German women are always slighted and kept back by our husbands; they humiliate us by the most insulting distrust, they treat us like slaves; they--" The professor's wife could not go on; as a realizing sense of her slavery and humiliation clearly dawned upon her mind, she began to sob aloud. Her husband was almost beside himself.

"Gretchen, my dearest Gretchen, do not weep," he said, entreatingly. "You know that I have no secrets from you which concern me alone, but these secrets concern others, and I have pledged my word not to divulge them, not even to you."

"How can any one exact a promise from a married man to withhold secrets from his wife?" cried Gretchen, sobbing still more violently. "It is not right; it ought not to be required."

"I have for this once given my promise," said Fabian, despairingly. "Now control your emotion! I cannot bear to see you in tears. I--"

"Well, if this isn't a most beautiful display of petticoat government!" interposed the superintendent, who had entered unremarked, and had witnessed the pathetic scene. "My daughter errs in regard to the person who suffers humiliation and slavery. Do you allow yourself to be controlled in this manner, Emil? Do not take it ill of me if I say, that although you are an excellent scholar, you play a most pitiable part as a married man."

He could not more effectually have come to the aid of his son-in-law. No sooner had Gretchen heard the disparaging words, than she rushed to her husband's rescue.

"Emil is the noblest, the dearest, the most excellent of husbands," she said, and her tears straightway ceased to flow. "You need not reproach him, papa; it is only natural that he should love his wife."

Frank laughed. "Do not be so hasty, child," he said, "I meant no harm; and, after all, you excite yourself without cause. We are compelled to draw you into our plot, which you have rightly divined. News has just come that the princess and her niece will be here in the course of the afternoon. You must go over to the castle and receive them, as Waldemar is absent, and would naturally delegate that duty to his friend Fabian and his wife. Our aim is to disarm the suspicion of the servants, who well know that these ladies have not entered Villica for a year. The princess and her niece know what is going on, and will await the issue of events here. I shall drive over to the border-forester's, and wait there with my horses, according to agreement. Your husband will explain the rest to you, my child; I have no time."

He went, and Gretchen received full details of the plot for the count's release from her husband. Her ill-humor vanished, and her face and manner expressed supreme delight at the consciousness that she was at last treated with as much respect as even a Polish woman could demand, and allowed to have her share in the conspiracy.

It was night. The superintendent's house was wrapped in slumber, and the servants at Villica had retired. Lights still gleamed from some upper windows of the castle, and in the embrasure of one of them stood a tea-table, which had been laid as usual, although no one had tasted a mouthful. Gretchen's righteous soul was vexed; she was for the time being mistress here, and liked to see things go on in an orderly manner. She ere long compelled her husband to take a seat at the table, and there gave him a mild but very impressive lecture.

"Do not torture yourself so with anxiety, Emil! Would you see me also ill from excitement, like those ladies in the next room? Their pale faces frighten me. I cannot endure the sight of their silent anguish. I think they prefer for us to leave them alone. Our tea is ready; why should we not drink it together?"

Fabian pushed aside the obtrusive tea-cup.

"Your despondency is past comprehension," added Gretchen. "Waldemar Nordeck carries through all his undertakings; there must be something in the superstition of these Villica people which declares him bullet-proof. He will safely cross the line, and the count with him."

"God grant it!" ejaculated Fabian. "If that Hubert were not on their track, I should be more confident. If he should meet the count and Waldemar in any disguise, he would recognize them."

"Hubert has all his life been doing the most stupid things," said Gretchen, disdainfully; "he will not be likely to do anything clever at this late hour. He will make some blunder or other, you may rely upon that."

The princess and Wanda remained in the adjoining parlor; the lamp which was burning upon a side-table only partially lighted the lofty room, its depths remained in shadow. The princess sat motionless amid the dense shadows, in the same place she had occupied the morning when Leo's unblest return had drawn that fatal catastrophe upon himself and his family. The mother struggled painfully with the remembrances which came thronging around her. What had become of those daring plans, of those lofty hopes and glowing anticipations which had centred here? They all lay in ruins; Bronislaw's rescue was the only boon it was in the power of destiny to offer, but the rescue was only half accomplished, and perhaps at this very moment Waldemar was paying for his hazardous venture with his life.

Wanda stood in the niche of the large central window and gazed out with straining eyes, as if she would pierce the outer darkness. She had opened the window, but she did not feel the sharp night-air; she was not conscious how she shuddered at its chilling breath. No memories of the past, with its blighted plans and hopes, haunted this hour for her; she thought only of the danger of the two beings she loved best on earth, and her heart asserted its right; she trembled most for Waldemar.

It was a cold, foggy night, and no moon was visible. Only now and then a star gleamed forth, to vanish soon behind the clouds. No sound broke the profound silence all around the castle; the park lay dark and still; and amid the pauses, when the wind was lulled to rest, every falling leaf was heard.

Wanda started suddenly, and a half-suppressed cry passed her lips. The next moment the princess stood at her side.

"What is it? Do you see anything?"

"No; but I think I hear a sound of hoofs in the distance."

"I fear it is only imaginary, we have so often been deceived."

The two women leaned far out of the window, and listened in breathless silence. They fancied they heard a sound distant and half audible, but the wind rose anew and drowned it. After some ten minutes of agonized suspense, a sound of muffled footsteps was heard in an alley of the park which led into the forest. By straining their eyes to the utmost, Wanda distinguished amid the darkness two forms emerging from among the trees.

"They are here," whispered Fabian, with white lips, as he burst suddenly into the room. "They are coming down the side-steps, and will enter through the back gate which I opened half an hour ago." Wanda's first impulse was to rush to meet them, but Gretchen held her back. "We are not alone in the castle," she said; "we must be quiet and cautious."

A few moments passed, then the door opened softly. Count Morynski stood on the threshold, and behind him towered up Waldemar's stately form. That very instant Wanda was clasped in her father's arms.

The professor and his wife had tact enough to withdraw, and Waldemar also followed them, giving both a cordial greeting.

"What a desperate undertaking, you have been engaged in, Waldemar!" said Professor Fabian. "Supposing you had been discovered?"

Waldemar smiled. "Before engaging in any bold venture, we must count the chances," he said; "in leaning over a precipice, if we think of dizziness, we are lost. I went straight on to my purpose, looking neither to the right nor the left."

He threw aside his cloak, and taking a revolver from his breast-pocket, he laid it on the table. Gretchen, who was standing near, stepped back.

"Do not be frightened, madam," he said. "The weapon is not cocked; the affair has been carried through without bloodshed. We found an unexpected helper in Assessor Hubert."

"The new government counsellor?" asked Gretchen, in surprise.

"The very same. And so he has really become counsellor! Well, he can air his new dignity over in Poland. We drove across the border in his carriage with his pass and credentials."

The professor and his wife were speechless with amazement.

"O, but he did not grant us this favor of his own accord," continued Nordeck; "he will be sure to call us highway robbers; but necessity knows no law. Our freedom and life were at stake, and we had to act promptly. Yesterday afternoon we arrived at a Polish village-inn, only a dozen miles from the border. The landlord was a Pole, and warned us against pursuing our journey before dusk, as the officers were on our track. Both his sons had served the revolution under Count Morynski, and the whole family would have risked their lives to save him. Toward nightfall our horses stood saddled in the stable, and we were about to depart, when all at once Assessor Hubert appeared at the inn, making inquiries for us. His carriage had received some injury on the way, and he had left it at the blacksmith's to be repaired. The landlord concealed us in the garret, and pretended to know nothing of us.

We distinctly heard the assessor down-stairs haranguing, in his usual voluble style, about conspiracies and arch-traitors. In the course of his remarks he gave us the very information in regard to his plans for arresting us which we most of all wished to obtain. No choice was left us; we must leave as quickly as possible. Immediate proximity to danger gave me a happy thought, and I imparted it to the landlord, who at once informed the assessor that his carriage would not be ready for an hour. Hubert was exasperated at the delay, but he consoled himself in a measure by doing ample justice to the very excellent supper which was set before him. Meantime we slipped out at a back-door, and upon arriving at the smith's, we found the carriage in readiness. I stepped inside, my uncle, who passed for my servant, mounted the box, the landlord's son handed him the reins, and we drove out of the village by an unfrequented road.

"No sooner had I entered the carriage than I made an invaluable discovery. The assessor's overcoat lay upon the back seat, and in its breast-pocket I found his letter-case with his pass, his credentials for his present mission, and other valuable papers. I, with my giant stature, could make no use of the pass, but the other papers did me good service, for they contained minute directions in regard to the methods to be pursued in our arrest. We were, of course, unprincipled enough to use for our own benefit the documents issued against us.

"As the assessor had informed the people at the inn that he had passed through A---- that morning, we took a by-road to the next border station, and drove boldly through the town as Government-Counsellor Hubert and his coachman. I showed my papers, and demanded permission to pass on quickly as possible, for fear lest the fugitives I was pursuing might escape me. So great was my apparent haste, that my pass was not demanded. We left our carriage a few miles on this side of the boundary, pursuing the way to our border-forester's on foot. There Herr Frank met us with his horses, and--here we are!"

Gretchen, who had listened intently, could not conceal her delight at the trick which had been played upon her former admirer, but Fabian, always inclined to sympathize with the unfortunate, asked, anxiously, "What has become of poor Hubert?"

"He remains over in Poland, without a carriage and without credentials," replied Waldemar, dryly; "and he may think himself fortunate if he is not looked upon as an arch-traitor. Circumstances are very much against him, and he may even now be enjoying the pleasures he had destined for us."

"What a delightful conclusion of his official career!" exclaimed Gretchen, mockingly, and regardless of her husband's warning glance.

"We may as well let Hubert rest!" said Waldemar. "Shall I not see you both in Villica on my return? I am here to-night *incognito*, but in a few days I shall return from Altenhof, where I am supposed to be at present. Now I must greet my mother and my--cousin."

CHAPTER XXIX.

REUNION.

Waldemar re-entered the room where he had left his relatives. The count sat in an easy-chair; both his arms were around Wanda, who knelt before him, and leaned her head against his shoulder. He had aged greatly during these last twelve months. He had left Villica a strong, energetic man, in the prime of middle life; he returned old in body and in heart, broken down by mental and physical suffering.

The princess, who stood near her brother, was first to observe the young man's entrance.

"Are you here at last, Waldemar?" she said, in a reproachful tone, as she advanced to meet her son; "we began to think you was not coming."

"I did not wish to intrude," replied Waldemar, hesitatingly.

"Will you always insist upon remaining a stranger to us? Have you not been so long enough? My son," she added, extending both arms to him, "I thank you."

For the first time since infancy Waldemar was clasped in his mother's arms. In that long, fervent embrace years of estrangement, strife, and bitterness vanished; that cold, hostile barrier which had separated two beings who belonged to each other by the holiest and nearest ties of kindred, was broken down. The son had at last won his mother's love.

The count rose and offered his hand to his deliverer. "Thank him your whole life long, Maryna," he said; "you do not know what he has dared for me."

"The venture was not so great as it appeared," returned Waldemar. "I smoothed the way beforehand. Wherever prisons exist, bribery is possible, and golden keys sometimes unlock the strongest doors. I have hitherto set little value upon the wealth that came to me without any effort or merit of my own, but I have at last learned its worth."

Wanda still kept close to her father, holding him fast, as if she feared he might again be torn from her. She had not uttered a word of thanks, but her glance spoke more than words. Waldemar understood that silent language, and was content.

"The danger is not over," he continued; "Hubert's papers, which are now in my hands, authorize your arrest and extradition, even here. You must rest a few hours, and then we will leave for S----, which is the nearest seaport, and only a day's journey. An English ship has for four weeks lain there at my disposal; it is ready to sail at any moment, and will carry you directly to England. Upon your arrival there, France, Switzerland, and Italy will be open to you. When once upon the high seas, you are safe."

"And you, my nephew, will you not have to atone for this deed?"

"I have no fears," replied Waldemar; "I am a German, and as such your political enemy. If my connivance in your escape is discovered, it will hardly be considered a crime, since I am your nephew, and hope ere long to be your son."

As Waldemar alluded to the closer tie that would soon bind him to his uncle, the latter was deeply moved; his lips quivered, his features seemed convulsed by some inward struggle. He had fought against his daughter's love for this man with every weapon at his command. For the sake of rending a tie so hated he had consented for Wanda to accompany him into an exile that must be almost certain death. Never had the old national animosity been stronger in his heart than at this moment of shipwreck to all his hopes, but he looked upon the man who had rescued him, who had risked life for his sake, and then he bent down to his daughter.

"Wanda!" he said, softly.

Wanda gazed into his face. Never had she seen it so sorrowful as at this moment. As she read in his eyes what acquiescence would cost him, every selfish wish vanished, and filial love and tenderness alone ruled her heart.

"Not now, not now, Waldemar," she cried, imploringly; "you see what my father has suffered and is suffering still. You cannot ask me to leave him at the very moment of reunion. Allow me to remain a little longer at his side--one brief year more. Shall I let him go into a foreign land, into exile, alone and ill?"

Waldemar was silent. He could not at this moment remind Wanda of her promise; the count's bowed form and broken health pleaded powerfully for his daughter's request, but all the egotism of love asserted itself in the young man's nature. He had done and dared so much to win his beloved, and he could not endure the thought of having the prize longer denied him. His gloomy brow, his set lips, and downcast eyes expressed the protest he would not utter. The princess was first to break the painful silence.

"I will take care of your father, Wanda," she said; "I will go with him."

All started in surprise. "Do I understand you aright, Maryna?" asked the count. "Do you say you will go with me?"

"Yes, into exile," added the princess, in an unshaken voice; "we both know what exile is, Bronislaw; we have tasted it for long years, we will again share it together."

"Never," cried Waldemar, excitedly. "I will not consent to have you leave me, mother. The old strife is buried. The chasm that once yawned between us is closed up. Your place henceforth is at Villica with your son, who--"

"Who is at this moment seeking to Germanize his estates," interposed the princess, gravely. "No, Waldemar, you undervalue the Pole in my nature if you think I can now live in Villica. I love you at last wholly and unselfishly, as a mother should love her child. I shall maintain this love through distance and separation; it will be renewed and strengthened at our occasional meetings in the future; but we can never be one in national ideas and feelings, and did we attempt to live together, the old strife might again break out between us. Therefore let me go; it is best for us both."

"The old strife ought not to intrude into an hour like this," said Waldemar, reproachfully.

"We are not at war with you," replied the princess, sadly; "it is with the destiny that has condemned us to overthrow. My brother is the last of his race--a race which for centuries has been illustrious in the annals of our people. Wanda's name will soon be merged in yours. She is young; she loves you. She may forget the past for your sake. To you two belong life and the future; we have only the past."

"Maryna is right," added the count. "I cannot remain here, and she *will* not. Wanda, too, is the daughter of her people, and will not disown her lineage. I augur no happiness from the marriage of a Nordeck and a Morynski, but your hearts are set upon the union, and--I oppose it no longer."

The young pair had no joyous betrothal. A deep shadow brooded over that hour which is usually so full of sunshine and promise to plighted hearts. But they could not believe the count's mournful augury; they felt that the love which had fought its way through so many conflicts and surmounted so many barriers would bless and sanctify their lives, whatever trials might intervene--that it would remain a love lasting as time and changeless as eternity.

"Come, Bronislaw," said the princess, taking her brother's arm, "you are weary, and must rest. We will leave these lovers alone; they have scarce spoken to each other, and they must have so much to say."

Professor Fabian and his wife had remained in the adjoining room. Gretchen was ill at ease; every now and then she would throw a melancholy glance upon the tea-table, which she had arranged with especial care.

"Why must people, in giving way to their sentimental feelings, always forget what is proper and necessary?" she said, in an aggrieved tone. "The anxiety and excitement are over, so is the meeting; if they would only act like reasonable beings, we might all of us be cosily seated around the tea-table. I cannot persuade the princess or the count to taste a mouthful, but Wanda must certainly take a cup of tea. I have just made some fresh for her. Now I will go and see if she and Herr Waldemar are in the parlor. You stay here, Emil."

Emil, like an obedient husband, heeded his wife's command. He remained keeping guard over the tea-service, but the time seemed very long; ten minutes, at least, had rolled away, and his wife did not return. The professor began to be uncomfortable. He felt so superfluous here; he wished he could only make himself useful in some way, like Gretchen, whose practical nature always asserted itself. He must have the satisfaction of doing something, no matter of how little consequence, and so he poured out two cups of tea, and taking one in each hand, carried them into the next room. To his surprise, he found neither Waldemar nor Wanda there, but his wife was standing close to the library door, which was slightly ajar.

"Gretchen, my love," said Fabian, balancing the tea-cups as carefully as if they held the most precious life-elixir, "I have brought the tea. I was afraid it might become cold, and I thought--I had an idea that perhaps--they would like it."

The *Frau Professorin* had allowed herself to be surprised in a position not quite suited to her dignity. She stood close to the crevice of the door, evidently peeping into the next room, and listening also. Upon hearing her husband's voice, she started in alarm and confusion; but, quickly recovering her equanimity, she seized the professor by the shoulder, and marched him and the tea-cups back to the place they had just left.

"Set down the cups, Emil," she said; "the young countess doesn't want any tea; she won't require any for a long time. And you need have no further anxiety about your dear Waldemar; things are going on very nicely in the room over yonder--very nicely indeed! I may as well confess that I have done the young man wrong; he really has a heart. This cold, stiff Nordeck can actually kneel before a lady, and pour forth his love in the most eloquent and glowing words. O Emil, if you could only hear the sweet, nice things he has been saying to her! I certainly could not have believed it."

"But, dear child, how do you know all this?" asked the professor, who, in his scholastic innocence, had never dreamed that anybody could listen at doors or peep through key-holes. "You stood outside."

Gretchen's face flushed crimson, but her discomfiture was only for a moment; she looked her husband full in the face, and said, with an air of great superiority,--

"What an absurd question, Emil! You do not understand such things at all; you would not understand if I should tell you. As the tea is poured out, we will drink it ourselves."

CHAPTER XXX.

AUF WIEDERSEHEN!

The mild spring night which had enveloped the waters began to give place to the dawn. The stars were dying out one by one, and in the eastern horizon glimmered the first beams of day. The waves, lightly stirred by the rising breeze, murmured softly as in a dream.

A ship sped on through the ever-brightening morning twilight. It had left the harbor of S---- at midnight, and having passed the broad river's mouth, was about to enter the open sea. Count Morynski, with his daughter and Waldemar, stood on the deck. Wanda had insisted upon accompanying her father to S----, and remaining until the last possible moment at his side. The ship would pass Altenhof in its course, and here the final parting would take place. The count was now on the way to England, where his sister would join him after the marriage of her son and niece, which was to be solemnized in a few weeks. Upon reaching England, the exiles would decide upon their future residence.

It was broad day. A light, cold and colorless as yet, illuminated the waves. The strand of Altenhof hove in sight, and the dreaded separation was close at hand. The ship at length landed near the beech-holm, which was just discernible through the morning vapors. The parting between the father and daughter was full of anguish; the count could not control his emotion; he broke down utterly as he placed Wanda in the arms of her future husband. Waldemar, feeling that this torture must not be prolonged, hastily carried his betrothed to the boat that was waiting to convey them to the strand. It reached the beech-holm in a few moments. The ship was already in motion. A white handkerchief fluttered from the deck, and was answered by another from the shore. The distance between the father and his children grew wider and wider, and the ship steamed away to the north.

Wanda sank helplessly upon a stone seat under one of the beeches, and gave herself up to an outburst of passionate anguish. "My darling," said Waldemar, taking her hand in his, "the separation is not final; if your father cannot come to us, nothing hinders our going to him. You shall see him within a year, I promise you that."

"In a year's time I shall not find him living," sobbed Wanda.

Waldemar could not answer. He felt the same foreboding. When, years ago, the count had gone into exile, he had borne with him the mental and physical strength of a man in the prime of life, and hope for the future of Poland had still animated his breast. Now his strength was broken, his hope was dead; what more had life to offer him?

"Your father will not be alone," Waldemar said, consolingly; "my mother will be with him. You know her love for her only brother; she will comfort and sustain him."

Wanda's glance was still riveted upon the ship, which grew less and less in the distance.

"And you, too, must part from your mother," she said, softly,--"part from her when you have just found your true place in her heart."

"It will be a hard parting for us both," replied the young man, sadly, "and yet I feel that my mother is right. Away from each other, we may join hands across the abyss that lies between us, and feel that we are mother and son; but I fear that we cannot walk side by side. Separation alone can insure us peace."

Wanda raised her dark, tearful eyes to his. "Did you hear my father's gloomy prophecy?" she asked. "He thinks that because the married life of your parents was unhappy, ours also must be so."

"My parents were unhappy because they did not love each other," returned Waldemar, "because they entered from cold, sordid calculation into that closest union that can exist between two mortals. Their marriage was cursed from the beginning; it needed no old national antipathy to enhance its wretchedness. Our case is not a parallel one; our love has been tried in the furnace, and it has stood the test. What do we care for this slight difference in nationality, when we have chosen each other out of all the world? If our marriage is indeed a venture, we dare to make it."

The light morning clouds still floating in the sky began to disperse, and the eastern heaven was all aflame with the glory of the sunrise. The horizon was flushed with rosy hues, and the waves were bordered with liquid gold. Now, flashing and gleaming athwart the blue, came the first rays that heralded the advancing sun; now, slowly and majestically, he rose from the waters, mounting higher and higher, until he stood far above them in the clear, unclouded sky. A warm, roseate flush thrilled the air just now so white and cold, and the vast expanse of sea, that had been at night so dark and desolate, became tinged with a blue deep as that of the heaven above it. The sunrise had flooded sea and land with life and light.

Its first beams touched the beech-holm, dispersing the white vapors that still floated between the trees; they descended upon the dewy meadows; they diffused themselves over the forests, but only to blend there with the light shadows they could not dispel. The morning wind swept through the crowns of the mighty beeches, which in soft whispers bent down to one another; but they now murmured no mournful lament over the fading and dying of the beautiful, such as they had murmured that autumnal day by the forest-lake at Villica; and yet from that desolate forest, from out the twilight and its misty shadows, had risen that dream-picture, whose reality existed here--the beech-holm environed by the sea, bathed in the sunlight, and invested with the poetry of its fairy legend.

Waldemar and Wanda stood again in that very place where, years ago, the wild, impetuous boy had stood, the boy who then thought that he need but stretch forth his hand to win and to retain as his very own, the one being who had awakened his first passion, and the spoiled child who had made sport of that passion. Then neither knew anything of life and its problems. They had since stood face to face with its grave responsibilities, they had been involved in its bitter conflicts; it had placed between them every barrier that can sunder mortals. But the old sea-myth had spoken truth to them. Since that hour, when it had thrown its spell around these youthful hearts, it had held them under its thrall in spite of estrangement and separation, drawing them together when strife and hatred raged all around them, and bringing them through all opposing forces to this moment.

Waldemar threw his arm around his loved one, and gazed deep into her eyes. "Do you still believe that the union of a Nordeck and a Morynski can bring no happiness?" he asked. "We will dispel the shadows that once darkened such a union."

Wanda leaned her head upon his shoulder. "You will have to forgive and forget much in your wife," she said. "I cannot renounce all that has my whole life-long been holy and dear to me. Do not seek to separate me wholly from my people, Waldemar! A part of my life is rooted there."

"Have I ever been hard with *you*?" he asked, and his voice had that strange tenderness which one only being on earth could call forth from this cold stern man. "Your eyes long ago taught the unruly boy submission, they will know how to control the man. That unblest shadow may often obtrude between us, it may perhaps cost you many tears and conflicts, but I know that in every decisive moment my Wanda will stand where she stood that day when mortal danger threatened me, and where henceforth her place alone will be--by her husband's side."

The ship which bore the exile from his native land vanished in the nebulous distance. All around, the blue sea rose and fell in gentle undulations, and the beech-holm lay bathed in golden sunbeams. The waters sang again their old, eternal melody, a rhythm of whispering breezes and murmuring waves, and amid the pauses of the music came a far-off mysterious chorus like the chime of sweet-voiced bells--the spirit-greeting of Vineta from its ocean-depths.

Milton Keynes UK
Ingram Content Group UK Ltd.
UKHW030904151124
451262UK00006B/1017

9 789362 994462